Praise for

Introducing the
ANCIENT GREEKS

"[Hall's] book is a hearty, delightful voyage through 2,000 years of Greek history, written with wit and verve and deep insight."
—Mark Gamin, *Cleveland Plain Dealer*

"[Edith Hall's] insights into cultural history can be penetrating and acute. . . . Ms. Hall is an engaging writer and an acute scholar."
—James Romm, *Wall Street Journal*

"A wonderful book, which serves both as introduction to the Ancient Greeks and a hugely entertaining, informative and thoughtful discussion of what made them so important, in their own time and in ours."
—Natalie Haynes, *Independent* (UK)

"In Edith Hall's new and groundbreaking study of ancient Greek culture, society, and mentality over a millennium and more, from Agamemnon to Constantine, she acutely identifies and brilliantly explains why we simply cannot do without the ancient Greeks."
—Paul Cartledge, A. G. Leventis Professor of Greek Culture, University of Cambridge, and author of *The Greeks: A Portrait of Self and Others*

"Edith Hall's characteristically original approach to the world of classical antiquity is on full display in this introductory survey of the ancient Greeks and their enduring accomplishments."
—Froma Zeitlin, Ewing Professor of Greek Language and Literature, emerita, Princeton University

"In this vivacious and learned book, Edith Hall distills the essence of Hellenic culture to discover the secrets of its success and stamina. Filled with striking anecdotes and little-known facts, this book will delight any student of the ancient Greek world."
—Adrienne Mayor, Stanford University, and author of *The Poison King*

"*Introducing the Ancient Greeks* is informative and inspiring. With deep expertise and unabashed enthusiasm, Edith Hall surveys the whole history of the ancient Greeks and pinpoints the shared traits that explain their enduring achievements."
—Sheila Murnaghan, professor of classical studies and Alfred Reginald Allen Memorial Professor of Greek, University of Pennsylvania

A boy musician riding a dolphin. Detail of a red-figure Etruscan vase of the mid-fourth century BC in the National Archaeological Museum of Spain, Madrid. *(Photograph: Alberto Rivas Rodríguez. Museo Arqueológico Nacional, Spain N.I. 1999/127/3.)*

Introducing the
ANCIENT GREEKS

From Bronze Age Seafarers to
Navigators of the Western Mind

EDITH HALL

W. W. NORTON & COMPANY
New York London

For information about permission to reproduce selections from
this book, write to Permissions, W. W. Norton & Company, Inc.,
500 Fifth Avenue, New York, NY 10110

For information about special discounts for bulk
purchases, please contact W. W. Norton Special Sales at
specialsales@wwnorton.com or 800-233-4830

Manufacturing by LSC Harrisonburg
Book design by Cassandra Pappas
Production manager: Devon Zahn
Maps by Valeria Vitale

Library of Congress Cataloging-in-Publication Data
Hall, Edith, 1959–
  Introducing the ancient Greeks : from Bronze Age seafarers to navigators of the
western mind / Edith Hall. — First edition.
       pages cm
  Includes bibliographical references and index.
  ISBN 978-0-393-23998-0 (hardcover)
  1. Greece—History—To 146 B.C. 2. Greece—History—146 B.C.–323 A.D.
  3. Greece—Civilization—To 146 B.C. I. Title.
  DF214.H26 2014
  938—dc23

                                                2014005740

ISBN 978-0-393-35116-3 pbk.

W. W. Norton & Company, Inc.,
500 Fifth Avenue, New York, N.Y. 10110
www.wwnorton.com

W. W. Norton & Company Ltd.
15 Carlisle Street, London W1D 3BS

     5 6 7 8 9 0

To My Family

—As some grave Tyrian trader, from the sea,
Descried at sunrise an emerging prow
Lifting the cool-hair'd creepers stealthily,
The fringes of a southward-facing brow
Among the Aegean isles;
And saw the merry Grecian coaster come,
Freighted with amber grapes, and Chian wine,
Green bursting figs, and tunnies steep'd in brine;
And knew the intruders on his ancient home,
The young light-hearted Masters of the waves . . .

—MATTHEW ARNOLD, *The Scholar Gypsy*, 231–40

Contents

Preface

Between 800 and 300 BC, people who spoke Greek made a rapid series of intellectual discoveries that propelled the Mediterranean world to a new level of civilization. This process of self-education was much admired by the Greeks and Romans of the centuries that followed. As this book explains, however, the history of the ancient Greeks began eight hundred years before this period of accelerated progress, and survived for at least seven centuries afterward. When the texts and artworks of classical Greece were rediscovered in the European Renaissance, they changed the world for a second time.

The phenomenon has been called the Greek "miracle," as well as the "glory" or "wonder" that was Greece. Many books have been entitled *The Greek Genius, The Greek Triumph, The Greek Enlightenment, The Greek Experiment, The Greek Idea,* and even *The Greek Ideal.* But over the last two decades the notion that the Greeks were exceptional has been questioned. It has been stressed that the Greeks were, after all, just one of many ethnic and linguistic groups in the ancient Mediterranean world. Long before the Greeks appeared in the historical record, several complicated civilizations had arisen—the Mesopotamians and Egyptians, the Hattians and Hittites. Other peoples provided the Greeks with crucial technological advances; they learned the phonetic alphabet from the Phoenicians and how to mint coins from the Lydians. They may have learned how to compose elaborate cult hymns from the Luwians. During the period when the Greeks invented rational philosophy and science, after 600 BC, their horizons were opened up by the expansion of the Persian Empire.

In the late nineteenth and twentieth centuries, our understanding of the other cultures of the ancient Near East advanced rapidly. We know far more about the minds of the Greeks' predecessors and neighbors than we did before the landmark discovery of the *Epic of Gilgamesh* on clay tablets in the Tigris Valley in 1853. There has been a constant stream of newly published writings in the languages of the successive peoples who dominated the fertile plains of Mesopotamia (Sumerians, Akkadians, Babylonians, Assyrians). The words of Hittites on the tablets found at Hattuša in central Turkey and the phrases inscribed on clay tablets at Ugarit in northern Syria have been deciphered. New texts as well as fresh interpretations of writings by the ancient Egyptians continue to appear, requiring, for example, a reassessment of the importance of the Nubians to North African history.

Many of these exciting advances have revealed how much the Greeks shared with their predecessors and neighbors. Painstaking comparative studies have been published that reveal the Greek "miracle" to have been one constituent of a continuous process of intercultural exchange. The Greeks were innovators, but they could never have made the progress they did without adopting many of their skills, ideas, and practices from their non-Greek neighbors. It has become a new orthodoxy that the Greeks were very similar to their ancient Near Eastern neighbors in Mesopotamia, Egypt, the Levant, Persia, and Asia Minor. Some scholars have gone so far as to ask whether the Greeks came up with anything new at all, or whether they merely acted as a conduit through which the combined wisdom of all the civilizations of the eastern Mediterranean was disseminated across the territories conquered by Alexander the Great, before arriving at Rome and posterity. Others have seen sinister racist motives at work, and accused classicists of creating in their own image the Oldest Dead White European Males; some have even claimed that classicists have systematically distorted and concealed the evidence showing how much the ancient Greeks owed to Semitic and African peoples rather than to Indo-European traditions.

The question has thus become painfully politicized. Critics of colonialism and racism tend to play down the specialness of the ancient

Greeks. Those who still maintain that there was something identifiably different and even superior about the Greeks, on the other hand, are usually conservatives who have a vested interest in proving the superiority of Western ideals and in making evaluative judgments of culture. My problem is that I fit into neither camp. I am certainly opposed to colonialism and racism, and have investigated reactionary abuses of the classical tradition. But my constant engagement with the ancient Greeks and their culture has made me more, rather than less, convinced that they evinced a cluster of brilliant qualities that are difficult to identify in combination and in such concentration elsewhere in Mediterranean or ancient Near Eastern antiquity. After an outline of these qualities in the introduction, the ten chapters of the book take us on a chronological journey through important points in Greek history. These also involve a geographical journey, since the center of Greek activity and achievement shifted over time from the peninsula and islands that constitute the Greek nation today to significant communities in Italy, Asia, Egypt, Libya, and the Black Sea worlds. But most of the ancient Greeks, however scattered across time and space, shared most of these qualities most of the time. In this book I try to explain what I understand these qualities to be.

Taken singly, most Greek achievements can be paralleled in the culture of at least one of their neighbors. The Babylonians had known about Pythagoras's theorem centuries before Pythagoras was born. The tribes of the Caucasus had brought mining and metallurgy to unprecedented levels. The Hittites had made advances in chariot technology, but they were also highly literate. They recorded the polished and emotive orations delivered on formal occasions in their royal court, and their carefully argued legal speeches. One Hittite king adumbrated Greek historiography when he chronicled in detail his frustration at the incompetence of some of his military officers during the siege of a Hurrian city. The Phoenicians were just as great seafarers as any Greeks. The Egyptians told *Odyssey*-like stories about sailors who went missing and returned after adventures overseas. Pithy fables similar to those of Aesop were composed in an archaic Aramaic dialect of Syria and housed in Jewish temples. Architectural design concepts and technical know-how came from the Persians to the Greek world via the many Ionian Greek workmen, named *Yauna* in Persian texts, who helped build Persepolis, Susa, and Pasargadae. But none of these peoples produced anything quite equivalent to Athenian democracy, comic theater, philosophical logic, or Aristotle's *Nicomachean Ethics*.

I do not deny that the Greeks acted as a conduit for other ancient peoples' achievements. But to function successfully as a conduit, channel, or intermediary is in itself to perform an exceptional role. It requires a range of talents and resources. Taking over someone else's technical knowledge requires an opportunistic ability to identify a serendipitous find or encounter, excellent communicative skills, and the imagination to see how a technique, story, or object could be adapted to a different linguistic and cultural milieu. In this sense, the Romans fruitfully took over substantial achievements of their civilization from the Greeks, as did the Renaissance Humanists. *Of course* the Greeks were not by nature or in potential superior to any other human beings, either physically or intellectually. Indeed, they themselves often commented on how difficult it was to distinguish Greek and non-Greek, let alone free person from slave, if all the trappings of culture, clothing, and adornment were removed. But that does not mean they were not the right people, in the right place, at the right time, to take up the human baton of intellectual progress for several hundred years.

This book attempts to give an account of the ancient Greeks spanning two thousand years, from about 1600 BC to AD 400. They lived in thousands of different villages, towns, and cities, from Spain to India, from the freezing river Don in the northeastern corner of the Black Sea to remote upland tributaries of the Nile. They were culturally elastic, for they often freely intermarried with other peoples; they had no sense of an ethnic inequality that was biologically determined, since the concepts of distinct "races" had not been invented. They tolerated and even welcomed imported foreign gods. What united them was never geopolitics, either. With the arguable exception of the short-lived Macedonian Empire in the later fourth century BC, there never was a recognizable independent state run by Greek speakers, centered in and including what we now know as Greece, until after the Greek War of Independence in the early nineteenth century. What the ancient Greeks shared was their polysyllabic and flexible language, which still survives today, in similar form, despite centuries of serial occupations of Greek-speaking regions by Romans, Ottomans, Venetians, and others. The stamina of this language, by the mid-eighth century BC, was underpinned by the universal Greek familiarity with certain poems composed in it, especially those of Homer and Hesiod. The major gods celebrated in these poems were taken by the ancient Greeks wherever they settled, and worshipped in sanctuaries with sacrifices. But this book sets out to answer a single question: Beyond their cultural absorbency, their language, their myths and Olympian polytheism, what exactly did the ancient Greeks, living in hundreds of diverse communities scattered across so many coasts and islands, ever have in common?

Acknowledgments

I would like to thank Maria Guarnaschelli and Mitchell Kohles at Norton for their enthusiasm for the project and unending patience. Janet Byrne was a superlative copy editor who improved the book enormously. Paul Cartledge's incisive and humorous comments on the whole book proved indispensable, although I have stubbornly not heeded his advice on every single occasion. My father, Stuart Hall, read the last chapter in detail and provided me with invaluable suggestions for improving it. My mother, Brenda Hall, helped me with gathering the data for the maps and timeline. Valeria Vitale designed the maps. R. Ross Holloway and Laura Monros-Gaspar lent generous assistance with tracking down images. Yana Sistovari has been an unfailingly sympathetic and entertaining companion on visits to archaeological sites. My views on the ancient Greeks have developed in lively discussion with students over the last twenty-five years at the universities of Cambridge, Reading, Oxford, Durham, and Royal Holloway and at King's College, London. I thank them all. But the book could not have been written without the day-to-day support and encouragement of my husband, Richard Poynder, and the humorous commentary of our children, Sarah and Georgia.

Greeks of the
ancient Aegean Sea

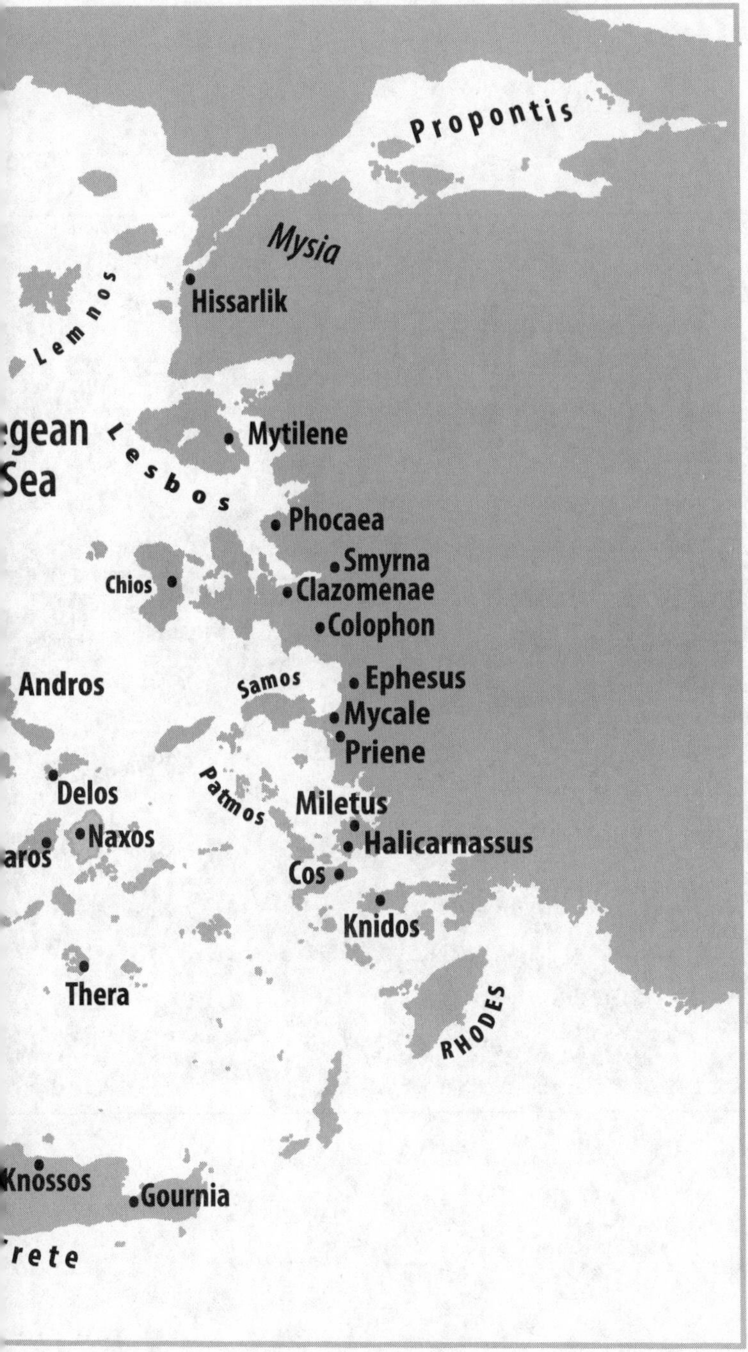

Propontis

Mysia

Lemnos

Hissarlik

Aegean
Sea

Lesbos

Mytilene

Phocaea

Smyrna
Clazomenae
Colophon

Chios

Andros

Samos

Ephesus
Mycale
Priene

Patmos

Delos

Miletus

Naxos

Paros

Halicarnassus

Cos

Knidos

Thera

RHODES

Knossos

Gournia

Crete

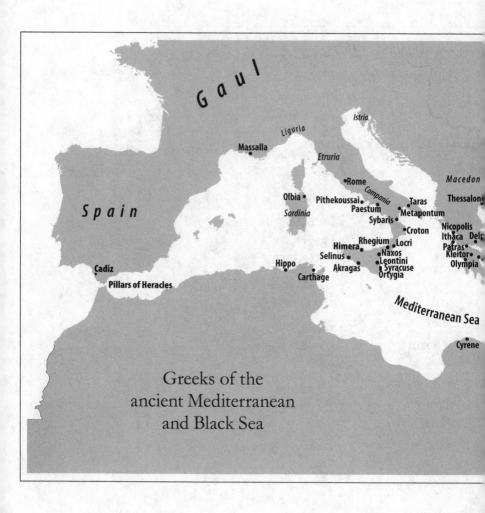

Greeks of the
ancient Mediterranean
and Black Sea

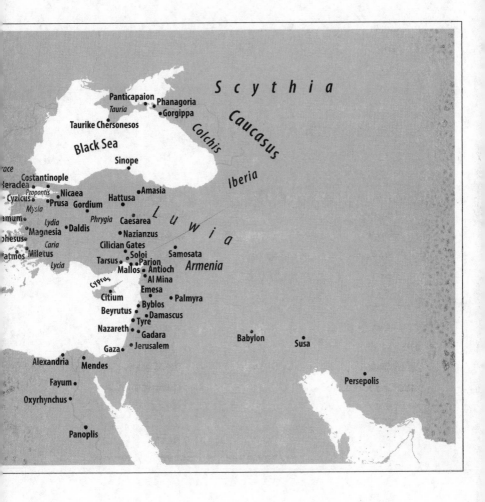

Timeline

BC

c. 1550   Mycenaean Greek civilization begins

c. 1450   Destruction of pre-Greek Minoan Palaces; the Mycenaeans, using Linear B script, are ascendant in mainland Greece and Crete

c. 1200   The collapse of Mycenaean palace civilization

c. 1050   Poseidon's sanctuary at Isthmia in operation

c. 950   Toumba cemetery built at Lefkandi, Euboea

776   Foundation of the games at sanctuary of Zeus in Olympia

c. 770   Greeks begin to use the Phoenician phonetic alphabet

c. 630   Foundation of Cyrene in Libya

c. 625   Birth of Thales of Miletus

594   Solon's reforms at Athens

582   Inauguration of the Panhellenic Pythian games at Delphi; Inauguration of Panhellenic Isthmian games at Isthmia

c. 575   Foundation of Massalia

573   Inauguration of the Panhellenic Nemean games at Nemea

c. 546   Cyrus the Great of Persia overthrows Croesus and conquers Lydia

c. 534   Foundation of Elea in south Italy

528   Death of Athenian tyrant Peisistratus

(continued)

(continued)

73–63   Third Mithridatic war ends with Mithridates ordering his
         attendant to kill him

   31   Cleopatra VII of Egypt and her husband and ally Mark
         Antony are defeated by Octavian (soon to become Augustus)
         at the battle of Actium

AD

c. 30   The crucifixion of Jesus

  50   St. Paul writes the first Epistle to the Thessalonians

c. 61   The Gospel according to Mark is written

66–73   Jewish revolt against Rome

  96   Assassination of the Roman emperor Domitian

c. 108   Arrian records the teachings of the Stoic philosopher
         Epictetus

131–32   Hadrian organizes a group of Greek cities under the heading
         Panhellenion

c. 160   Pausanias writes his *Description of Greece*

161–66   War between Rome and Parthia

267–74   Zenobia is queen of Palmyra and revolts against Rome

  301   Armenia adopts Christianity as official religion

  312   Constantine's soldiers fight under standards bearing the
         Christian monogram

  325   Constantine invites Christian bishops to the Council of
         Nicaea

  349   Libanius is appointed Sophist of Constantinople

  354   Libanius settles in Antioch

  363   Death of the last pagan emperor Julian (the Apostate);
         Libanius's obituary for Julian

  365   Earthquake and tidal waves destroy Alexandria

380–91   Edicts of Theodosius I forbid pagan religious practices

  395   The Delphic oracle is closed down; final partition of the
         Roman Empire

Introducing the
ANCIENT GREEKS

Drawing of the Tomb of the Diver at Paestum by Alice Walsh, reproduced from p. 366 of R. Ross Holloway, "The Tomb of the Diver," in *American Journal of Archaeology* 100, no. 3 (2006): 365–88. (*Courtesy of Archaeological Institute of America and American Journal of Archaeology*)

Ten Characteristics of the Ancient Greeks

M ost ancient Greeks shared ten particular qualities most of the time. Of these, the first four—that they were seagoing, suspicious of authority, individualistic, and inquiring—are tightly interconnected and the most important. They were also open to new ideas, witty, and competitive. They admired excellence in talented people, as well as being wildly articulate and addicted to pleasure. But here we run up against a problem in modern attitudes toward writing about the past. Some scholars prefer to downplay the role of individual excellence in the shaping of history, instead emphasizing economic, social, or political tendencies manifested across populations or social strata. This type of account assumes that history is uncomplicated enough to be understood without acknowledging individual brains as well as broad contexts, and asking how they interact. Let me explain how my account differs. If the philosopher Aristotle, for example, had not been born into a medical family favored by the Macedonian monarchs, whose power was based on new wealth from gold mines, he might never have enjoyed the leisure, resources, travel, and education that went into his intellectual formation. He certainly would not have encountered men like Alexander the Great, with the military power to change the world. But that does not mean that Aristotle's intellectual achievements are not, frankly, awe-inspiring.

Throughout this book I try to show the connections between the contribution made to the emergence of outstanding individual Greeks—Pericles and Leonidas, Ptolemy I and Plutarch—by the social and historical contexts into which they were born, and by the ten features of the ancient Greeks' mind-set that I think defined them as an ethnic group. The ten contexts in which the narrative of ancient Greek history is here discussed are the Mycenaean world from 1600 to about 1200 BC (chapter 1), the emergence of the Greek identity between the tenth and the eighth centuries (chapter 2), the era of colonization and tyrants in the seventh and sixth (chapter 3), the early scientists in Ionia and Italy in the sixth and fifth (chapter 4), democratic Athens in the fifth (chapter 5), Sparta in the early fourth, Macedonia in the later fourth (chapters 6 and 7), Hellenistic kingdoms in the third to first centuries (chapter 8), Greeks under the Roman Empire (chapter 9), and the relationship between pagan Greeks and early Christians leading up to the triumph of the new monotheistic faith at the end of the fourth century AD (chapter 10). In each chapter, starting with the Mycenaeans' skill as mariners, I also give special attention to the aspect of Greekness among the ten I here identify that I consider, in that context, particularly conspicuous. This is not to say that other ancient Mediterranean civilizations did not share some of the characteristics I think in combination defined the Greeks. The mystery of the debt owed by Greek culture to the literate trading Phoenicians, for example, is necessarily addressed at some length in this introduction. But almost all of the ten "Greek" characteristics were present, to a varying degree, in most Greeks most of the time.

It is incontestable that the ancient Greeks were enthusiastic seafarers. In 490 BC the important Greek city of Eretria was burned to the ground by the invading Persians, and its population taken captive, never to return. The Persian king made the Greek prisoners found a colony far inland, between Babylon and Susa. A poem attributed to the philosopher Plato imagines their collective tombstone inscription in Asiatic exile:

We left the deep roar of the Aegean Sea
And lie here in the central plain of Ecbatana.

We salute you, Eretria, once our famed fatherland.
We salute you, Athens, neighbour of Eretria. We salute you, beloved sea.

The Eretrians' destroyed fatherland had been a harbor town. But ancient Greeks hardly ever settled more than twenty-five miles—a day's walk—from the sea. Early Greeks lived in hundreds of small communities that were autonomous and independent-minded, practicing a way of life that was the inevitable response to their physical environment. Most of the farmable land in the Greek peninsula and islands is isolated by mountains, or sea, or both. There are only twenty-five thousand square miles in Greece today, which means it is smaller than all but ten of the states in the United States and much smaller than Portugal or Scotland. But Greece contains no fewer than twenty-six areas where the land rises higher than three thousand feet, making travel by land endlessly challenging. Moreover, the number of headlands, inlets, and islands makes the proportion of coastline to land area higher than in any other country in the world.

The Greeks felt trapped when they were far inland, and traveled hundreds of miles to find places to build towns that had easy access to the sea. Their communities therefore came to line many of the shores of the Mediterranean and the Black Sea and their islands. They were one of the most littoral peoples the planet has ever seen. Their preferred mode of transport was by ship, although they also preferred not to sail too far from land. As Plato put it, they chose to live "like frogs or ants around the pond." They were cultural amphibians. The notion of the creature that is at home on land and in the sea was imaginatively displaced, in myth, onto the sea's actual inhabitants, who were usually imagined by the Greeks as half human and half beast—Glaucus, once a fisherman, ate a special herb and became the original merman, half man and half fish, with green-blue skin.

At the end of the thirteenth century BC, the Egyptian king Merneptah had an inscription set up at the Karnak temple complex to celebrate his victory over a group he calls "Peoples from the Sea," who almost certainly included Greeks. Seafaring was intimately bound up with the ancient Greeks' own sense of identity. In the epic *Iliad*, Homer introduces the earliest account of the people who were the ancient

[handwritten margin note: situated on the shore of the sea or lake]

Greeks. It is a list of the communities who in the mid-eighth century regarded themselves as being united because they could enjoy poetry in Greek and had long ago fought together in the siege of Troy. It formed the very core of the Greek sense of self for at least twelve centuries subsequently. But it is not structured as a list of geographical places, or tribes, or dynastic families. It takes the form of a catalogue of *ships*.

Nearly fifty years ago, in June 1968, a beautiful image of a diver was discovered in a tomb of the early fifth century BC excavated at Posidonia (Paestum) in the part of southern Italy that Greeks had colonized. Indeed, they were Greeks who had moved on, having already built one colony farther south in Italy, the city of Sybaris, famed for its luxury. The diver was painted on the underside of the lid of a rectangular tomb. On its four walls were painted equally beautiful scenes of men enjoying themselves on couches at a symposium. The man buried in the tomb, surrounded by his drinking companions, would be able to look forever at a picture of a diver suspended between a stone-built diving board and the inviting turquoise water into which his outstretched hands are about to plunge.

Some have said that the dive has an erotic message. For others, the scene of diving is a metaphor for dying, for the leap between the known and the unknown worlds, between the elements, perhaps with occult resonances connected with Orphism or Pythagoreanism. But the painter has taken the trouble to add just a slight growth of hair to the diver's chin in specially diluted paint. The diver is touchingly young. Did he look at all like the deceased? Could he simply have been famous for his skill at diving?

The Greeks' sense that they were masters of the sea is also expressed in their attitude to swimming. The Athenians believed it was the duty of every father personally to teach his sons how to read and how to swim: The proverb characterizing the most uneducated type of man said he could "neither read nor swim." The Assyrians and Hebrews both portray their enemies drowning, but the Greeks' conviction that they were the best swimmers in the world was a core constituent of their collective identity. They felt this was proved during the Persian Wars in the fifth century BC, when many of the enemy had drowned; the Greeks also celebrated the notable exploits of two expert

Greek divers—Skyllias and his daughter Hydne—who had sabotaged the enemy fleet from underwater. The Greeks had developed the science of diving to a sufficiently high level to enable practitioners to stay below water, for considerable lengths of time, with the aid of inverted air containers lowered to them by force.

The heroes of Greek myth whom the young were trained to admire were outstanding divers and swimmers. Theseus, the son of Poseidon and mythical founder of the Athenian democracy, proved his mettle on the voyage to Crete before he even met the Minotaur. He accepted a challenge to dive down to the depths and retrieve Minos's ring from the palace of his father. But even Theseus's feat was outdone by Odysseus's distance swim after his raft broke up. He used raw muscle power to resist the line of breakers crashing on the shore of Scherie and keep away from land the coast he could find a landing-place free of rocks and turbulent winds.

Unsurprisingly, the Greeks used metaphors to do with the sea, ships, and sailing for almost every sphere of activity. In the *Iliad*, when the Greek army goes into battle it looks "like a wave rearing close-ranked out of the sea under the blast of the west wind." The sight of Odysseus to his lonely wife, Penelope, who has not seen him for decades, is like the first glimpse of land to a shipwrecked mariner. But the seashore was also a place where Greek heroes like to think, which perhaps made it inevitable that maritime imagery would become common in descriptions of thought processes. Nestor, the wise old counselor in the *Iliad*, faced with a strategic problem on the battlefield, pondered the alternatives deeply, "like the vast sea when it darkens with a silent surge before swift shrill winds arise, but it doesn't roll forward at all nor to either side until Zeus brings the gale to a critical point." The king in a tragedy by Aeschylus, faced with an international crisis, says he needs to engage in profound deliberation, "like a diver descending into the depth." To read a treatise on philosophy was to go on a voyage: When Diogenes the Cynic philosopher came to the end of a long and unintelligible book, he said with sardonic relief, "I can see land!" In Plato's *Republic* Socrates is trying to persuade Glaucon of his controversial views on women and children. To express the difficulty of the philosophical challenge, he chooses a swimming analogy.

"Whether someone falls into a small swimming-pool or into the middle of the largest sea, he must still swim all the same." Dealing with a philosophical challenge requires argumentation regardless of the triviality or weightiness of the topic.

The very earliest Greek literature, dating from four centuries before Plato, already shows ethical issues such as guilt and responsibility being explored at an extremely sophisticated, proto-philosophical, and indeed *politicized* level. The second outstanding feature of the ancient Greek mind-set that we shall encounter repeatedly is their suspicion of authority, which found expression in their advanced political sensibility. This quality receives special attention in chapter 2, "The Creation of Greece." In the *Iliad*, the right of any one individual or group to determine the whole community's actions is questioned more than once by members of the Greek army at Troy. When the Greek soldier Thersites, who is not a king, wants to persuade his compatriots at Troy to return home, we are told that he uses his customary tactic of "railing at all who were in authority." He tries to make the others *laugh* at their leader. But Odysseus pours expert scorn on Thersites and manages to get the army's laughter directed at the protestor rather than at Agamemnon, Thersites' target. Although Thersites' mutiny fails, the inclusion in the *Iliad* of his criticism of Agamemnon's privileges hurls the epic's audience into political consciousness.

Leaders are consistently scrutinized by Greek authors and usually found wanting. Odysseus faces a near-mutiny in the *Odyssey*, on Circe's island. He had sent out a reconnaissance cadre of twenty-two men led by Eurylochus, who returns to report that all the others in the advance party have been turned into swine. Eurylochus, reasonably enough, discourages the remaining crewmen from taking such a risk themselves and issues a stern rebuke to Odysseus. Even the Spartans, who were no democrats, suspected rulers who gave themselves airs and graces. When two Spartans named Sperthias and Bulis were on an embassy to the Persian king, whose court was hierarchical and run according to elaborate ceremonial protocols, his courtiers tried to make them perform the prostration or *salaam* before him that he expected of his subjects. The Spartans absolutely refused, explaining that Greeks reserved such obeisance for images of gods, and, besides, it was not for this reason that they had come.

The undoubted "stroppy" streak in the Greek character raises the question of whether it was shared by their women. In classical democracies, where the rebellious tendency became constitutionally actualized, there is evidence to support this view. Thucydides tells us that during the revolution in Kerkyra (Corfu), the women of democratic families climbed the roofs of their houses, joining in the fight and hurling down tiles onto the heads of their oligarchic opponents below. The speeches that survive from the ancient courts of law also show that although their legal rights were shockingly few, women operated in determined and devious ways to maximize their influence. Ancient Greek men may have wanted their women to be docile and retiring. But the force and frequency with which they enunciated this ideal of femininity suggest that women did not always embrace it.

How the Greeks reconciled their suspicion of authority with their almost universal acceptance of slavery presents a greater challenge. The slaves in Greek comedy "talk back" to their masters, and critics of democracy complained that slaves in Athens enjoyed so much license that it was difficult to distinguish them from the free. Brutally mistreated slaves, for example the helots at Sparta, escaped or revolted the minute they were able. But there is another factor that needs to be taken into account, and that is the paradoxical link between the Greeks' independent streak and their ownership of slaves. The word for freedom, *eleutheria*, means the opposite of the word for slavery. It meant collective freedom from rule by another people, such as the Persians, but it also meant individual liberty. Even the poorest citizens of Greek states possessed precious rights as free men, *eleutheroi*, which they would lose if enslaved. Moreover, the fear of slavery was an ever-present reality for everybody in antiquity; the earliest private letter by a Greek that has survived is a desperate plea by a father, about to be enslaved and deprived of his property, to his son Protagoras. It was written on a plate of lead by a Greek living in the north of the Black Sea in the early fifth century BC. We must wonder whether a society that did not have slave ownership at its core could ever have produced such a strong definition of individual freedom, as Orlando Patterson asked in *Freedom in the Making of Western Culture* (1991).

The idea of individual freedom underlies the third characteristic of the ancient Greeks instrumental in their intellectual progress: a marked sense of individual independence, of pride in their separate selfhood and individuality, which I explore in chapter 3 in connection with the age of colonization and of the replacement of monarchies by tyrants. In a treatise entitled *Airs, Waters and Places*, the medical writer Hippocrates even suggested that the physical variation between individuals in Europe (especially Greece) as opposed to Asia was connected with the greater extremes of climate and landscape. These produce, Hippocrates argued, rugged individualists with powers of both physical and psychological endurance, preparedness to take risks for individual self-advantage but not on behalf of someone else, independence of mind, and intolerance of kings.

Hesiod's *Theogony*, or *Birth of the Gods*, perhaps the oldest surviving Greek poem, begins in the first-person plural, "let *us* begin to sing." Yet we are soon introduced by name to Hesiod, to whom the Muses "taught glorious song while he was shepherding his lambs beneath sacred Helicon." Two lines later, "Hesiod" is in turn replaced by the first-person singular: "and this word first the goddesses said to *me*." The songs of the lyric poets of the seventh and sixth centuries revel in the individual names, personae, and subjectivity of their authors. Archilochus the soldier makes poetry out of his personal preferences in a military leader: "*I* do not like my general to be tall or mincing or proud of his hair or clean-shaven. For *me*, let him be short, bow-legged, his feet firmly planted, full of heart." Sappho tells us her name, how she feels physically when watching her lover, and that she has a treasured daughter called Cleis. The ancient Greeks, moreover, invented the self-conscious *theorizing* of the "I" voice, in Plato's assault on the speciousness of direct speech in his *Republic*. Greek philosophy also encouraged individuals to develop their interior selves as moral agents. This in due course produced the first surviving extended literary constitutions of the self-through-writing in St. Paul's *Epistles* and the Stoic emperor Marcus Aurelius's *Meditations* (actually entitled *To Myself*). Both these seminal texts were written, of course, in Greek.

These twin imperatives of subjecting leaders to criticism while celebrating strong individuals were sometimes contradictory. The tension between them occurs in another of the large number of maritime images used by Socrates as portrayed in the writings of Plato, the acknowledged founder of Western philosophy. Although he did not invent the metaphor, Plato gives Socrates the most famous instance of the analogy of the ship of state. If there is not to be a mutiny, a ship *requires* an individual captain to steer it (our word *govern* is etymologically connected with the same root as the Greek for steer a ship, *kubernan*), but he must be endowed with superior competence in several branches of knowledge. Other kinds of ruler were seen as ships' captains. When the Greeks imagined Zeus ruling the world, they sometimes conceived him as "the helmsman" of Olympus, just as he has an epithet, "sitting high on its benches," as if Mount Olympus was a ship, in Homer. Nor was it just political theory that attracted naval analogies: so did cosmology and eschatology. The Greeks imagined the entire universe as being constructed like an enormous trireme. At the climax of the *Republic*, Socrates tells the story of Er, who had visited the land where dead souls go before miraculously returning to life. Er's description of the constitution of the universe was that it was held together by an absolutely straight column of light, which extends right through the whole of heaven and earth, binding them and reinforcing them "like the central under-girders of a trireme, thus holding together the entire revolving vault." One Greek trying to explain to another how the universe was held together here intuitively felt that it was an enormous, carefully crafted ship.

The inquiring minds of the ancient Greeks—their fourth definitive characteristic, and here discussed in relation to the first scientists and philosophers in chapter 4—were intimately connected with their experience of seafaring. The sail on a ship represents not only the understanding of the behavior of an elemental force of nature ("pure" science) but its practical application ("applied" science). The sail is the earliest human device that harnesses a non-animal force found in nature to provide energy, and remained so until the invention of the water mill, almost certainly by a Greek, in the third century BC. The energy with which a ship could speed along encouraged the Greeks to imagine that it was alive, a large animal on which they were riding, and from which they had a privileged view of the littoral world flashing by and towns they could see lining the coast. Ancient Greek ships were all given an eye or eyes, a custom that stretched back as far as the late Bronze Age. In the sixth century, Attic black-figure vase paintings often show a warship, complete with offensive ramming prow, which resembles a wild boar. In these, the eye of the ship is the eye of a charging wild animal, crashing through the waves as if through forest undergrowth to strike foes with his alarming tusks. But on other vase paintings, ships are shown that have two large, arresting eyes, one on either side of the prow, just above the waterline. The sighted ship is alive, observant, and vigilant, gathering information from both underwater and the world above as it glides toward the horizon.

Poseidon, the Greek sea deity, was connected with horses, and in this aspect he reminds us that the Greeks, regardless of the degree to which it is fair to claim that they were the first philosophers, were neither the first nor the most expert Mediterranean mariners. They had certainly seen the great horse heads decorating the prows of the ships sailed by their eastern and southern maritime rivals, the Canaanites, whom the Greeks called Phoenicians after the precious crimson-purple dye they procured from seashells. The Phoenicians had long since pioneered the trading routes of the Mediterranean. From the Levant they had sent out port settlements to secure the routes by which large cargoes of metals were moved around on slow, stable, round-hulled merchant ships, allowing them to dock in Cyprus, Carthage, Sardinia, and as far west as the Atlantic coast of Spain. They were always seeking new sources of timber with which to maintain their fleets. They were intrepid explorers and long-distance sailors: By around 600, according to a source quoted by the classical Greek historian Herodotus, the Phoenicians had even circumnavigated Africa.

The mystery of the acceleration of intellectual progress by Greek speakers in the eighth century and onward may lie at the bottom of the sea, in Phoenician shipwrecks yet to be discovered. The Phoenicians were inventive and technologically resourceful, alone among the ancient Semitic peoples in becoming expert seafarers. Like the

Greeks, they lived in independent city-states, building maritime port cities along the fertile crescent—Sidon and Tyre, Byblos and Berytus. Like the Greeks, the Phoenicians had always been adept at cultural borrowing; their surviving artifacts—carved ivories, metal bowls, razors, stone monuments, terra-cotta masks—are recognizable precisely because their styles are so eclectic, fusing elements from Greek, Assyrian, and especially Egyptian idioms.

Alongside Ba'al, the most prominent Phoenician divinity was Melquart, a hunter with special powers over the sea, whom the Greeks identified with Heracles. Herodotus even calls a temple he visited in Tyre, dedicated to Melquart, a "temple of Heracles." Within it Herodotus saw two sacred pillars of gold and emerald, and some scholars think that the double pillar was a distinctive symbol in the Phoenician religion, imitated in the Jewish temple at Jerusalem by Solomon. The Jewish monarch summoned Hiram of Tyre, a Phoenician architect and mason, who "cast two pillars of brass, of eighteen cubits high apiece" to set up in the porch of the temple (I Kings 7:15). The distinctive double pillar may even explain the ultimate origin of the idea of the Pillars of Heracles at Gibraltar. It may well be, though it cannot be proved, that beneath the famous Greek stories about Heracles' labors, especially those set in the west, there lies unknown Phoenician storytelling. Heracles' far western labors are the quests for the apples of the Hesperides and the cattle of Geryon. The remoteness of the second task is underlined by Heracles' means of transport there—he uses some kind of vessel, but it may have traveled through the air rather than on water, since it is lent to him by the Sun. When the Greeks started thinking about the ends of their known worlds, their imagination here, as often, fused sailing the sea with aerial flying. The fusion was assisted by the visual similarity they perceived between a ship being propelled along by rows of flashing oars and the rhythmical beating of a bird's feathered wings—a favorite comparison in Greek poetry.

The Greeks may have taken some of Heracles' labors from stories the Phoenicians told about their own or their god Melquart's expeditions. But there are serious obstacles to understanding the relationship between Greek and Phoenician culture. It is often claimed, for example, that the Greeks learned everything they knew about ships from the Phoenicians. Evidence for this is sometimes drawn from the eulogy of Phoenician ingenuity by the Greek Xenophon, expressed in a text from the fourth century BC in which a man is explaining the virtue of domestic tidiness:

> The most attractive and precise arrangement of equipment I have ever seen, Socrates, was when I was given a tour of the great Phoenician merchant ship. I saw a vast amount of equipment lodged separately in the smallest of spaces. . . . For a ship needs a huge number of wooden implements and ropes in order to moor safely or put out to sea; to sail she needs a great deal of what they call rigging, and she must be armed with numerous pieces of machinery to defend her against any enemy vessels, and weapons for her crew to fight with. Then there are all the cooking utensils which people use at home that are needed for each of the different messes on board.

But this beautiful description of the ship's interior does not mean that the Greeks copied the achievements of Phoenician shipwrights wholesale. None of the words for parts of ships in Greek derives from a Semitic root. More recently, naval historians have developed a revised picture that presents the two peoples as engaged in a centuries-long competitive race to outstrip each other, which inevitably involved mutual imitation.

The crucial technological innovation took place in the eighth century BC. In previous centuries, the ships of both Greeks and Phoenicians were all rowed from the single deck at the level of the upper edge of the vessel. But after adding a platform on which armed sailors could stand, the ancient shipwrights realized that they could also add one more layer of oarsmen, with longer oars, to make a bireme. The ship could be made much faster without being made longer and more difficult to maneuver. But we have no way of knowing whether it was a Phoenician or a Greek mind that first made this important discovery. There are also conflicting claims about the introduction of the ship with three layers of rowers, the trireme, a prerequisite of the rapid development of Greek navies in the fifth century BC and therefore of the Athenian empire. Some Greeks at the time claimed that the trireme was invented by a Corinthian named Ameinocles, but later sources may well be correct that it was borrowed by them from the Phoenicians of Sidon.

Another problem is the inaudibility of the Phoenicians' own voices, either from the Levant or from their Punic colony at Carthage, where there was a library, destroyed by the Romans in 146 BC. This is frustrating, because the Phoenicians and their Carthaginian offspring were literate. St. Augustine wrote in the fourth century AD, when Phoenician could still be heard in the streets of North Africa, that "many scholars attest to there having been much virtue and wisdom in the Punic books." Although the earlier Canaanites of Ugarit in the late second millennium BC wrote down myths and narrative poetry, notably a cycle of texts about Ba'al, as well as more everyday records, the relationship of these texts to the later Phoenicians remains obscure. The failure of the Phoenicians of Carthage to leave substantial written records of themselves for later historians to read has even produced a paranoid scholarly myth that they adopted a state policy of secrecy.

A few phrases in ancient Phoenician survive for us to read. A king named Kilamuwa left an inscription near the border between modern Turkey and Syria in the ninth century BC, perhaps in verse, chronicling how he had protected his people. At Pyrgi, north of Rome, inscribed golden leaves record, in both Etruscan and Phoenician, a dedication made in about AD 500 to a Phoenician goddess. But we just can't have a dialogue with the Phoenicians as we can with most ancient Near Eastern peoples. The sole candidate for a substantial text first written in Phoenician is actually in ancient Greek. It claims to be a translation of a treatise connected with a voyage that took place in the fifth century BC, *A Report of the Voyage of Hanno, King of the Carthaginians, to the Parts of Africa beyond the Straits of Gibraltar, which he dedicated in the temple of Baal.* The first half names places that can still be identified in Morocco. The second half includes fantastic ethnography, involving the flayed skin of hairy women, and is the source to which we owe the zoological term *gorilla*. Its authenticity and date have been fiercely debated, although there is no reason why it should not contain at least an echo of Hanno the Navigator's original Punic-language report.

What most obscures the picture, however, is the ambivalence of the Greeks—and Romans—toward the southern maritime super-power. They thought the Phoenician language sounded hilarious, and included characters speaking it at nonsensical length in their comedies (for example, Hanno in Plautus's Latin *The Young Carthaginian*, modeled on a Greek original). They thought that the Phoenician language had magical powers and sometimes wrote spells in a pseudo-Phoenician patois. The Phoenicians appear in early Greek literature in contradic-tory ways. The Homeric Phoenicians, realistically enough, are seago-ing traders, although Homer was presumably being unfair in implying that they were any more immoral than the Greeks. Some echoes of the Phoenicians can be also heard in Plato's fantastic story of Atlantis, Poseidon's land, the center of a seagoing confederacy that had once dominated the Mediterranean from beyond the Pillars of Heracles. The Greek apprehension of Phoenician culture informs the semisu-pernatural Phaeacians of the *Odyssey*, expert seafarers who can travel from Phaeacia to mainland Greece and return in a single day. In one fascinating passage, the Phaeacian king Alcinous (whose name means "mighty in mind"), son of Nausithous ("swift in ships"), tells Odysseus that their ships are mentally conscious and can steer themselves by their own intelligence: "Phaeacian ships have no helmsmen nor steer-ing oars, but instead they understand the minds and thoughts of men; they also know the way to all human cities and fertile plains." These verses play on the aural similarity of "ship" and "mind," which both begin with *n* and end with *s* and may ultimately have derived, in the distant past, from the same Indo-European root.

The Greeks certainly saw the Phoenicians as having taught them important skills. To explain their adoption of the Phoenician phonetic alphabet, they said that it had been introduced to Greece by Cadmus, the founder of Thebes. He originally arrived, they remembered or decided, from Phoenicia. Greeks frequently claimed themselves that their sages had connections with Phoenicia, including the first philos-opher of all, Thales of Miletus. Thales was also held to have written about navigation by the stars, and in later antiquity, strenuous attempts were made to use the Phoenicians' skill at navigation to justify the belief that the origins of rational thought had something to do with them. A Greek geographer called Strabo insisted that the Phoenicians' maritime expertise and the birth of scientific and rational thought were related. "They are philosophers in the sciences of astronomy and arithmetic, having begun their studies with practical calculations and with night-sailings; for each of these branches of knowledge concerns the merchant and the ship-owner." There is no doubt, of course, that the Greeks intimately connected the stars and ships. They had magnetite and iron but as yet no compass, and so Odysseus's sailors mostly travel at night, gauging their route by the stars. Archaic astronomical lore was turned into an oral poem by Hesiod, who had undertaken at least one voyage himself. But we can't be sure whether it was from the Phoenicians that he and his compatriots had learned about navigation, astronomy, and mathematical calculations.

In Odysseus the Greeks had a glamorous hero with expertise in navigation: Even on a humble raft, he can steer his route by the constellations. But Odysseus is a hero who symbolizes Greek intellectual prowess in other ways. He is inherently curious about the world and investigates interesting phenomena just because he encounters them. Two of the most famous incidents in the *Odyssey* explore the rewards and the dangers of wanting knowledge for the sake of it. Only once does Odysseus allow uncontrolled curiosity to get the better of him, and the ultimate consequence is the death of every single one of his men. There is no reason at all for him to visit the Cyclopes' island. He and his fleet have succeeded in catching a large number of animals on the adjacent Goat Island, which is uninhabited and unvisited, since the Cyclopes do not sail. The Greeks have access to unlimited supplies and are safe. But they have heard voices drifting over the sea, and Odysseus just can't control his desire, carefully signaled by Homer, to try the voices' owners out, "to learn who they are, whether they are insolent and wild and wicked, or hospitable and god-fearing." He takes one crew with him, and not only raids Polyphemus's cave but lingers on out of curiosity to see what the giant is like. Although he escapes with some of his men, it is the blinding of Polyphemus that causes Poseidon to curse Odysseus and eventually results in the loss of all his ships' crews.

What a difference, therefore, by the time Odysseus succumbs to his second serious bout of curiosity! Symbolizing the entire future of philosophical inquiry, he is determined to hear the Sirens, who "know all that happens on the rich earth," thus transcending all normal limitations of time and place, even though this could put him into mortal jeopardy. So Odysseus negotiates a compromise between curiosity (there is no actual need for him to hear the Sirens' omniscient song) and *applied* intelligence, or scientific inventiveness. He asks himself how he can intervene to stop the Sirens' song from endangering him and his crew, and comes up with practical solutions; he makes his men insert wax stoppers in their ears to prevent them from hearing the song at all, and orders them to bind him to the mast so that he cannot jump out of the ship to destruction. Odysseus here conducts a controlled experiment to test the hypothesis that the Sirens can increase his knowledge, but without jeopardizing his men's lives. It is implied that with sufficient forethought, preparation, and caution, uninhibited curiosity even about the most dangerous of topics can indeed be indulged. This is why, for the Greeks, to voyage was to gain knowledge. The third line of the *Odyssey* says that its hero "had seen the cities of many human beings and learned about their *minds*."

Before we leave the Greeks' inquisitiveness, there is a quartet of features of ancient Greek analytical thought that seem to me to have helped them understand the "cities and minds" of all the peoples they encountered and thus facilitated their rapid intellectual progress. The first is that their flexible tongue gave them a wider range than most modern languages of ways to express causality, consequence, and sophisticated grades of overlap between them. The second is their love of analogy—of looking for resemblances between different spheres of activity or experience that would mutually illuminate one another, such as all the metaphors equating maritime and intellectual motion. The third is the opposite love of polarity: The Greeks apprehended the world whole by breaking it down into polarized entities and had a special pair of syntactical markers that they inserted into clauses that they wished to be understood antithetically. These syntactical markers are used, for example, to heighten the impact of the two perfectly balanced clauses of the proverb that the Lydian king Croesus uttered when regretting that he had waged war on Persia: "In peacetime sons bury their fathers, but in wartime fathers bury their sons." One of the first philosophers, Pythagoras, even drew up a "table of opposites" to help his students analyze phenomena: odd vs. even, light vs. dark, male vs. female, etc. The Greeks' love of polarity was so strong that instead of a collective term they often simply referred to the two opposing parts of a single phenomenon: Instead of "the whole human race," for example, they almost always preferred to say "both the Greeks and the barbarians."

The fourth type of argument that was more instrumental in their philosophy than any other is the principle of the *unity* of opposites. Two things or forces that look to be in opposition or contradiction may also be unified, or indeed it may be the very contradiction between them that determines their permanent state of interaction. Centripetal force can only be understood in combination with centrifugal force; concave in relation to convex. The ancient Greek mind really does seem to have had fewer problems with the concept of the interaction and unity of opposites than the modern Western mind, at least the modern Anglo-American mind, which is doggedly empirical. The unity of opposites is easier to understand in terms of myth and religion than in terms of philosophy. Take the figure of the prophet Tiresias, who is blind because he can actually "see" far more of the truth than sighted people. Or consider the dichotomy of crime and punishment: Christianity presupposes an all-virtuous father god, whose Messianic son was also virtuous, and he punishes his opposites—the wicked. But in ancient Greece, the heroes and gods responsible for policing particular misdemeanors tend to have been perpetrators of similar crimes themselves. The incestuous father-killer Oedipus, for example, became a cult hero involved in *preventing* incest and parricide. The mother Medea, who founds a cult near Corinth in which women can pray for the safety of their children, is actually a child killer herself: Good mother and bad mother are mutually defining, and therefore unified, concepts. They are "two sides of the same coin." The origins of this manner of thinking may be connected with euphemism, in its original, technical sense. Since naming a feared power could activate it or arouse its enmity, the Greeks addressed as "Kindly Ones" the hideous female personifications of violent revenge or curses, the Erinyes (Furies). Curses are obviously blessings when they are not activated as curses.

The unity of opposites, already articulated in myth and cult, explains one tendency in early Greek philosophy. It was Heraclitus who saw that the sea is both pure and polluted, encompassing opposites. For fish it is pure and therefore beneficial; for humans it is harmful. It was Empedocles who argued that the physical world, which lives and dies, is in a constant state of alternation between separation and coming together, under the influence of two opposing but dialectically unified forces that he called Love and Strife. It was Aristotle who saw that you did not have to *act* to be guilty of doing something unethical: By *omitting* to do something you could do just as much damage as by *committing* something else. Culpability can rest both on Doing and on Not Doing.

One manifestation of the ancient Greeks' inquisitiveness was the fifth characteristic, which, I believe, in combination with the others, made them distinctive: a certain mental *openness*. Because they loved to travel and habitually lived close to the sea, they consistently put themselves in positions that maximized their exposure to other cultures and took swift advantage of the chance to learn skills from other peoples and to experiment with completely new techniques and ideas themselves. The ancient Greek word for "opening," *anoixis*, which lingers on in the modern Greek word for the season of spring, which "opens" the year, has several meanings. It can mean the moment when a ship sails clear of the land and finds its route on the open sea, and it can also designate the arrival *or first full understanding* of an idea in the human mind. Enlightenment and control of the sea were inseparable constituents of Athenian identity. But when ancient Jewish and Christian authors wrote in Greek, as they so often did in the Mediterranean world, they sometimes used the word *anoixis* as an equivalent of the key concept of "equality in the right to speak," *parrhesia*, which was a core element of many Greek constitutions, especially identified with Athenian democracy—which is why I have chosen to focus on openness in connection with classical Athenians (chapter 5). Having a society sufficiently open to hearing honest expressions of different points of view is an idea that many Greeks cherished. It has had a long future.

Openness to foreign influence, novelty, and candid expressions of conflicting opinions are all associated with a tendency toward emotional honesty. A reason why ancient Athenian drama has enjoyed such a revival in the theaters of the modern world is that its pre-Christian ethics often seem refreshingly honest about emotions. Baby boomers and their children have generally preferred to deal with their darker urges—anger, revenge, lust, envy—by admitting to them rather than by repression or denial. Early Greek thinkers had the advantage of a degree of clarity about human passions that did not become possible again until after Freud. The Greeks, for example, had a profound respect for sex, which they talked about frankly, and knew exactly how far it could make people go, as their obscene comedy and some tragic myths illustrate. Many of their myths portray warriors—trained killers—failing to cope with anger. When a general named Gylippus addresses the Syracusans before they joined battle with the invading Athenians, he urges them that "in dealing with our enemy it is both just and lawful to claim the right to slake the fury in our soul." In chilling words that provoked moral outrage in Christian scholars, he adds that vengeance provides the "most acute of all pleasures." In Plato's *Republic*, Socrates makes his interlocutor acknowledge the murderous hatred that slaves, at any rate those held in large numbers, inevitably felt toward their owners. But the Greek emotional term for which I most wish there was an English equivalent is *phthonos*—or envy, mixed with delight in the misfortunes of those one envies: envy plus Schadenfreude. No Greek would ever deny that a beggar would enjoy seeing a rich man in trouble. As Dionysius of Halicarnassus put it, "No generous thoughts can occur in a man deprived of the daily necessities of life." The Greeks' emotional honesty can make them seem callous and mean, but they hardly ever come across as hypocritical.

It is easier to practice psychological honesty about dark aspects of human existence with the protective shield of laughter, and humor is the sixth of the Greek characteristics I emphasize, in the context of the Spartans (chapter 6). They used pointed Laconic wit to help maintain the morale of their warrior culture. But the Spartans were not the only amusing Greeks: In classical Athens there was a special drinking club whose members were all famous raconteurs. Philip II of Macedon, who enjoyed a laugh, once offered them a talent, or silver money bar, and asked them to write down their jokes and send them to him, presumably so he could perform them at one of his uproarious palace banquets. The Greeks invented the idea of the joke collection, and one example of such a book survives from the third century AD, the *Philogelos*, or Laughter-Lover. Incompetent professionals form one group about whom jokes were told: An incompetent schoolteacher, when asked the name of the mother of Priam, king of Troy, said, "I suggest that you call her Madam."

When the Greeks imagined the immortals living blissfully on Olympus, they were rocking forever with "inextinguishable laughter." In an archaic hymn to Demeter attributed to Homer, the goddess of arable farming is inconsolable because her daughter Persephone has been kidnapped by Hades and dragged down to the underworld. Demeter boycotts Olympus and goes to Eleusis, but nothing can ease her pain. Then her hostess, the queen of the surrounding territory, has a brainstorm. She enlists the help of the only female stand-up comic in ancient mythology, whose name was Iambe after the rude iambic jokes she recited. Demeter finally bursts into laughter. Iambe the comedian gave her name to the poetic meter that the Greeks always used for poems of insult and satirical abuse; it probably had its origins in prehistoric festivals, in ritual obscenity and jesting. But the Greeks acknowledged many different types of drollery. If the Inuit have twenty different words for snow, the Greeks had as many that translate as "mock" or "laugh at," implying fine gradations of mischief or malice, although Aristotle argued that laughter in some circumstances was actually a sign of moral virtue. Central to the method of Socrates was humorously pointing out the absurdity in other people's philosophical arguments—*eironeia*, or "irony." The Cynics, who practiced an austere way of life and had contempt for all trappings of wealth and power, gave us the word *cynical*, which we still use to describe an attitude combining distrust and derision. Hilarious anecdotes were told in antiquity about the most famous Cynic, Diogenes. When Plato said that Socrates had defined men as "featherless bipeds," Diogenes ridiculed the notion by taking a plucked chicken into the Academy and announcing, "Behold! I bring you a Man!"

Sometimes the Greeks' use of ridicule is tiresome, especially when the target is (as often) womankind. We unfortunately do not know exactly what jokes Iambe told Demeter. But we do possess conventional satirical tirades against women, whom ancient Greek men typically professed to despise. One of Theophrastus's studies of commonly encountered personality types, in his *Characters*, is the "tactless man" whose fault is not that he likes to perform conventional rants against the female sex but that he tactlessly performs them *at weddings*. On the other hand, wit and mockery are used against the powerful—whether gods, kings, or commanding officers—in stunning displays of irreverence and moral courage that help to explain why the Greeks invented democracy as well as comic theater.

Comedies were written to be performed in festival competitions, and every comic writer aimed to beat his rivals and win the prestigious prize. The seventh characteristic component of the Greek mind-set, discussed in chapter 7 and especially pronounced among the rivalrous, bickering Macedonians, was an almost obsessive competitiveness. At Olympia, where the Olympic Games were held, there stood a statue of *Competition*, personified as a man holding jumping-weights. The Greek term for a public contest was *agon*, which came to mean "struggle" and thence produced our term *agony*. But the Greeks conceived everything, not just athletics, agonistically. Odysseus tells the most important of Penelope's suitors that he could beat him in a plowing competition. Teenage girls singing hymns to Artemis at Sparta made claims and counterclaims about which of them was the loveliest. Plato subtly sets up Socrates' dialogues with the Sophists as verbal *contests*. The competitive approach assumed a fundamental social equality between contestants, who improved their own skills by mutual emulation. One of the most resonantly Greek passages in archaic poetry is Hesiod's description, in *Works and Days*, of the two types of strife, personified in the goddess Eris. One kind leads to war and is harmful. But the other Eris "is far kinder to men. She stirs up even the lazy to labor." Farmers work hard when they see their neighbor grow rich. Potters vie with potters, craftsmen with craftsmen, and bards with bards. Even beggars compete between themselves.

The Greeks saw a logical connection between the benevolent form of strife and their passion for excellence (*arete*) in every sphere of activity, the eighth of the ten features that I believe defined their mind-set, and which motivated the Hellenistic kings of Egypt, the Ptolemies, to conceive the idea of a library at Alexandria to house the best books and the best scholars the world had ever produced (chapter 8). At Smyrna, in what is now northwest Turkey, other Hellenistic rulers even built a temple in honor of the goddess Excellence. Hesiod said that *arete* could not be achieved without much sweat. Women could cultivate *arete* in the appropriate departments: attractiveness, weaving, self-control, and fidelity. Land and animals could also possess their own kind of excellence. But the epitome of excellence in Greek myth was usually Achilles, "the *best* of the Achaeans," because he is the bravest warrior, the fastest runner, and the most beautiful. A Greek epic poet described the designs on the shield of Achilles: Excellence, a personified female, was depicted as difficult to reach, bestriding a palm tree itself planted on the summit of a mountain. But the poet with whom *arete* is most strongly associated is Pindar, author of exquisite songs in praise of victors in athletics and musical contests. The world of the victor is forever shaped by his outstanding performance at the Panhellenic games. Excellence is a divine and therefore inborn gift, but, according to Pindar, needs to be cultivated by training. Finally, the resulting display of excellence needs an excellent poet to immortalize it in an ode (which is where Pindar comes in): "*arete* lives long in splendid songs," he claims, in his third *Pythian Ode*.

The beautiful body of the champion athlete was therefore celebrated in the beautiful poetry of the champion poet. "Language is to mind what beauty is to body," said Aristides, and the Greeks' finest asset was surely their articulacy, the ninth of their qualities to strike me as defining them, manifested above all in the extraordinary flowering of Greek prose writing—of both nonfiction and fiction—under the Roman Empire (chapter 9). The Greeks themselves believed that they were incomparable at talking. They often said that it was this that made them superior to all "barbarians," a word that originally meant "people who don't speak Greek but speak unintelligibly." (Paradoxically, Greeks borrowed this word from "barbarians," since *barbaru* is a word for "foreigner" in ancient Sumerian and Babylonian.) A Homeric hero could assert his status by his oratory: The best talker of all was Odysseus, who stood absolutely still, his eyes on the ground, before he spoke in the assembly. "But as soon as he let his great voice forth from his chest, and words like snowflakes falling in winter, then no other man alive could contend with Odysseus." One of the first skills the Greeks decided could be learned systematically was the art of speaking persuasively, or rhetoric, on which the fifth-century Sicilian lawyers Tisias and Corax wrote the first of many ancient Greek specialist handbooks. The Greeks' sensual delight in their words underlies the advances they also made in the field of poetic expressivity. Along with action narrative and direct speech, even the earliest poetry shows the Greeks practicing description at the highest level. The first *locus amoenus* in Western literature, the god Hermes' description of Calypso's cave in the *Odyssey*, appeals to all five senses, including those difficult to reproduce in words—smell and taste:

There was a big fire blazing on the hearth, and through the whole island wafted the scent of burning spliced cedar wood and juniper. She was inside, singing in her lovely voice as she went to and fro at her loom, weaving with a golden shuttle. A luxuriant wood sprang up around her cave—alder and poplar and sweet-smelling cypress. Long-winged birds nested there, horned owls and hawks and cormorants with their long tongues, whose sphere of operation is the ocean. Over the arching cavern there spread a flourishing cultivated vine, with abundant grapes. There was a row of four adjacent springs, with gleaming water, their streams running off in different directions, surrounded by soft meadows that bloomed with violet and parsley.

In the twin verbal arts of rhetoric and poetry, the Greeks put words at the center of their culture. As Gorgias the Sophist put it, words were a form of enchantment that could abduct the human soul.

Tenth and last of the Greeks' core characteristics—but by no means the least—was their attitude—or, rather attitudes—to joy. Their capacity for enjoyment underlay their unabashed commitment to the pursuit of happiness, or at least to asking what made people happy. The repeated experience of founding new colonies made them think harder than permanently settled communities do about the circumstances conducive to human flourishing. The Greek philosophers liked to debate what the ideal state would be like, and their creative writers to imagine utopias and dystopias, precisely because they were incessantly creating new polities and drawing up laws, often in reaction to an unhappy situation in the cities they had abandoned. Even the most unapologetically wealthy and autocratic of the Hellenistic Greek kings liked to surround themselves with philosophers to discuss these issues. Most Greek voices we can hear, moreover, are laudably insistent that money could not buy you certain happiness (*eudaimonia*). Solon the Athenian told Croesus, the richest man in the world, that the happiest man he had ever known was an apparently ordinary Athenian named Tellus. Tellus lived to a ripe age, saw all his grandsons survive into adulthood, and died in combat for his country. By the fifth century BC, the philosopher Democritus was systematically arguing that happiness is not to be looked for in property such as a herd or gold, for one's state of mind is a property of the *soul*.

The Greeks knew that an intense form of joy was an attribute of certain kinds of transient sensory or sensual experience: In late antiquity, the luxury-loving citizens of Antioch commissioned a mosaic for their bath complex depicting a female personification of *Gethosune*— Pleasure, or Delight—to smile on them. With only the mildest tone of censure, the Greeks collected stories about the extremes to which the pursuit of pleasure could go and attached them to the city of Sybaris, the short-lived colony of fabled wealth in south Italy, which loved food so much it offered prizes to local chefs. Greeks adored organized entertainment, which is why they invented theater. They debated whether the goal of literature and art was to edify or simply to confer the maximum gratification, *hedone*. I discuss the Greeks' love of pleasure in chapter 10, "Pagan Greeks and Christians," because it is in the written texts recording the battle between Christianity and paganism that the Greeks' love of pleasure is most richly illustrated. The pagans delighted in theater, wild music, and dancing, but the Christians banned them as immoral. The pagans' religion entailed spectacular, extravagant public sacrifices condemned as diabolical by the austere Christians. The pagans worshipped gorgeous painted pictures and statues of their gods, condemned as sacrilegious idols by the new religion. Worst of all, the pagan Greeks attached no intrinsic shame to the hedonistic enjoyment of wine and recreational sex.

This book's ten periods of Greek history, each paired with a fundamental Greek characteristic, are localized in ten dissimilar geographical areas, since the center of Greek cultural gravity shifted around the ancient Mediterranean, Asia, and the Black Sea. But I need to emphasize from the outset that the Greeks' distinctive personality seems to have been mature well before this history begins. It is apparent from the moment that their first words recorded in the phonetic Phoenician script (from which the very alphabet I am using here is directly descended) burst into our historical record.

The two earliest specimens of Greek phraseology both date from the mid-eighth century BC. The first is inscribed on a wine jug of the style known as "geometric," called the Dipylon jug because it was found near the Dipylon gate in Athens. It seems to have been the prize in a dancing competition. In a line of the hexameter verse used in the Homeric and Hesiodic poems, the inscription reads, "Whoever of all the dancers now dances most dynamically . . ." There are other marks that can't be read, but the sentence calls out to be completed, along the lines of "then he will win this prize." In just a few words, we catch a thrilling glimpse of Greeks who danced for pleasure, drank from ornamental wine vessels, and above all competed with one another.

The other example is a competition in witty one-liners, inscribed on the so-called cup of Nestor. This vessel, of geometric decoration and probably Rhodian manufacture, was found in a tomb on Pithekoussai, an island later known as Ischia, in the Bay of Naples. The writing, three lines of poetry, each in a different hand, was added at some point after the cup was made, but still during the eighth century. The writers seem to have been playing a party game in which the cup was passed around and each one added a single line to the poem. It reads:

I am the cup of Nestor good for drinking from.
Whoever drinks from this cup, on him straightaway
will come desire for Aphrodite of the lovely crown.

This is a deliberate joke. The humble clay cup speaks in a mock-solemn adaptation of Homeric verse. It stakes a humorous claim to be the magnificent metal cup of Nestor famous from the *Iliad*. The next two lines say that it will make the drinker feel sexy (and Nestor, as the oldest of the Greek chieftains at Troy, was not generally regarded in an erotic light). The drinkers competed in making their friends laugh.

Nestor's cup communicates most of the elements that made the ancient Greeks distinctive. It was inscribed by competitive people who had quickly learned a new skill, an alphabet, from foreigners. They used wit irreverently, debunking someone of high status and a solemn genre. They talked frankly about sex. They loved pleasure, specifically the recreational use of wine, which was inseparable from their identity; sometimes they defined foreigners by what they drank instead—beer (the Egyptians) and milk (northern nomads). The drinkers were seafaring traders from Euboea in mainland Greece, partying on a small island where they had established a trading post. Since the cup is Rhodian, it is in itself a sign of the connectedness of their culture across islands separated by large stretches of sea. It shows that shared knowledge of particular myths and poetry acted as social glue across that sea. The Greek inscribers of Nestor's cup at that remote island drinking session were already absolutely typical Greeks.

Drawing by Asa Taulbut of a fresco from Akrotiri, depicting a naval expedition and a town, in the Archaeological Museum of Thera, Cyclades. *(Reproduced by permission of the artist)*

I

Seafaring Mycenaeans

G reek history begins with the mysterious, seafaring, well-organized Mycenaeans. By the time of the first surviving literature, the long poems of the eighth century BC that have come down to us under the names of Homer and Hesiod, the Mycenaeans had vanished. Yet they were ever present, just beneath the surface. They had worshipped by and large the same gods, and the poems—the Homeric epics—in which they took the leading roles as heroes and heroines were without exception the most important part of the ancient education throughout antiquity. All Greeks of the archaic, classical, Hellenistic, and Roman Imperial eras spent their days in dialogue with their Mycenaean ancestors. But they felt separated from these ancestors by a wide chasm. The civilization had disappeared, leaving fragmentary but fascinating material remains.

Our relationship with the ancient Greeks is in some ways similar to the ancient Greeks' relationship with the Mycenaeans. Only samples (however rich) of the ancient Greeks' artifacts survive to remind us of the psychic intensity of the seafaring society that produced them. Because pagan ancient Greek culture was little understood for so many centuries preceding the Renaissance, at least west of Byzantium, when we approach the Greeks it is always with a sense that there has been a break with the past, that we must bridge a gulf in order to rediscover the Greeks, rather than a feeling that there has been a process of accumulation or smooth continuum. It must have been rather similar for eighth-century Greeks looking back on the Mycenaeans.

Since the Mycenaeans used a form of writing and built imposing structures, they left evidence, although it is patchy. In this chapter we visit the remains of some of the palaces in Crete and the Peloponnese and decipher some of the lists they used to help them in household and official administration. We can reconstruct something of their economy, their diet, their status system, their occupations, their religion, and their intense relationship with the sea. We can approach the question of why their society collapsed. We can ask if there is any evidence at all for cultural continuity between the end of the Mycenaean palace civilization in the twelfth century BC and the introduction of a new alphabet in the eighth. Most importantly, we ask what they were like as people and how closely they resembled their later Greek-speaking descendants in anything but their obvious confidence as mariners.

Near the beginning of the *Odyssey*, first written down in around the eighth century BC but set in the imagined Mycenaean past, there is a description of the first of many voyages in the poem. The hero, Odysseus, has been absent from his home island of Ithaca for nearly twenty years, and the baby son he left behind, Telemachus, is now approaching adulthood. Telemachus sets sail in search of news of his father, from Ithaca to the Greek mainland, the southwestern coast of the Peloponnese. He leaves in the evening and arrives in the morning. This is a fast rate of progress for a distance of about 120 nautical miles, but feasible since the goddess Athena has granted him a favorable wind. At dawn he puts in at the sandy bay at Pylos but finds it surprisingly crowded: "The people of Pylos were offering sacrifices on the seashore, black bulls for the Earth-Shaker with his blue-black hair. There were nine groups, and five hundred men sat in each one, and each group was putting forward nine bulls for sacrifice." Even the capacious sands of Pylos would have been challenged to accommodate 4,500 men as well as 81 bulls. The people of Pylos clearly had a high regard for the god of the sea and the earthquake, Poseidon of the blue-black hair.

Telemachus has picked Pylos because he hopes that Nestor, its elderly king, may have information about Odysseus. Nestor is one of the few Greek warriors to have survived the Trojan War. He was already old when he joined that expedition. In visiting him, the teen-aged Telemachus gains access to eyewitness memories of a much earlier stage of Greek mythical prehistory even than the Trojan War. One of Nestor's functions in the *Iliad* had been constantly to remind the generation of famous heroes in their prime—Achilles and Agamemnon, Menelaus, Ajax and Odysseus—that they were standing on the shoulders of giants. Nestor is also an experienced sailor, indeed the only Greek warrior at Troy who had once been an Argonaut, sailing with the superheroes Jason and Heracles to the remote Black Sea in search of the Golden Fleece. He thus personifies the earliest generation of mortal heroes in Greek mythology. He embodies accumulated wisdom; his memories of mythical feats are the same memories celebrated by the godlike bard, and it is through Nestor's experiences that he has acquired his famous sagacity. He is a rounded character in Homer: Too old and wise to take sides in partisan quarrels, or in direct combat, he leads his warriors into battle from his chariot and dispenses friendly advice to younger men. He is an outstanding horseman and orator. We can imagine how the Greeks visualized him from an ancient description of a famous (lost) painting by the unrivaled artist Polygnotus, which was later exhibited at Delphi: Nestor, wearing a cap and with a spear in his hand, stood with a horse about to roll in the dust, on a pebbled beach right by the sea.

Nestor's seaside kingdom of Pylos in the *Odyssey* not only supports a large population but has substantial accoutrements of civilization. Pylos is described as "sandy" or "sacred," and its citadel "well-built." Although nowhere near as splendid as the palace in Sparta, farther east, which is to be Telemachus's next destination, its sacrificial cups are made of gold, its palace contains row upon row of high seats at the banquet table, the wine that is opened for special guests is of a precious vintage, and the paving stones of the courtyard where Nestor likes to deliberate are polished white and glistening with oil. When a heifer is sacrificed to Athena, her horns are specially gilded with gold by a skilled blacksmith to delight the goddess. The poetic account of the civilization at Pylos, as we shall see in the next chapter, is in essence the way that Greeks in the eighth century BC imaginatively re-created their own past of several centuries before, much as we might re-create the world inhabited by King Arthur or Robin Hood. Some of the phrases in the epics were, however, certainly handed down over several previous centuries. Scholars will always argue about how much of the *Iliad* and the *Odyssey* was inherited from the songs that Greek-speaking minstrels had undoubtedly sung in Mycenaean palaces in the fifteenth to thirteenth centuries BC.

This debate changed irrevocably, however, as a result of the archaeological recovery of the Mycenaeans, which has been ongoing since the mid-nineteenth century. Mycenaean structures have been excavated at several of the sites so important in Greek myth—Thebes, Tiryns, and Therapne (a few miles from Sparta), as well as Pylos, Mycenae, and Crete. It has also been discovered that the Mycenaeans' inscribed writings, in the script known as Linear B, were in a recognizable forerunner of the classical Greek language. The Homeric Nestor indubitably represents a type of *historical* Mycenaean monarch. He exemplifies exactly the kind of leader who had really lived in a palace at sandy Pylos, with its superb natural harbor, in the late Bronze Age—that is, in the period between the mid-sixteenth and mid-eleventh centuries BC that modern archaeologists term "Late Helladic."

It is therefore fitting that the earliest "real" ancient Greek voice we can hear speaks to us not from Athens or Sparta, nor even Mycenae, but from near the palace of the venerable Nestor. The voice was recorded on a clay tablet between 1450 and 1400 BC. All the Linear B tablets were inscribed with signs drawn from left to right on a malleable gray clay, and they were not baked or fired. The ones that survived to be deciphered today were hardened by being accidentally burned. They now appear brown or red, depending on the heat of the fire, which, in each case, accidentally baked and preserved them. The tablets are mostly the size and shape of a small palm leaf. That first voice from around Pylos resounds from the rubbish dump into which it was discarded, all those centuries ago, near another Mycenaean palace slightly inland at a site named Iklaina. The Iklaina palace, now being excavated, was itself a substantial residence, with terraced walls, murals, and an advanced drainage system. The scribe's actual words on the tablet are not in themselves particularly exciting. One side records the last part of a man's name, followed by the numeral sign for "one"—he seems to head a list of personnel. The other side records part of a word related to manufacturing. This mundane clay object, discovered in 2011, is significant because it pushes back the use of writing to record the Greek language into the fifteenth century BC. But it has another significant implication.

It had previously been thought that writing was only used in major centers of Mycenaean power, such as Mycenae itself. The previous holder of the record for the oldest recorded example of the Greek language was a tablet from Mycenae, dateable to a hundred years later. The new find changes our understanding of Mycenaean life because it shows that advanced bureaucratic systems, including the writing of inventories, were being used not only in the major centers of Mycenaean power but in much smaller communities. It may mean either that writing was in more common use, lower down the social hierarchy, than was previously thought. On the other hand, it may be evidence for a sophisticated and surprisingly extensive network of communities with a shared regional administration.

In Crete, the main stronghold of Mycenaean culture away from the Greek peninsula, our understanding of early Greek speakers is rather more complicated. Long before the Mycenaeans had begun building their palace complexes on the Greek mainland, a people whose name we do not know, but whom we conventionally call Minoans after the mythical king Minos of Crete, had established a similar civilization on his island. Crete played a dominant role in the Aegean and exerted a cultural and possibly political influence on the Mycenaeans. The classical historian Thucydides may not have been far wrong when he claimed that Minos "was the first person to organise a navy. He controlled the greater part of what is now called the Hellenic Sea. He ruled over the Cyclades, in most of which he founded the first colonies." This sentence underlies the scholarly theory that the Minoans actually ran a thalassocracy, or political system dependent on their domination of the sea (*thalassa*). Minoan civilization reached its apex in the two and a half centuries between 1700 and about 1450 BC. The ethnicity of the Minoans is disputed. They spoke another language altogether and it was almost certainly not Indo-European. They also used writing, a syllabic script known as Linear A, but this has not yet been satisfactorily deciphered or translated. Although the palace at Knossos excavated by Sir Arthur Evans in the first years of the twentieth century is by far the most famous, there are several other important Minoan palaces and building complexes on Crete, mostly around the coast of the eastern half. They include Phaistos (the second largest) and Gournia, excavated by two American archaeologists, Harriet Boyd Hawes and Edith H. Hall, between 1901 and 1904. The Minoans also settled on smaller islands, mostly near Crete, including Thera (now known as Santorini).

In the mid-fifteenth century BC, however, the Minoan palaces were destroyed by fire. The chronology is much disputed. There are complications caused by the evidence for more than one catastrophic volcanic eruption on Thera, possibly resulting in tidal waves that engulfed the coast of the Cretan mainland. The fires may have been connected with the volcanic eruptions; on the other hand, they may have been caused, aggravated, or exploited by aggressive invaders. Most of the palaces were rebuilt. But one thing is certain: Soon after the fires, the script in which the palace inventories were recorded changed from Linear A to Linear B. Greek speakers, very likely from the Mycenaean palaces of the mainland, had taken over the administration of Minoan Crete. Thucydides suggests that the Mycenaean empire had indeed had a large navy in the late Bronze Age, at the time when he thought it was ruled by the Agamemnon who sailed to Troy.

When the Greeks sail south to make their entrance into Cretan history, they are therefore already absorbing, if not rapaciously expropriating, the achievements of an earlier civilization. The reason we can call them Greeks is that they used their own distinctive language. But we will never know either how much the mainland Mycenaeans had borrowed from the Minoans or the precise process by which Greek became the language of power on Crete. The issue is much debated by archaeologists in the context of the magnificent Thera frescoes. In 1967 the archaeologist Spyridon Marinatos, who wanted to discover what had destroyed Minoan civilization, began digging near the modern Greek farming village of Akrotiri, on the southern coast of the island of Santorini (ancient Thera). The results were astounding. Buried under many feet of volcanic ash, Marinatos discovered an entire town, "the Pompeii of the Bronze Age." The visitor can walk along the route of the paved ancient street that led into the center. The residents lived in impressive villas, some with three stories, bathrooms and plumbing linked to the town's public drainage system. Workshops and larders containing rich finds of pottery lined the streets. That they were commercial and utilitarian in function, and possibly dominated by men, is suggested by the lack of fresco decoration in most of them. But upstairs, the domestic living rooms, perhaps the domain of women, boasted elegant furniture and plaster walls painted with some of the most widely reproduced of visual images from all antiquity: the Akrotiri frescoes. Those from the West House have such a maritime focus that it used to be assumed that the house belonged to a rich sailor; it was referred to as the House of the Admiral. It contains several frescoes, including one of an arresting young woman with large eyes and earrings, and a head shaved except for a pigtail. She is often identified, on no evidence, as a priestess. But the richly painted panels of Room 5 make it the one of the most famous rooms in the world.

Two large panels in Room 5 depict youths, naked and carrying blue and yellow fish. Around the upper parts of the three surviving walls runs a border that consists of frescoes painted on a smaller scale. One depicts military activities. The middle fresco is a landscape that has rather misleadingly been called Libyan or Nilotic because it depicts a winding river and palm trees. The third, the south mural, shows a seascape with towns and ships sailing between them.

I gasped when as an undergraduate I first saw the south wall fresco, with its splashing dolphins and seven ships propelled by neat ranks of oarsmen. Their rhythmic rowing is conveyed almost audibly by the imagined shouts of the standing figures at the stern. The smaller town, on the left, portrays an island scene almost exactly like the images that reading about Odysseus's homeland of Ithaca had always engendered in my mind. Craggy mountains form the backdrop to a landscape where wild animals hunt one another, and a shepherd converses over a stream with a man of the town. Their clothes appear quite rough and functional. Other people stand at the harbor, watching the ships sail off to the larger city. The scene is full of movement and energy. Its topic, moreover, is precisely the boundary between life on land and life at sea, or rather the *lack* of any real boundary between them existing in the ancient Mediterranean islander's mind. But was either the person who painted the fresco or the householder who commissioned it Minoan? Or were they Mycenaean Greeks? Art historians simply can't agree on the answer to this question, although the pendulum has recently swung toward seeing them as incoming Mycenaeans, partly because the narrative storytelling in this picture is so reminiscent of the narrative style of Homeric epic. The frescoes of Pylos are less well preserved but suggest that their scenes were similarly action-packed and suggestive of Homeric storytelling: One shows warriors fighting men dressed in animal skins.

Every year that passes reveals further how momentous for our understanding of both the Mycenaeans and later Greeks was the decipherment of Linear B. Finalized in the early 1950s by Michael Ventris and John Chadwick, who built (rather more than they admitted) on the earlier work of the Americans Alice Kober and Emmett L. Bennett Jr., the decipherment has allowed us to listen directly to the Mycenaeans themselves. Where before we had only excavations and artifacts, now there are records, however limited, of thoughts that took shape inside Mycenaean Greek heads. We even know some of the Mycenaeans' names, including that of Philaios, a goatherd at Pylos.

A remarkable fifty-eight names are the same as, or similar to, names of warriors in Homer. Astoundingly, some Mycenaean Greek men bore the names of the top heroes on the Greek and Trojan sides, Achilles and Hector. Other names paralleled in the Homeric texts include Antenor, Glaukos, Tros, Xanthos, Deucalion, Theseus, Tantalos, and Orestes. Sadly, the proper name Nestor has not yet appeared, although many more tablets in Linear B undoubtedly remain to be discovered. A name, *ke-re-no*, found at both Pylos and Mycenae, moreover, looks similar to Nestor's recurring epithet in the Homeric poems, where he is the "Gerenian" horseman. The only proper name that it may be possible to associate with a historical figure known from other sources is the last king of Pylos, who from Linear B seems to have been called something like Echelaos. It is enormously suggestive—although it can be no more in the present state of our knowledge—that this happens to be the name of the traditional colonizer of the island of Lesbos, far across the Aegean Sea, who was also a son of the Mycenaean mythical hero Orestes.

A striking feature of the proper names in Linear B is how many of them contain elements connected with the sea or with sailing: one of the early Greeks named in this script was Fair Voyage (*Euplous*); others were called Fair Ship (*Euneos*), Oceangoer (*Ponteus*), Famous for Ships (*Nausicles*), and perhaps Swift Ship (*Okunaos*). In other respects, too, Linear B confirms the Homeric picture of Greeks to whom sailing and rowing were second nature. Among titles designating occupations, both coast guards and craftsmen who specialized in constructing ships receive separate labels. At Knossos, rowers are included in a list of officials supplying or receiving cattle; at Pylos it is possible that some rowers were conscripted, and perhaps the sons of slave women. There is even a specific mention in one Pylos tablet of a naval expedition: Thirty men's names, perhaps the personnel to man the oars of a single ship, are designated "oarsmen to go to Pleuron." This is likely to be the city called Pleuron, on the north shore of the Gulf of Corinth, which is named in the *Iliad*. A likely reason for sailing expeditions, besides trade, was the acquisition of slave labor. Some of the tablets at Pylos indicate that the labor force was recruited by raids in which captive women and children were brought home and taught trades. The places where the women are said to have come from are across the sea in the eastern islands and Asia Minor: Lemnos, Knidos, Miletos, and perhaps Chios.

What sort of religion was practiced by these seafaring people, with their Homeric names and squadrons of female slaves from overseas? By and large, the gods who have turned up in Linear B are exactly the ones whose appearance we would have predicted. The Poseidon to whom Nestor makes that vast sacrifice in the *Odyssey* was worshipped in reality at Pylos and Knossos and may even have been the senior god of the Mycenaeans. He was not only the deity of water but the spouse of Mother Earth: His name means Earth's Husband or Earth's Lord. Offerings to Poseidon include a jar of honey dedicated "to the Earth-Shaker." Besides Poseidon and Earth, named recipients of offerings in the Mycenaean tablets are the ones we would expect to be honored by any pagan Greeks—Zeus, Hera, Athena, and Artemis. A big stir was created by the discovery of Dionysus's cult at Pylos, since the Greeks themselves thought that he was a relatively late import to the Greek pantheon from Asia, the story dramatized in Euripides' *Bacchae*. Disappointment has so far awaited those who want to find Apollo or Aphrodite, although that does not mean that they will never turn up in the future. Other divinities greatly honored by the Mycenaeans include the childbirth-goddess Eileithyia, the Winds (who have their own priestesses), and perhaps a dove-goddess.

Unfortunately, the nature of the evidence as inventories means that the gods are only mentioned when they are to receive offerings. But the offerings they receive are rich and varied: they include not only the cattle that Nestor's sacrifices would have led us to expect but pigs and sheep, wheat and barley, oil and wine, figs and cheese, honey and spice tablets. Offerings of a nonedible form include sheepskins, wool, and a golden cup, as well as at least one woman. Women seem to have played an important role in religion in other functions than as animate votive offerings: They are priestesses, "key bearers," and probably cultic slaves. Other individuals were designated cup bearers, perhaps to perform their duties at sacrificial meals.

The Mycenaean Greeks begin to look different from their descendants only when we look at their monolithic political structures. By the eighth century, when ancient Greece emerged as a constellation of independent city-states on islands and lining some of the shores of the Mediterranean, the desirability of living in a strictly hierarchical system under an all-powerful hereditary monarch was already being questioned. The Mycenaeans, however, still lived under a monarchical system, as we can see from their term "king" (*wanax*, the Homeric *anax*). The *wanax* has some kind of lieutenant or second-in-command, who may or may not have been a military officer, and whose title was *lawagetas*, or "people leader." At Knossos there is not much information about military matters, unfortunately, but the situation seems to have been approaching an emergency at Pylos, which was preparing for an attack when it collapsed, and men were being distributed around local leaders. This implies that each leader was preparing a small army to defend his territory. The *wanax* may also have had a special group of courtiers or attendants (*hepetas*). Some tradesmen seem to be designated as working for or belonging to the king—a fuller (wool washer), a potter, and possibly an armormaker. At Pylos, there was a royal council called something like a *gerousia*, implying that it consisted of men of a mature age. At Pylos, too, we catch a glimpse of a category of officials who held a substantial portion of land, and also landholders of a lower status, perhaps suggesting a system not dissimilar to feudal peasantry. There is plentiful information about the amounts of wheat to be sown on each Pylian field. The *wanax* may have governed satellite towns farther afield through men designated by a term similar to the Homeric term for the "king" at Troy, *basileus*. There are other status terms connected with particular regions that may mean something like "mayor" and "shareholder," but this is by no means certain.

In all later periods, pagan ancient Greeks owned slaves, often in large numbers. Although we can tell that there was a clear-cut division of types of labor among the Mycenaean lower classes, unfortunately it is impossible to be sure whether most of the male workers were technically free or not. It is rather surprising that no term has been deciphered designating people responsible for farming crops, although there are both shepherds and fullers. It has been suggested that the men who worked with livestock were understood to do other kinds of work on the land as well. There are words meaning "slave man" and "slave woman" at Pylos, but most of them are "slaves of the god," which could designate an honorific status or a category of publicly owned religious functionaries or cult attendants. Regardless of their status, however, it is clear that most Mycenaeans did a great deal of often backbreaking work and that there were numerous different occupations. Public servants included messengers and heralds (although unfortunately no word for "scribe" or "accountant" for any official responsible for inscribing the tablets has yet been found). At the upper end of the spectrum of crafts, there are goldsmiths and boilers of ointments or perfume, and a medical doctor. Other early Greeks who have appeared in Linear B include bronze smiths, cutlers, and bow makers. Besides the shepherds and goatherds there are huntsmen, woodcutters, masons, and carpenters. It is not surprising that shipbuilding is a distinct craft (*na-u-do-mo*). The women in the palaces worked at carding wool, spinning, and weaving, while both men and women seem to have been involved in making clothes and working flax, which would also have been crucial for equipping ships with sails and both fishermen and hunters with nets. Women ground and measured grain but men made the bread. Male stokers and ox drivers, and female bath attendants and serving maids, are also attested.

Linear B has told us a good deal about the plants with which the Mycenaeans flavored their food: celery, beetroot, cumin, sesame, fennel, mint, pennyroyal, and safflower. It is interesting that some of these have names borrowed from Semitic languages, suggesting that they were originally imported from Syria—cities like Ugarit, Byblos, and Tyre. These exotic tastes will have added variety to the basic diet attested to by material finds: wheat, barley, pulses, almonds, fish, shellfish, octopus, and grapes. Named timbers include elm, willow, and cypress; furniture is decorated with kyanos, horn, and ivory. Horses are mentioned, but not often, which implies that they were used for chariots rather than plows and farm carts; deer and asses make appearances, and dogs are implied from the word for a huntsman, *kun*-*agetai*.

A fascinating material context in which to read these earliest of ancient Greek words is provided by the archaeology of the Mycenaean sites. One of the most important finds at Pylos have been several *tholos* tombs. These are underground circular stone rooms with vaulted roofs, where the late Bronze Age elite buried their dead. One of them is in a tumulus raised over a wooden platform to give it extra prominence on a headland overlooking the sea. There is also a cave containing Mycenaean pottery, in antiquity known as Nestor's Cave; it was said that Nestor and his father used to assemble their cattle there. Pylos is not as well known to tourists as either Mycenae or Knossos, but its excavated palace is in the best physical condition and conveys a strong sense of what it was like for the Greeks who lived there. Its Linear B tablets have confirmed that it was indeed named Pylos, and that the building was begun in the fourteenth century and completed in the thirteenth, never to rise again. It was soon afterward destroyed by the fire that accidentally baked and preserved the inscribed tablets.

The complex was built on an acropolis, with steep enough sides to deter assault and a long wall on one side. It was constructed out of mud bricks and rubble, pressed onto a wooden framework, with wooden pillars to support the ceilings, planted in fixed stucco mounts. It consisted of more than a hundred individual rooms contained in four main buildings or blocks, together forming a large rectangle. The smallest one seems to have been a wine store. The next largest seems to have been equivalent to a garage—at least, chariots were repaired there. The second largest building may have been used to eat in, since it contains a substantial hall of its own and a good deal of pottery. But it is the main building, in the center, that clearly constituted the social and psychological center of the building complex.

The visitor who arrived at Nestor's two-story palace, as Telemachus did a decade after the Trojan War, was taken through a series of ever-more stately rooms before he arrived in the presence of the king. He would first have passed through doors on the eastern side of the building and entered an imposing entrance hall (*propylon*). A large proportion of the Pylos tablets were found in rooms on its left, suggesting that this was the administrative and accounting center, where people and products that entered or left the palace could be systematically recorded. The visitor next entered a court but would not have minded if he was kept waiting, because it opened onto two adjacent rooms containing a bench to sit on, wine jars set in special holders, and a large choice of different cups. When summoned to the royal presence, the visitor would next have passed through a porch into a vestibule and only then into the large, square throne room, in which the plastered walls were decorated with dazzling frescoes. The throne was positioned at one side, and in the center there was a massive circular hearth, more than thirteen feet in diameter. Although in winter this would have helped keep the monarch warm, it is designed to make a statement, perhaps a ritual one. It would also have illuminated the gorgeous decorated walls with flickering firelight.

A luxurious lifestyle was enjoyed by the royal family. In this palace, as in Nestor's Pylos in the *Odyssey*, wine flowed abundantly. The Pylos excavators were amazed by the several thousand drinking vessels stored in rooms on the west side of the main building. The palace held plentiful supplies of olive oil, and also assigned a room to making perfume. On the upper floor, accessible by a staircase, there were many more rooms. On the ground floor there were at least two independent suites of apartments, one with a grand terra-cotta bath, and another a toilet and drain.

When Telemachus left Pylos, he traveled on overland in a horse-drawn chariot to Sparta, to the gorgeous palace of Menelaus and his wife, Helen, who had been forgiven after the Trojan War. Homer calls the Spartan homeland of Lacedaimon "hollow" but also "full of gorges," an accurate description of the Eurotas valley beneath its towering mountain ranges. Two Mycenaean mansions were built, in the fifteenth and fourteenth centuries BC, respectively, adjacent to the site of the later Menelaion, or hero shrine, for Helen and Menelaus at Therapne on a ridge near Sparta. The earliest dedications at the shrine are from the eighth century, but the mansions were out of use by then, destroyed by fire in the thirteenth or twelfth century. On a smaller scale, their architecture resembles that of the palace at Pylos. They could have been the residence of the "real" (that is, Homeric) Menelaus.

No Mycenaean palace is as well preserved as the one at Pylos. But a commanding impression is still created by the enormous walls at Tiryns, near the port town of Nafplio. No wonder the Homeric epithet for Tiryns was "walled." When Pausanias, a traveler, visited Tiryns in the second century AD, he was astounded by the walls. The ancients called them "Cyclopean," believing that only giants could have achieved the task. Tiryns, says Pausanias, "consists of rude stones, each of which is so big that a team of two mules is unable to move even the smallest of them from the spot." The stones are massive: 6 feet long and 3 feet wide, creating a wall of 148 feet in height. During the Persian Wars, a group of rebel slaves who had escaped from Argos held out behind these walls for months before being recaptured. Perhaps it was living inside this oppressively fortified edifice that made Antaea, Queen of Tiryns, according to the *Iliad*, fall so madly in love with the handsome guest Bellerophon from nearby Corinth that she accused him of rape when he refused her. Her husband, Proitos, was incensed.

The story of Bellerophon in the *Iliad* contains the sole reference in Homer to what seems to be writing. Poor Bellerophon's punishment for his chastity was that Proitos packed him off to Lycia in Asia Minor with a missive addressed to the king there. It consisted of a "folded tablet," and Proitos "wrote in it many signs of misery, life-destroying signs." The Lycian king interpreted this as meaning that he needed to have Bellerophon killed, and sent him to fight deadly foes including the monstrous Chimaera. But what did those deadly signs look like? The word for "write" here does not help, since it is *graphein*, which in classical Greek means both "write," in the phonetic alphabet, and "incise," a line or a picture. Perhaps the poet of the *Iliad* was trying to make sense of examples of Linear B he may have heard about or even come across. Since his contemporaries could not understand what the script was saying, the strange, spiky, semigeo-metric symbols, which actually correspond to particular syllables, must have looked sinister indeed.

The most famous Mycenaean palace is at Mycenae itself, less than an ancient day's journey from Nafplio. It is accessible from the west only, and the people who lived there enjoyed breathtaking views over their rocky kingdom in the Argolid. Like Tiryns, Mycenae was built on an acropolis, the citadel surrounded by massive "Cyclopean walls," and one of its Homeric epithets, or descriptive adjectives, is "well built." But the fabulous treasures which the archaeologist Heinrich Schliemann found in its graves, and which are now on display in the Athens Archaeological Museum, explained the other Homeric descriptor for Mycenae, "rich in gold." Schliemann conducted the first systematic excavations at Mycenae in the 1870s, with the eyes of the world fastened upon him after his sensational finds at Troy. Some of the visual images from Mycenae have come to define the Greek Bronze Age in the popular imagination, such as the Lion Gate, the largest remaining Mycenaean sculpture. This had been visible to tourists before Schliemann's dig, but it was his genius at publicity that brought it to the world's attention. Even more famous are the golden burial masks that Schliemann discovered in shaft grave circle A, one of which he liked to think revealed the contours of the "face of Agamemnon."

Sadly, we have not yet found the equivalent "face of Oedipus" in Thebes, the setting of some of the most famous Greek tragedies, even though a Mycenaean palace has been found there, too. In 1906 our

modern picture of Thebes was transformed by the discovery of a pala-
tial building, richly furnished with fresco paintings and artifacts made
of gold, agate, and quartz. More astoundingly, it also housed jars, of
a shape designed for transporting their contents in wagons or ships,
inscribed with administrative notations in Linear B. Classical Greek
literature had always provided a picture of Thebes in the heroic age
of myth, the Thebes of Tiresias and Antigone, as a sophisticated and
mighty culture, but this poetic image had suddenly materialized as a
historical reality. The archaeologist, Antonios Keramopoullos, sug-
gestively identified the august building as the House of Cadmus, the
residence of the legendary founder of Thebes, grandfather of Pentheus
in Euripides' *Bacchae*, and great-great-grandfather of Oedipus himself.

In the introduction to this book, I outlined qualities that later
defined the Greek mind-set and can help us to understand why the
Greeks made such rapid intellectual progress between 800 and 300
BC. Some of these characteristics are plainly shared by the earlier
Greeks who inscribed their lists on clay tablets in Mycenaean palace
complexes. The Mycenaeans' own voices tell us that they were seafaring; their curiosity about the world was a factor in the long distances
they sailed to both Greek and non-Greek lands for trade and slaving.
The wine and perfume consumption at Pylos suggests that they were
joy-loving. That they were as emotionally honest, articulate, and witty
as later Greeks is impossible to prove, although the names they gave
their cattle suggest a love of words and a sense of humor: One yoked
pair at Knossos were called *Aiolos* and *Kelainos*, Shiny or Nimble and
Blue-black; others were named, perhaps with a Mycenaean tongue
slightly in cheek, *Xouthos* (Swift), *Stomargos* (Talkative), and *Oinops*
(Wine-dark or Wine-faced), like the Homeric sea.

The hierarchical palace culture does not suggest that the Greek
suspicion of authority was yet well developed, although even here
there are occasional suggestive scenarios, such as the rowers who
have gone "absent without leave" from Pylos, and the agricultural
worker at Knossos who has been ordered to confiscate the ox from
another. We can never know what emotional trauma was undergone
by all those imported slave women, whose sons (some of whom were
presumably fathered by their Mycenaean owners) were conscripted

into the navy. But the admiration for excellence and competitiveness are well illustrated by the Thera fresco depicting the young boy boxers aggressively punching one another; they can scarcely be more than twelve years old.

Yet the Mycenaean Greeks, whose surviving words are so limited, remain enigmatic. The lack of fortifications does not imply any sense of vulnerability or fragility—indeed, it creates an atmosphere of peace and orderliness. The walled palaces and clay jars consolidate the feeling of careful organization and placement of objects in space. The frescoes and the evidence for the perfumed oil industry, especially at Pylos, suggest sensuality and the love of physical beauty, of ornamentally exaggerated difference between the sexes, of bright color, and of the sea. But the modulated voices that speak from the clay tablets may be more misleading: They somehow suggest a slow, deliberate pace of life, and a lack of vitality and emotion. It may be that these Greek speakers did not talk fast and loud and argumentatively. It is possible that they did not use sarcasm and did not display passion. But if that is so, then they were different from every other community of Greek speakers who have followed them in recorded history.

Recent discoveries have just begun to challenge the idea that the Mycenaean era in Greek history was followed by a Dark Age at all. The label has conventionally been applied, since the first Victorian excavations of the Mycenaean palace civilizations at Mycenae and Knossos, to the several hundred years between their collapse and the eighth century BC, when the Greek "miracle" began. Yet some Greek communities continued to flourish—albeit without leaving written records—in the tenth and ninth centuries, for example in Euboea. This long, narrow island is so close to the eastern side of the mainland that it does not feel like an island. In antiquity, as in scholarship, Euboea suffered from a reputation as a peasant backwater. Even its name is tame, referring to the excellence of its cows. But the Euboeans of the so-called Dark Age have recently been cast into a glamorous light. The excavations by the British School at Athens at Xeropolis, which may be the original site of the city of Eretria, have shown that it was inhabited continuously from the Mycenaean period to the eighth century and beyond, including the "dark" period from 1100 to about

750. Many other Mycenaean communities collapsed completely, their sites never to be rebuilt. Xeropolis therefore raises vital questions about the transmission of culture—especially the heroic poems and the gods they celebrated—from the time of Nestor's palace and the Mycenaean takeover of Crete to the introduction of the Phoenician alphabet.

Not far away from Xeropolis, on a hillside overlooking the fishing village at Lefkandi, the remarkable Toumba cemetery has made it possible to enter the world of the tenth century BC with unprecedented vividness. A three-roomed tomb, its thatched roof supported by a row of wooden pillars, was built to honor the memory of two people. One was buried and the other cremated. In the shaft graves in the middle room, there lay luxury Phoenician items, pottery and bronze urns. These Euboeans traded and were prosperous. The cremated remains, bronzes, and immolated horses are reminiscent of the culture depicted in the *Iliad*.

The building had been covered with a mound. Other funerals, perhaps for members of the same family, were conducted in the adjacent cemetery. The most arresting item these sophisticated people have bequeathed to us is a clay statuette of a centaur, over a foot high, exquisitely decorated with a geometric dog-tooth pattern. The centaur's head and body were found in separate tombs, suggesting that they had been considered precious enough by two members of the same family for mourners to bury the broken parts with their respective bodies. These people were fond of each other. The centaur is hollow, was made using a potter's wheel, and dates from the tenth century BC. Although tenth-century images of centaurs have been found in Cyprus, none shares the same quality of manufacture and design. With this centaur, we are looking at something much loved by a tenth-century Euboean family who did not feel they were living in a Dark Age. I suspect that they already knew from their poems that the first medical doctor was a man-horse, Cheiron, "the wisest of the Centaurs, teacher of Achilles," as he is in the *Iliad*.

The so-called Dark Age Greeks continued to worship the Mycenaean sea god, Poseidon. His sanctuary at Isthmia, easily accessible by sea and also the place where Greeks could cross by land into the

Peloponnese, was established as early as 1050. The inhabitants of the villages that would eventually coalesce into the port city of Corinth could all meet at Isthmia to sacrifice in Poseidon's honor, and from 582 BC to compete in the Panhellenic games. The archaic temple had a ninety-eight-foot altar, reminding us of the vast sacrifice Nestor conducts at Pylos in the *Odyssey*. Yet we have no written record of the tenth-century words spoken by the Poseidon worshippers of the Isthmus or the sophisticated residents of Euboea. How many of them had seen the ruins of the palaces that had still been inhabited elsewhere in Greece only nine or ten generations previously? We cannot ask them whether they had ever seen a Mycenaean fresco or a sample of Mycenaean script. But it is impossible that they did not tell stories about their ancestors, their voyages, and their wars, combining memories handed down over the generations with creative fantasy.

The discovery of the tenth- and ninth-century Euboeans reminds us of the association between Euboea and Hesiod, the author of the early poems in the same epic meter as the *Iliad* and the *Odyssey*. In *Works and Days*, Hesiod tells us that he once sailed to Euboea and went to Chalcis (the other major town of Euboea besides Eretria), where games were being held in honor of the deceased leader Amphidamas. Hesiod says that he won the competition between singers and the prize of a tripod with handles. How far back in history had the Euboeans been holding such contests? Bards could have been competing in Euboea through all the long centuries since the Mycenaeans. At least parts of the poems of both Homer and Hesiod may date back into prehistory. The people whose graves have been found in that Lefkandi cemetery may have listened, enraptured, to a poet singing songs about Odysseus's adventures, Achilles, and the centaur Cheiron.

It was also in the supposedly dark eleventh, tenth, and ninth centuries that several cities were founded on the coast of Asia Minor, in what is now western Turkey. A wave of settlers arrived by sea from regions of mainland Greece, including Euboea, Phocis, Thebes, Athens, and the Peloponnese. This movement eastward is conventionally labeled the period of Greek "migrations" rather than "colonization," to differentiate it from the larger-scale expansion across the Mediterranean and Black Sea that ensued in the later eighth century. Most of the earlier migrants were Ionian Greeks, distinguished from members of the other Greek tribes, Dorians and Aeolians, by dialect and to an extent by way of life. The new Ionian settlements included Phocaea, Priene, Miletus, Ephesus, Colophon, and Clazomenae, and ties were naturally maintained between them, as with the most easterly of the Aegean islands, Chios and Samos. Twelve of them came together to form the Ionian League or Panionic League. The god symbolizing their shared ancestry and identity was Poseidon, who ruled the element that allowed them to travel in their ships to create their new towns, and to come together at his sanctuary, the Panionion. This was built on the rocky peninsula of Mycale, stretching northwest of Priene in an arc toward Samos; archaeological finds there may date from the sixth century BC, but the cult must have dated from centuries earlier.

If we knew more about life in the Ionian cities of Asia in the tenth to ninth centuries BC, we would understand better why it was among the Greeks that the intellectual "miracle" was soon afterward to occur during the "archaic" period between the eighth and the sixth centuries. Cultural interaction with the ancient peoples they encountered in the east must have played a crucial role. Since we have no written records of their experiences, we can only speculate. But relationships with the Carians, the inhabitants of the area around Miletus and speakers of an Indo-European language, were cooperative and involved intermarriage. Herodotus said that the residents of Miletus spoke Greek with an audible Carian accent. The Lycians must have been an impressive people, to judge from the fight they later put up when the Persians attacked their city of Xanthos in around 540 BC; Sarpedon, one of the Lycian leaders in the *Iliad*, is notably belligerent. The Greeks probably learned to worship Apollo from the Lycians, as the god's Homeric epithet "Lycian" suggests; the only two figures who pray to Apollo in the *Iliad* support Troy—the priest Chryses and the Lycian hero Glaucus, who says that the god's "home" is the rich land of Lycia. From the Phrygian mother goddess Matar, who had connections with an even more ancient Hittite goddess, the Greeks acquired some of the attributes of the goddess they knew by the name of either Mother or Cybele—her lions and *tympana* (kettledrums). From the Luwians they

borrowed the worship of stones representing gods (*baetyls*), often fragments of asteroids.

But no written records of their interactions with their neighbors
were left by the Greeks of the tenth and ninth centuries BC. This
silence compromises our understanding of their forebears in the
Mycenaean era. Unless the situation changes dramatically in terms of
the available evidence, we can never inhabit the insides of the Mycenaeans' minds nor become familiar with individual Mycenaean personalities. Their importance for getting to know the ancient Greeks
lies in what they meant to the Greeks whose sustained talk we *can*
begin to hear, from the time of the poets of the eighth century. For
the Greeks of antiquity from Homer and Hesiod onward, the Mycenaeans were a distant memory.

The Greeks always knew that their ancestors in the Peloponnese,
Thebes, and Crete had lived seagoing lives that adumbrated their own
and yet in important ways radically differed. They may have seen examples of Linear B, for they knew that these forefathers had used strange
inscribed signs to record important information. Yet no archaic Greek
could read the Mycenaean script. They knew that Mycenaeans had
lived in grand palaces, often with many rooms, and husbanded their
ample stores. They knew that these men of old had enjoyed kingdoms
and wealth that could only be envied by the often hungry peasant of
the eighth and seventh centuries. In the next chapter we ask how they
used this semi-forgotten past in their own self-definition, at a time
when inherited monarchies were becoming less likely to be tolerated
by Greeks of independent spirit but much more modest means.

Polyphemus the Cyclops hurls a boulder at Odysseus's ship. Engraving of a painting by Louis-Frédéric Schützenberger (1887). (*Author's personal collection*)

2

The Creation of Greece

Life was changing fast for the Greeks of the eighth century BC. They explored farther afield and traded with distant peoples, opening up ever-more remote horizons. In their homeland, the sparse and scattered coastal and island settlements of the centuries since the collapse of the Mycenaeans waged war on one another. They began to become more centralized into city-states and to hold regular meetings at shared religious centers, such as the sanctuary of their supreme god, Zeus, at Olympia. But there was a crucial additional development, related to the Greeks' inherent distrust of authority. In some Greek city-states a radical new idea emerged of the free male who was fundamentally equal in status to his peers, even if he possessed no inherited wealth or aristocratic identity whatsoever. The free Greek man was able to call, moreover, upon men of the same status to show solidarity with him in defense of his rights and privileges. By the late sixth century this vision of the ideal citizen of the polis (city-state) was to lead, after grueling struggles, to democracy.

These tendencies—expansion abroad, centralization at home, conflict between social and economic classes—were in some ways contradictory. Yet they collectively resulted in the creation of an ethnic identity based on those fundamental aspects of life that any one Greek speaker intuitively felt he shared with any other, despite remoteness of residence or disparity in wealth and status. They included the cherished ideal of individual self-sufficiency, often by making a living from a small farm. It went in tandem with competitive values and a distinctive pride in the independence of the free individual. Men with this outlook were clear-eyed about the inevitability of conflict between rich and poor, those privileged by heredity and those who had to win wealth and respect by simply being excellent at what they did. This value system was in turn tied to the ideal of political autonomy for individuals and communities, who, however, subscribed to a joint set of practices agreed on by Greeks everywhere. In the fifth century, these are defined by Herodotus's Athenians as sharing a genealogy, language, ritual sacrifices, and *nomoi*—laws or customs, agreed-upon rules of conduct, taboos and imperatives, such as the protection of vulnerable people conducting embassies, and rights of the dead to burial.

The outlook of the Greeks of this era is crystallized in the earliest Greek literature: four long poems. They are the *Iliad* and the *Odyssey*, epic narratives that have come down to us under the name of Homer, and Hesiod's *Works and Days* and *Theogony*. The rebellious, independent element of the Greek character is fundamental to all of them. It is the motor of the wrath of Achilles, which drives the *Iliad*—the contradiction between traditional values, embodied in Agamemnon's insistence that he deserves the greatest rewards from the Trojan War because he is by bloodline the supreme king, and rebellious, meritocratic ones, embodied in Achilles, a lesser king by birth status but a far greater warrior. The meritocratic and egalitarian tendency may have been an inevitable result of the near-subsistence economy of much of archaic Greece, which could not support the extreme wealth that the Greeks noticed among Near Eastern neighbors, especially the Lydians and Egyptians, and which they envied. In the *Odyssey*, for example, the property of even the king of Ithaca amounted to only fifty-nine herds of livestock and one chamber of treasure.

In this chapter I use these four early poems to explore both the internal political tensions and the emergent collective ethnic self-consciousness of these proud, self-determining Greeks, whose name for themselves was Hellenes. The poems offer an imagined backstory, with some history mixed in, for the contemporary situation in the eighth century. The Homeric epics narrate the story of the Trojan War and raise the question of the location of Troy and the reality of the war. Hesiod's *Theogony* traces the history of the Greeks much further back, to the origins of mankind after the creation of the physical and moral universe. But all four poems offer unforgettable scenes of fighting, sailing, and farming—the three activities central to the archaic economy and to the archaic Greek male experience of life. They were performed at festivals where self-governing Greeks, from diverse communities, met as equals in shared sacred spaces to worship their shared gods and, in doing so, invented the competitive athletics festivals of which we possess a descendant in the Olympics. The poems recited at these gatherings were the collective cultural property of the independent-minded Greek warrior peasants wherever they sailed and were fundamental to the transmission of their values. They remained so until the end of pagan antiquity.

The poems' core constituents—heroic narrative and wisdom literature—had originated in oral composition and had been developed in the process of being memorized, repeated, supplemented, and adapted over the course of decades and (parts of them, at least) centuries. But between 800 and 750 BC, Greek culture changed forever. Some resourceful speakers of Greek, probably traders, borrowed the signs used by the ingenious Phoenicians to represent consonantal sounds, adopted some other signs to indicate vowels, and used them to write down in Greek their already canonical authors. In inscribing them, no doubt the poet-scribes (perhaps individuals really called Homer and Hesiod) made changes that ornamented the language and improved the poems' structure. The classical Greeks knew that the *Iliad* was aesthetically superior to other epic poems because it is not made up of episodes loosely strung together. It is unified by one incident during the Trojan War, a period of a few weeks when Achilles became angry with both Agamemnon and Hector. But it looks backward and forward in time to engage the listener with the war's antecedents and consequences. Older inherited material—heroic lays about heroes, animal fables, proverbs and maxims, astronomical lore—was also shaped to express the concerns of the self-reliant eighth-century

Greek male, as well as (in Hesiod's case) personal information. In writing down these poems, the freedom-loving Greeks, newly empowered by Phoenician technology, invented themselves and their collective past.

Hesiod and Homer composed in a distinctive meter, the dactylic hexameter, consisting of lines of six feet, or emphases. These long lines create a rolling, insistent rhythm, which Victorians liked to imitate in English, as in this translation of line 8 of the *Iliad*: "Who of the great gods caused these heroes to wrangle and combat?" Every line is in the same meter, and there are no subdivisions into groups of verses or stanzas. But the rhythm is flexible, since half of each foot can consist of either short or long vowel sounds. Homeric and Hesiodic dactyls can dance and sparkle with a light, tripping rhythm of seventeen syllables, most of them short, or groan plangently in just thirteen mostly long ones. Poetry that is originally produced without the aid of writing is qualitatively different from the work of literate poets, and the distinctive features of Homeric and Hesiodic verse derive from its oral nature—lists, repetitions, mirror scenes, and the use of formulae. A "formula" sounds off-puttingly clinical, but it is just the name given to the marrying of two or more words in a recurrent rhythmic cluster—"rosy-fingered Dawn," for example, or "thus spoke swift-footed Achilles."

The *Iliad*, "Poem about Ilium (Troy)," created for the Aegean Greeks, west or east, a picture of their obstreperous warrior forefathers. It provided them with a detailed narrative of voyage over the Aegean to Asia of the Greek-speaking men of the heroic age, outraged by the insult to their reputation when one of their wives—Helen—ran away with the Trojan Paris. The poem begins in the Greek camp ten years into the war, which has reached stalemate. Helen is living with Paris inside Troy, and neither Greeks nor Trojans have gained the upper hand on the battlefield. But Agamemnon, the Greek commander, quarrels with his best warrior, Achilles, who withdraws his goodwill and refuses to fight at all. This allows Hector, son of the Trojan king Priam, to lead the Trojans to score some important military successes. Achilles only comes back onto the battlefield when he is thrown into despair by the death of his best friend, Patroclus, killed in a duel with Hector. At the climax of the poem, Achilles kills Hector and desecrates his corpse by tying it to his chariot and dragging it around the walls of Troy. Although he does give the body back to the Trojans for burial eventually, the death of Hector marks the decisive moment in the war when Greek victory becomes inevitable. The Greeks will conquer Troy.

The *Iliad* does not call the Greeks "Hellenes" but makes the story sound archaic by using the ancient clan names Achaeans, Argives, and Danaans; the name Hellas still only designates one small district in Thessaly. The word Panhellenes, or All Greeks, which occurs only once, may still refer only to the population of northwest Greece, not the Peloponnese. The *Iliad*, however, provided the charter myth of Greek ethnicity for at least twelve centuries. The catalogue of Achaean ships in the poem enacts a roll call, designed to suit the eighth century BC, of the twenty-eight contingents of Greeks, in more than a thousand vessels, who participated in the Trojan War centuries before. The Greeks come from mainland strongholds including Pylos, Lacedaemon, Mycenae, Argos, Athens, and Boeotia (although no northern districts) and several islands, including Ithaca, Rhodes, and Crete.

The list has been scrutinized by historians seeking a straightforward account of Mycenaean Greek populations, but this reading cannot succeed. The catalogue may contain much older, inherited Mycenaean material, but it was given its present form *after* the Greek migrations to Asia, and this must interfere with the way that it portrays the distant past. Imagine a screenplay writer and film director who are planning a movie about, for example, the reign of the English king Alfred the Great in the ninth century AD. They want to film a spectacular scene at his court in Wessex, where the camera pans delegations from Mercia, Anglia, Wales, Kent, and so on, summoned for a council to organize defensive operations against the Vikings. The cinema professionals would be able to draw on some historical records, including the *Anglo-Saxon Chronicle*. But they would interpret these, to an extent, in the light of twenty-first-century viewers' knowledge of their country, the names of its counties, and their regional boundaries. The invention of Great Britain in 1707 under the terms of the Act of Union would also interfere in the reconstruction of Arthur's world.

Similarly, by the eighth century BC, many Greeks lived in new settlements on the Asiatic seaboard, and this is where the relationship between the social geography of the *Iliad* and that of the eighth-century epic poets becomes opaque. The *Iliad*'s list of forces mustered to defend Troy includes the Bronze Age residents of the areas in Asia Minor in which the Greeks later built cities, but it describes them *as they were retrospectively visualized in the eighth century*. The largest contingent by far is furnished by the Trojans and their immediate neighbors the Dardanians, both of whom share language, culture, religion, and protocols with the Greeks. The Phrygians, Lydians, and Thracians who lived farther away, but also in the northern part of Asia Minor and across the Hellespont, fight for Troy. But the poet of the *Iliad* carefully includes allies who "speak other tongues" from regions that lay to the south of Troy down the coast—Mysia, Caria, and Lycia—which his audience knew were in their own day heavily populated by Greeks. Listening to the *Iliad* required them to engage in the act of remembering, or more likely imagining, Asia before the Greeks came. Perhaps, for them, the Greek conquest of Troy, regardless of its historicity, *symbolically* represented the Ionian forefathers' arrival on the Asiatic seaboard, during the putatively dark centuries, from the Greek mainland and islands. The ambiguous ethnicity of the Iliadic Trojans themselves, similarly, may have functioned to represent the *fusion* of cultures, Greek and Asiatic, that had necessarily resulted.

This raises the problems of the location of Troy and whether the Trojan War actually happened. There is no contemporary historical documentation of Homer's Trojans, except a handful of controversial references in tablets inscribed by the Hittites, who from the eighteenth to the twelfth centuries BC ran a massive empire approximately coextensive with modern Turkey. Hittite tablets refer to places named Wilusa and Taruisa, which may be Ilium and Troy. One precious Hittite text, known as the Tawagalawa letter, may even mention the Trojan War. Written by a Hittite king, probably in the thirteenth century, it is addressed to the king of the Ahhiyawa (perhaps the Achaeans, one of the names of the Greeks in the *Iliad*) and refers to an incident in the past, now resolved, when the Ahhiyawa were involved in hostile military operations. One of the allies of Troy in the poetic tradition was Eurypylus, said in the *Odyssey* to be leader of the Keteioi, who might be the Hittites.

The archaeological evidence is tantalizing. The Persian king Xerxes, the Greek Alexander the Great, and the Roman Julius Caesar all later visited Troy. They identified it with the ruins of the deserted settlement they could see at what is now called Hissarlik, near the Dardanelles. But archaeologists today distinguish between many levels of occupation on the site. The two levels that have most often been identified with the Troy of the *Iliad* are technically known as Troy VIh (fifteenth to thirteenth centuries BC) and Troy VIIa (thirteenth to twelfth centuries BC). Troy VIh, which had imposing bastions and sloping walls, was destroyed in the mid-thirteenth century. This can be made to correspond with the assumed date of the Trojan War. But trying to fit the story told in the *Iliad* to thirteenth-century history is not the best way to understand it. The story told in the *Iliad* is how the Greeks of five hundred years later liked to *imagine* their past. They would have been able to see ruins at Troy, and no doubt durable antiques—armor, for example, or shards of pottery—could help them elaborate the tale. But the concerns addressed in the Homeric epics are those that occupied the minds of the Greeks of the eighth century, transposed into their fictionalized prehistory.

How should we visualize the audiences of these poems when they were first written down? The epics themselves provide several pictures of bards in action. Phemius, Odysseus's minstrel in Ithaca, is already singing about the Trojan War and plays at banquets to entertain aristocrats. Demodocus, in Phaeacia, performs to mark the climax of a day of athletics competitions. In the *Iliad*, Achilles himself whiles away his self-exile from the battlefield at Troy by strumming a lyre and singing "of the glories of heroes." But the picture of epic performance that corresponds to the experience of most Greeks in the eighth to sixth centuries features in another text attributed to Homer. It is a hymn to Apollo of Delos, the tiny central Aegean island where the god Apollo, along with his mother, Leto, and twin sister, Artemis, received one of his most important cults. The island, which lies near the center of the "circle" of the Cyclades, was the traditional site of the birth of the god. From as early as the ninth century, Ionian Greeks were meeting there to dedicate offerings to him and his sister in the famous sanctuary. In the Homeric hymn, the authorial voice describes the audience at a festival of Apollo on Delos, where Ionian Greeks have assembled after arriving in "their swift ships":

> The Ionians, in trailing robes, gather in your honor with their children and decorous wives: holding you in their minds, they delight you with boxing and dancing and song, whenever they hold their contests. If someone came across the Ionians assembled in such crowds, he would say that they were immortal and did not age. He would see how graceful they were, and enjoy gazing at the men and well-girdled women with their swift ships and numerous possessions.

The poet then describes the famous Delian Maidens, mysterious women who perform choral songs for Apollo; in "a hymn commemorating men and women of past days" they "charm the tribes of men." But finally, perhaps in a bid to win the bardic competition at the festival itself, the poet tells us more about the hymns that male soloists performed on the island. First, he tells the Deliades that if asked the identity of the sweetest singer to visit the island, and their favorite, they are to respond, "He is a blind man, who lives in craggy Chios, and his songs are supreme forever." Since Chios is a traditional birthplace of Homer, and one of the chief Ionian islands, this text shows that the participants at Ionian festivals on Delos *believed* that Homer had sung for them or their ancestors there. The voice singing the hymn adds that he will spend his life spreading the fame of Delos and "far-shooting Apollo, god of the silver bow, whom rich-haired Leto bore." He travels between sanctuaries praising the Panhellenic gods.

The Delian sanctuary became one of the richest in the ancient world, attended not only by Ionians but all the Greeks. It later became a major trading post where people of every Mediterranean ethnicity congregated. But that Homeric hymn shows Greek identity being consolidated, during the archaic period, at the shared sanctuaries to which the Greeks traveled to meet each other in their swift ships. It is from the eighth century that much of the earliest evidence dates for the worship of Greek gods in many other sanctuaries, always open-air spaces marked off as sacred, with low walls or rows of stone, and an altar on which to burn offerings. Many sanctuaries soon gained a temple and a dining room. Sanctuaries could be inside cities and could provide a focus for the community (Athena and Apollo were popular choices as "city-protecting" gods). Or they could be outside, used by a city in negotiating the limits of its territory or as venues for formal meetings with members of other states. A few sanctuaries were truly Panhellenic in that they belonged to all the Hellenes in a neutral space. Zeus, the supreme god of the Greek pantheon, presided over several key sanctuaries of "all the Greeks." At Dodona, for example, his prophecies were decoded from the rustlings of the leaves on his sacred oak trees. Of the four major Panhellenic centers in Greece that were, from early on, the venues for big athletics festivals, two were sanctuaries of Zeus—Olympia and Nemea.

The Nemean games in the northern Peloponnese were the last to become established, in the early sixth century, but Olympia was already in use as a sanctuary of Zeus in the ninth or even tenth century. According to ancient tradition, it was in 776 that the famous Olympic Games were founded. Archaeological evidence shows that by 800 BC, leaders of Peloponnesian communities were meeting at Olympia to consult the oracle of Zeus and compete in athletics contests. Impressive votive offerings, especially bronze tripods, show that Olympia and its games began to attract Greeks from ever farther afield. A similar pattern applies at Delphi, where the earliest competitions in honor of Apollo were in musical performance rather than sport. When Greeks of different tribes accomplished something together, they began to name it a "Hellenic" achievement. In the seventh century BC, eastern Greeks and men from Aegina arrived at what was then the principal port in the Nile Delta, which they called Naucratis (Ship Power); they offered their services as mercenaries to the pharaoh, exchanged silver, oil, and wine for Egyptian grain, linen, and papyrus, and created a crucial site of cross-fertilization between Egyptian and Greek culture. Some of the Greeks there built a joint shrine, which they naturally called the Hellenion, thus defining their joint Greek identity despite coming from nine different cities.

The Panhellenic shrines arose to fulfill two functions. Through the oracles they pronounced, they mediated relationships between the emerging states of Greece, who were as keen to maintain independence from one another as individual Greeks were anxious to be self-sufficient, autonomous, and indebted to no one. But they also provided a venue for aristocrats and parvenu tyrants to compete in the display of their wealth through athletics and the dedication of fabulous offerings to the gods. In their home communities, powerful families may have been under pressure not to indulge in excessively ostentatious self-promotion; at the Panhellenic shrines, they could compete with their peers in other city-states, thus declaring their joint membership in a Panhellenic elite class. The games at Olympia, held only every four years, did not satisfy their desire for such opportunities. Games were established at Delphi in the early sixth century (the Pythian games), and at Nemea and the Isthmus. The games were arranged to occur sequentially so that there was a Panhellenic gathering every year.

In the twenty-third book of the *Iliad*, Achilles holds games to honor the funeral of his comrade Patroclus. These epic games would have felt evocatively Panhellenic to archaic audiences because the competitors in the poem, like them, came from many Greek regions and islands. Games, Panhellenism, military funerals, and war formed an associative cluster in the archaic Greek mind. The foundation myths of all four festivals with major games claimed that they were associated with funerals, and athletics events in ancient Greece were *all* developed out of military training exercises. In the *Iliad* the death and funeral games of Patroclus provide the climax to many scenes of bloody combat. These gave the Greeks a way to think about the exciting aspects of war, of the mustering of armies and the clanging of armor, but the audience is never allowed to forget that this excitement comes at a terrible price. In episode after episode, strong, sympathetic characters enunciate their emotional pain. The *Iliad* shows young men dying on the battlefield, to be lamented by parents and widows. It shows the last parting of Hector from his wife, Andromache, and little son. It shows the elderly Priam and his supposed enemy Achilles weeping together over their respective losses. It foreshadows the extreme situations and moral crises of Athenian tragedy in the dilemma of Achilles, who had to choose between dying young but gloriously, or old but in obscurity.

It adumbrates the harsh metaphysical conditions under which mortals in tragedy live, utterly vulnerable to the fickle whims of vindictive and childish gods.

If the *Iliad* gave the Greeks their sense of a collective past as warriors, the *Odyssey* gave them their archetypal descriptions of sailing, and provided its itinerant hero with more diverse challenges. For the free Greek male of the mid-eighth to sixth centuries, identification with the seafaring, resourceful, soulful Odysseus and his overseas adventures must have been profound. Odysseus may be a king, but he is also the definitive self-sufficient farmer whose small island produces all that his personal household requires, and who asserts his rights to autonomy as a result. Odysseus is also exciting company but by no means perfect. His mistakes include boasting to the Cyclops, falling asleep when in charge of the bag of winds, and arguably losing his head during the bloody slaughter of the suitors. But as the philosopher Aristotle pointed out, we identify better with a hero who is neither too virtuous nor too wicked—that is, with a hero rather like ourselves.

The cast of the *Odyssey* is an expression of the egalitarian streak in the Greek character in that its characters are not confined to an elite, aristocrat group. Besides the significant slave characters (Eurycleia, Eurynome, Melantho, and Eumaeus), the poem includes an ordinary rower (Elpenor) and the beggar Irus. Men and women, rich and poor, and old and young were offered sympathetic characters with whom they could identify. The poem also includes stories about lowlife merchants and pirates, and much backbreaking peasant labor, in the fields, in the orchards, and at the loom.

In the practical, resourceful, wily Odysseus, archaic Greek men could enjoy a hero who was a glorified version of their own self-image. A competent all-rounder, gifted with a brain as well as brawn, he possesses the skills to survive anything life on land or at sea can throw at him. He is a supreme orator and world-class warrior, seen in fighting action in books 22 and 24 of the *Odyssey* and as an expert city-sacker in book 9. Odysseus is an excellent navigator and swimmer, the ideal pioneer, frontiersman, and colonizer. Besides his moral qualities (diplomacy, courage, self-control, patience, self-reliance, and so forth), Odysseus has surprising skills, grounded in the life experience of the seagoing archaic Greeks. These contribute to a picture of masculinity that has proved perennially attractive. He is a shipwright who builds a sizable raft in four days, from tree felling to sailmaking. His expertise at carpentry is also exemplified in the bedroom, with its built-in bed, which he made for himself and his bride, Penelope. Odysseus is no slouch as a farmer, either; he is an expert behind the plow, and his father promised him trees and vines of his own to tend when he was a boy (thirteen pear trees, ten apple trees, forty fig trees, and fifty rows of vines). But the *Odyssey* also celebrates its hero's status as a prize-winning athlete. He not only wins the discus-throwing competition at the Phaeacian games but is an able wrestler, javelin thrower, and, of course, archer. His amazing feat with his bow at the contest organized by Penelope heralds his return to the Ithacan throne. We learn that Odysseus could easily have been the victor in his boxing match with Irus had he so desired.

Odysseus's success with women will have endeared him to many archaic Greek males. He had the asset of a loyal wife, Penelope, whose resourcefulness matched his own. But he has affairs with two gorgeous supernatural females, Calypso and Circe. He is attractive to the much younger Phaeacian princess Nausicaa, and even the goddess Athena flirts with him when he awakes on a beach in Ithaca. The *Iliad* offered ancient Greek men a model of idealized love between men in the relationship between Achilles and Patroclus, but Odysseus is one of antiquity's few exclusively heterosexual heroes. This is part of the poem's anthropological dimension, which defines, among other things, the patriarchal social structure of archaic Greek communities by sending Odysseus into encounters with feminine power from which he invariably emerges with the upper hand. The *Odyssey* defines the male psychology that went with patriarchy by presenting various versions of the feminine—as desirable and nubile (Nausicaa), sexually predatory and matriarchal (Calypso, Circe), politically powerful (Arete, queen of the Phaeacians), domineering (the Laestrygonian king Antiphates has a huge daughter and a wife "the size of a mountain"), monstrous and all-devouring (Scylla, Charybdis), seductive and lethal (Sirens), but also as faithful, domesticated, and maternal (Penelope). In the "real" world of Greek island peasant farming, a good wife protects her husband's interests and in his absence keeps her legs crossed for twenty years.

The distinction between the supernatural world of Odysseus's wanderings and the reality of Ithaca defines other aspects of the archaic Greek's life. In Ithaca, men toil to produce food, whereas the Phaeacians are magically supplied from nature. The Cyclopes drink milk, but Greeks drink wine. Greeks abhorred the idea of eating human flesh, in contrast to the cannibalistic habits of both the Cyclopes and the Laestrygonians. But perhaps the strongest contrast with the Greeks is provided by the mysterious people whom Tiresias says Odysseus must visit on one more journey. They live so far inland that they have never heard of the sea, do not use salt, and know nothing of ships or oars. There Odysseus is to plant his oar in the earth and sacrifice to Poseidon, before returning to meet a gentle death that will come to him, mysteriously, "from the sea." It would be hard to imagine any story more profoundly Greek in its symbolism.

The other portrait of the fiercely independent farmer in the earliest Greek poetry is Hesiod's self-portrait in his agricultural poem *Works and Days*. Hesiod is the first author in world literature we feel we can understand as an individual. He exemplifies several of the ten characteristics that I think collectively constituted the distinctive ancient Greek mind-set, especially his strong authorial "I" voice and the emotional directness and mordant humor of his advice. "Do not let a flaunting woman coax and flatter and deceive you: she is after your barn." He despises his idle, litigious brother, Perses, and scathingly suggests that he stop worrying about legal disputes and do some work: "the man who has not laid up a year's store of food, Demeter's grain, has no business concerning himself with quarrels and courts of law."

Hesiod was a farmer in Ascra, a village in Boeotia he describes as "dismal in winter, excruciating in summer, never pleasant." Ascra lay below Mount Helicon, a name that became associated forever with poetic inspiration and idyllic visitations by Muses, since it was there that Hesiod realized his poetic vocation. The climate was indeed hot and airless in summer and cold in winter. Hesiod's father came from the trading city of Kymai in Asia Minor but had been driven to move by poverty. Hesiod was thus an archetypal ancient Greek: His family had undergone sea voyages, deracination, and transplantation, and he was a farmer. The leitmotif of his *Works and Days*, from which we learn about his personal situation, and which furnished the Greeks with seminal aspects of their collective identity, was the ever-present threat of hunger.

More than three-quarters of citizens in almost all Greek states, at least in the archaic and classical periods, eked out their living from the land (Sparta, where the ruling class forced slaves to do the agricultural labor, was in this, as in other ways, an exception). The three essential crops were grains, vines, and olives—the plants sacred to Demeter, Dionysus, and Athena, respectively, all of whom have appeared in Linear B. Hesiod gave the Greek farmer, everywhere he went, this memorable instruction: "Strip to sow, and strip to plough and strip to reap, if you want to harvest all the fruits of Demeter in due season." The farmer's priority is to "get a house and a woman and ploughing ox—a slave woman, not a wife, to follow the plough." The image of the cantankerous old Boeotian poet, asserting his independence by stripping naked to the waist and sweating behind his plow, speaks volumes about the reality of life for the less wealthy Greek— and his slave woman—everywhere. If poor Greeks were to avoid starvation or enslavement, they must do all Hesiod advises, and "add work to work and yet more work." The early Greeks had little help from mechanical devices or power not supplied directly by humans and animals. It was not until Hellenistic Egypt that sophisticated water-lifting devices were developed to aid irrigation, under the influence of the treatise *On Pneumatics*, by Philo of Byzantium. The water mill also dates from this later period.

The farmer's calendar began in late autumn with the plowing of a fallow field. Hesiod advises plowing the soil three times. The plowing needed to be repeated because the ancient plow, rather than turning the soil, simply drew a line with a bronze or iron plowshare. Wheat, barley, corn, and cereals were sown with hand and hoe, and the field needed to be weeded through the winter and spring. In May or June, unremitting labor commenced. The reaper stood with his back to the wind and cut every clump and stalk near the roots with a sickle, before binding them into portable bundles. These were carried to the threshing floor and trampled by oxen until the precious seeds were released. Even then they had to be winnowed hard, with basket and fan or shovel, to remove every fragment of chaff.

The olive has been cultivated in the eastern Mediterranean since 3000 BC, and the Mycenaeans used olive trees when designing decorations for their golden cups. In mainland Greece the olive lay at the heart of the economy, because it thrives in a climate with long summer droughts. The olive is hard work and requires planning and intelligence. It takes years for trees to come to fruition, so a man who planted them might expect to benefit not himself but his son or grandson. They require rigorous pruning, watering, and fertilizing. They can only be harvested every other year. Creating olive oil is labor-intensive. Harvesting the olives required several workers to cooperate in shaking and beating the tree, with one of them climbing to the top to get the highest fruit, before the olives were gathered as they fell on the ground. These were then processed, from fruit to sealed jar of oil, in work areas near the groves where they were grown. A wealthy household might have owned between two hundred and three hundred olive trees. Olives were not only the dietary staple they were once thought to be—olive oil was also a luxury, both as a condiment and as a toiletry. It was used for cleaning precious wooden statues and marble tiles. Until the Hellenistic era, it was usually produced on a small scale for domestic use, by farming families themselves, on unsophisticated presses.

The other plant at the center of Greek identity was the grapevine. Like olive farming, viticulture requires brains to supplement intensive labor. The Greeks planted grapevines wherever they settled, except when the climate would not allow it. Vineyards were dug in spring, and vines were grown from cuttings planted in carefully prepared holes. Barley or pulses (legumes) were grown between the vines to maximize yield in relation to land available, especially while one waited for the vines to mature. Once the vines were well established—which could take three years—they needed to be pruned hard every autumn and trained on stakes. The new leaves and shoots were thinned by hand. The ripening grapes were coated with dust in order to delay their maturation and thus increase their sugar content. The soil needed to be hoed regularly and parasitic weeds removed. The vintner picked the grapes and put them in baskets. The juice was extracted by treading the grapes in a wickerwork tray over a board or vat with a spout, through which the juice flowed into jars. The Greeks were not alone in drinking wine. The Mesopotamian elite imported wine from farther north, and Egyptian kings as early as the fourth dynasty (circa 2613–2494 BC) were buried with supplies of wine. The Phoenicians also seem to have been vintners. But wine was not an elite luxury for ancient Greeks: It was integral to their religion and ethnic identity everywhere.

In *Works and Days*, the eighth-century Greek peasant farmer's life is a relentless struggle to survive, and this is contrasted with a mythical age long ago when men of the "golden race" lived in primordial bliss. Pandora—the first woman—caused their fall. They did die, but painlessly and without aging first. They lived like the gods, did not have to work, and feasted constantly. But the gods replaced them with the second, silver race. Silver people took a hundred years to emerge from childhood and then did not last long, because they constantly wronged one another and did not honor the gods with sacrifice. The third race, made of bronze, was enormously strong, but so addicted to war and violence that they wiped each other out. The fourth generation were actually an improvement. They were the heroes of myth— Cadmus and Oedipus at Thebes; the heroes of the Trojan War. But the fifth race, of which Hesiod and his audience are members, the race of iron, know nothing but work, sorrow, and death. Only further decline awaits the iron men in the future. They will all become incapable of agreement, dishonor their parents, break oaths, and bear false witness. Men will no longer feel ashamed of themselves or indignant at malefactors. They will become entirely amoral. Hesiod's view of mankind's existence through time places remarkably little emphasis on the gods, making humans themselves largely responsible for their own terminal moral decline.

This lapsarian, or Fall, myth describes humanity's past in ways that foreshadow the Greek historians. Hesiod is interested in the earlier races of men because they may help to explain the world he inhabits himself. Herodotus and Thucydides both stressed that they did not just want to record events but to explain the nature of the present and help to understand the future. But Hesiod's myth of the Fall also adumbrates Greek rational philosophy. His vision of the races of man is on a universal scale. It has a secular tendency—humans' choices about actions determine what happens to them just as much as divine intervention. The information communicated in this myth is also given unity by its overarching moral lesson: the importance of moral decency and of living an upright life.

Hesiod's vision of history explained aspects of Greek ethnic identity. In a poem about famous heroines, which has unfortunately survived only in fragments, Hesiod related how heroes were often descended from male gods' sexual encounters with mortal women. He traced the heroic families' genealogies to their three tribal ancestors—Dorus (the Dorian Greeks), Xuthus (the Ionians), and Aeolus (the Aeolians). They were all sons of Hellen, the original Greek and the son of the only couple to survive the Greeks' version of the Flood myth, Deucalion and Pyrrha. But the human race itself crashes into world history in the Greeks' Creation story, told in Hesiod's *Theogony*.

In the beginning there was only Chaos (the word means something more like "void" than "chaos" implies nowadays). Chaos is followed by five primordial entities: Earth, who contained Tartarus (the lowest region of the cosmos) within her, Eros, Erebos (Shadowland), and Night. From Night and Earth the other residents and elements of the universe sprang: Night mated with Erebus and produced Aether (Air) and Day. But it was Earth who became the mother of most primary beings. By parthenogenesis she created a son, Ouranos (Heaven), the Mountains, and Pontus (Seawater). But then she lay with her son Ouranos, and conceived numerous children, representations of both elemental principles and more ethical or cultural ones.

So, by this stage, male and female constituents of the universe are being brought together sexually, and the physical and material scenography of the world has already been created—earth, air, mountains, sea. Earth produces beautiful daughters, including immaterial concepts that distinguish (the Greeks believed) human experience from that of animals: belief in gods (Theia), morality (Themis), and an ability mentally to transcend the here and now of bodily experience to move around in time (Memory). But the first, shocking conflict is about to afflict this elemental, dominantly feminine, and womblike world of mountain summits, watery beings, and incipient consciousness. The next child whom Earth bears by Ouranos is a "terrible" boy, Cronos, who, for no reason, detests his father. Without justification, long before Freud invented the Oedipal complex, this boy-child sets up the first intergenerational antagonism within the first nuclear family.

Cronos bides his time before attacking the father he loathes, by whom Earth now conceives six further male children. Three mighty one-eyed Cyclopes are followed by three overpowering monsters with fifty heads and a hundred arms each (Hecatoncheires). These six hideous youths are all "terrible" and, according to Hesiod, "hated immediately by their own father." Earth and Ouranos's large brood have now set the stage of the universe for the ethical conflict that became the stuff of Greek myth. Cronos feels for his father the first *unmotivated* hatred to corrupt the peaceful coexistence that had characterized the earlier world. Equally, the Cyclopes and their hundred-armed brothers may be unpleasant to look at but do not deserve their father's odium.

To make matters worse, Ouranos thrusts the last six children back inside Earth the minute each is born, delighting in what Hesiod calls his "evil deed." The unfortunate mother of his children, distended to bursting point, decides that enough is enough. Ouranos is now abusing her as well as the six of their children "straining" to leave her womb, which is what their Greek title, Titans, means. Here we see conflict between parents enter the history of the world. Earth invents flint, makes a sickle, and asks her sons to punish their father. The all-important principle of revenge now arises. Ouranos has done a bad deed, and one of the sufferers (Earth) wants retribution. But even this first retaliatory violence is not a simple case of a victim punishing her persecutor. The only son who offers to help her is *not* an injured party. It is the son and elder brother of Ouranos's victims. Cronos's motive, as we have seen, was an *unaccountable* loathing of his father felt from birth.

Hesiod shows through their cosmic origins that conflict and revenge are nuanced. Hatred, like Cronos's for his father, can be irrational. Sometimes hatred, like Ouranos's dislike of his six monstrous sons, is unfair but understandable. Some cruelty is arbitrary and—worse—

can give the cruel party pleasure, as interring his children inside Earth gave pleasure to Ouranos. Some victims do not attempt revenge: The Cyclopes and Hundred-Handers did not dare defy their father. Other victims may use surrogates, who are not victims themselves, in order to exact revenge, as Earth uses Cronos to punish Ouranos.

She lets Ouranos lie with her again so that Cronos can perform his ambush. He slashes off his father's genitals and throws them down behind him. The bloody drops that fall from them engender new entities. Drops falling onto Earth produce the Erinyes (Vengeance Spirits or Furies), the Giants, and the Ash Tree Nymphs. Drops falling onto the sea produced foam from which Aphrodite—sexual desire— emerged near the island of Cyprus. For the Greeks, not only was Aphrodite the first Olympian god to be created, but she is born from the same ejaculation as her half-sisters the Erinyes, personifications of revenge—the dark impulse that often accompanies sexual passion in human experience.

After this cataclysmic showdown—the cruelty of the father-husband, the revenge of the hate-filled son, the genesis of Revenge and Lust— cosmic reproduction accelerates. Night establishes a dynasty of vile entities including Doom, Fate, and Death (*Thanatos*). Seawater is the progenitor of the aquatic deities. Monsters (many of them destined to be killed by Heracles) are the offspring of Ocean's daughter Callirhoe. A daughter of Earth produces the Sun, Moon, and Dawn; Dawn in turn gives birth to the winds and stars. Ocean begets the rivers, both those in Greece and those in the rest of the world, such as the Nile, the Ister (Danube), Phasis (Rioni in Georgia), and several in modern Turkey—the Granicus, Parthenius, and the Scamander at Troy. Cronos begets six major Olympians by Earth's daughter Rhea: Hestia, goddess of the hearth, Demeter, Hera, Hades, Poseidon, and Zeus. In due course Zeus vanquishes his father, Cronos, assumes supremacy in the universe, gives Hades and Poseidon their portfolios, and puts the navel stone beneath the earth at Delphi.

Hesiod introduces humans abruptly. The third generation of gods has been born, including Death, although it is not yet clear who is subject to this dread divinity. Political affiliations between the immortals are tense. Zeus has dislodged Cronos from power and established the first cult center, at Delphi. But relationships are strained between the Titans (Earth's children), including Prometheus, and the aerial Olympians. The ascendancy of the gods over other supernatural beings (giants and monsters) is not yet settled, either.

Gods require humans to worship them. The historical development that Hesiod is about to explain is sacrifice—the slaughter of animals to provide burnt gifts for the gods, the ritual that defined pagan religion for all antiquity. Within this politically unstable world, Hesiod suddenly presents human beings. Rather, he introduces us, specifically, to "*mortal* humans"—beings vulnerable to death—who will all turn out to be male: "For when the gods and mortal humans were contending at Mecone, Prometheus with forward thinking cut up a great bull and set out portions, trying to deceive the mind of Zeus." Mecone is in the heart of Greece, near the Gulf of Corinth. It is here that the scene of the primordial sacrificial feast is set. But before the meat is sliced, gods and mortals are already *contending*. The verb here, *krinein*, related to the modern terms *crisis* and *critical*, is both problematic and astonishing. It is problematic because it encompasses a range of meanings in English. It could, with equal legitimacy, be translated "were distinguishing themselves from each other" or "were in the process of coming to a legal settlement." Just how hostile were the negotiations at Mecone? Gods and mortals are *equally* involved in determining their relative positions. They are both *agents* of the identical verb. The relationship between the divine and human inhabitants of the universe seems surprisingly balanced. It is also, undeniably, politicized.

The issue is dealt with—though by no means resolved happily—by Prometheus's invention of animal sacrifice and establishment of the customary way of dividing the meat among participants. Parts of the animal, however, are more desirable than others. Prometheus tries to trick Zeus into accepting a portion that contains not meat but bones cleverly dressed in fat. Hesiod is providing an etiology (a mythical explanation) for a traditional practice: The meat was always allocated to the humans, while the aroma of burning bones and sizzling fat was sent up from the altars to the gods. Zeus does not fight over the meat. But he is wrathful, and refuses to give mortals fire (which they would need, among other things, to conduct more sacrifices). But this time

Prometheus, the original rebel, successfully deceives Zeus, stealing fire in a fennel stalk and carrying it to man. In the myths of the Greeks, ever suspicious of established power, the origin of human progress is thus made to depend on a primeval flouting of authority.

When Zeus realizes that men have fire, he punishes them with the creation of Pandora, beautiful but deceitful, foremother of the race of women who brought suffering to mankind, especially poverty and labor. There are large differences between this account of the creation of humankind and the story told in the Judeo-Christian tradition. Humans—at least male ones—are on the cosmic scene and already in arbitration with the gods, before the power politics have been fully settled on the divine level. At least one immortal—the Titan Prometheus—favors mortals: He gives them not only superior servings at the first sacrifice but also fire, the emblem of mental and technological advancement. At Mecone there is no primordial state of innocence, no temptation by serpents, no woman's sin of biting an apple of knowledge, no shame and no expulsion from paradise. There are preexisting power struggles, in which men are implicated; as a result of Mecone, they receive the means by which to communicate with the immortals (sacrifice) and to develop technology (fire), but they also are introduced to marriage and endure labor and misery. Unlike Eve, Pandora is given little sympathy. Eve, as Genesis acknowledges, will have her own sufferings in childbirth. Pandora is just there to harass men. But the way that Hesiod presents human's relations with Zeus and the other gods is also radically different. It is *politicized*. The mortals who are already "contending" with the immortals, on their first appearance in history, are the forefathers of all the philosophers, scientists, and democrats who subsequently put the distinctive, striving, and often rebellious dynamism into Greek society.

By the end of the eighth century BC the Greeks knew who they were as a group and what they had in common. They treasured their independence both as individuals and city-states but met in joint sanctuaries to affirm their bonds by sacrificing and competing in athletics and musical performances. In their epic poems, which they transported as written texts across the sea, they possessed a portable library of images that affirmed that identity. The *Iliad* gave Greek men images of iconic warriors, battles, and military funerals that sustained them in their constant fighting. But it also offered them a poetic idiom of melancholy and grandeur, a picture of their shared heroic past and—however mediated by myth and fantasy—their sense that they had achieved conquests in Asia. The *Odyssey* gave them scenes of sailing and a charismatic quest hero who embodied an idealized version of the self-reliant, versatile farmer-seafarer of the archaic period, sufficient unto himself and equipped with advanced mental, practical, and social skills. Hesiod's psychologically astute poems outlined the Greeks' joint family tree leading back to Hellen, but also crystallized their relations with the gods, their ethical outlook, the power of hatred, revenge, and sex, their identity as farmers who might have to move because of poverty, their wit, and their contentious streak. Above all, the archaic period put *human* experience—of sea and land, war and travel, sex and work, food and drink—at the center of its cultural output. In the pictures painted on Athenian pottery, by the mid-eighth century, the human figure becomes increasingly dominant, but also glamorized, as if there was a conscious effort among the artists to create generic scenes that lent human activities prestige and heroism. With the eighth-century self-invention of the disputatious Greeks, the stage had finally been set for their expansion across the entire Mediterranean and Black Sea worlds.

Greek colonists welcomed at Massalia (Mar-
seilles). Engraving by Alphonse de Neuville,
originally created to illustrate F. Guizot's
L'Histoire de France (Paris, 1775). (*Author's personal
collection*)

3

Frogs and Dolphins
Round the Pond

Odysseus the mariner is a mythical avatar of all the real-life Greeks who, in the archaic age, sailed their ships into unknown waters across the Mediterranean and the Black Sea in search of new land and adventure. When he describes the Cyclopes' island, he speaks with the discerning eye of the colonist:

> The land is not at all bad, and could produce every kind of seasonal crop. There are luxurious irrigated meadowlands along the coast, by the white-topped sea, which would support vines throughout the year. The soil would be easy to plough, and tall ripe crops could always be harvested, for underneath the topsoil the earth is very rich. There is also a good natural harbour there. . . .

The "frontier mentality" articulated in the *Odyssey* is related to archaeologically identifiable manifestations of Greek colonization, reflecting the outlook of "proto-colonial" Greek traders, who needed to amass money and influence before they could launch an expedition aimed at creating a completely new settlement. Many Greeks from the eighth to sixth centuries were restless and on the move. Intrepid individuals left established communities in mainland Greece and on the western coast of Asia to form settlements far away, thus creating the distinctive map of ancient Greece, the connect-the-dots network of townships strung along so many coasts and islands of the Mediterranean and the Black Sea.

Greek colonizing activity intensified in the seventh and sixth centuries BC and is inseparable from the developments outlined in the previous chapter, especially the increasing determination of less wealthy Greeks, at a time of scarce resources, to secure themselves economic independence and political self-determination. The drive for independence—the rebellious quality in the Greek character—was in turn tied up with their developed sense of individuality. In this chapter, we learn how the Greeks transplanted their distinctive way of life—their gods, their songs, their vines, their drinking parties—to almost every corner of the Mediterranean and the Black Sea. We meet a remarkable number of Greeks with defined personalities and goals, who saw themselves not just as members of a colony or class but as important entities in their own right. Some, the founders of colonies and the "tyrants," belong to new categories of leader, but other colorful individuals who wanted their names known to posterity included poets, athletes, mercenaries, priestesses, entrepreneurs, vase painters, and explorers. Some of their stories are interlinked, because individuals who desired fame would commission a famous poet such as Pindar to promote their reputation and even to invent for them a family tree that would trace their descent from one of the rugged individuals of myth, such as Heracles or another Argonaut. The age of colonization is also an age of Greek individualism.

The proliferation of individual Greek communities can make the study of this period confusing. The confusion is exacerbated by the ancient Greeks' habit of reapplying old names to the new settlements they founded—Heraclea, Megara, Naxos. But the proliferation is what made this period so important. The Greeks exponentially increased the number of communities they lived in and the ethnic groups with which they had contact. They expanded their shared horizons fundamentally and forever. By the early fourth century, when Plato explains the physical nature of their environment, the Greeks' sense of their geospatial relationship to the world was dramatically different from that implied by the Aegean-focused map drawn by the catalogue of ships in the *Iliad*: In Plato's *Phaedo*, Socrates says that "the earth is very large and we who dwell between the pillars of Hercules and the river Phasis [the Rioni, in modern Georgia] do so in only a small part of it around the sea, like frogs or ants round a pond."

Some of the first enterprising long-distance sailors round the pond came from Euboea, which, as we saw in chapter 1, had flourished in what has been called the Dark Age. One of the earliest places where the Euboeans traded was Al Mina, in the estuary of the Orontes River near the modern border between Turkey and Syria. Al Mina has produced Euboean pottery and examples of Greek in the Phoenician script that may date from even earlier than the eighth century. Greeks competed commercially with the Syrians and Phoenicians at this crucial crossroads between the worlds of the Aegean, the Levant, and the many peoples of the Asiatic interior. But other Greeks soon traveled just as indomitably south, west, and north, to found cities in what are now Libya, France, and the Crimea, cheek by jowl with Africans, Gauls, Iberians, Thracians, and Scythians. The Milesians penetrated the Black Sea even to the remote estuary of the River Don to trade with tribes who were in turn in contact with southeastern Asia. Wherever the Greeks settled, they stayed near to the sea, their preferred thoroughfare and their escape route. When they did occasionally settle inland, it was always with a firm connection to an established coastal city.

This is how Thucydides summarizes the process, looking back from the late fifth century: "The Athenians settled Ionia and most of the islands, while Italy and Sicily were settled for the most part by the Peloponnesians, who also made some settlements in Greece itself. All these foundations took place later than the Trojan wars." The origins of the colonists mattered even though the mother city did not retain political control over the new settlements (Corinth attempted to do so, but with little success). All the new colonies, most of which were founded by enterprising men from a single town, took with them their tribal identity, inherited loyalties and enmities, dialect, preferred style of clothing and architecture, musical idioms, and even genres of song.

In their new settlements they continued worshipping the same gods at the same festivals and using the same names for months as they had in their mother city. Southern Italy and Sicily (together known as Magna Graecia), as Thucydides noted, were predominantly Doric, although Achaeans from the northern Peloponnese founded three cities on the sole of the Italian "boot"—Croton, Sybaris, and Metapontum. Since the Dorians' calendar revolved around festivals of Apollo, and they had a special regard for Heracles, the new cities in Italy honored these two figures. Croton had one temple of Apollo, another for his attendants the Muses, and it imprinted the tripod, symbol of his oracle at Delphi, on its coins. Sybaris claimed to house the original bow and arrows of Heracles, but so did Metapontum, which also built two temples to Apollo in the sixth century.

For all the Greeks, not only the Dorians, Apollo was implicated in the project of expansion overseas as god of the oracle at Delphi, on the Greek mainland at the "navel" or epicenter of the world encircling the pond. As we shall see later, the aural connection the Greeks heard between the name Delphi and the word for dolphin, *delphis*, made the link between the oracle and maritime expeditions enticing. Delphi was already the site of a sanctuary of Apollo in the eighth century BC. In the *Odyssey*, Agamemnon is said to have consulted the god about the expediency of going to war against Troy. Greek myth placed the foundation of the cult center in the earliest prehistory, before even the Olympian males—Zeus and Apollo included—had taken over the universe. Apollo was believed to have usurped the previous incumbent(s)—Mother Earth and/or her daughter, a massive snake or dragon called the Python. This means that the Greeks believed, rightly or wrongly, that the oracle was of great antiquity, functioning already in the Bronze Age. The oracle was certainly consulted by the Spartans in the archaic period, and the original temple was built in the seventh century; the Pythian games were inaugurated in 582 BC. By this time, Greek colonization had been in full swing for decades, and every colonizer wanted the approval of the Pythian Apollo.

Gaining a consultation with his priestess was a challenge in itself.

She only operated on certain days in the year, and so it was necessary to plan ahead. The climb up the rocky hillside to the sanctuary of Apollo is arduous. Once at Delphi, if the priests could not elicit a propitious response from a ram by making it tremble when they sprinkled it with water, then the priestess would not deliver a response. The priestess, ritually bathed, awaited visitors in a rock chamber below the temple, into which they descended. She sat on a tripod, perhaps over a fissure in the floor, or possibly astride equipment under a false floor that allowed smoke or steam to arise. Holding twigs of bay, and under the inspiration of Apollo, she theatrically delivered her oracles. It is not clear whether she gave them directly to the questioners herself, or whether they were "translated" into verse riddles by one of the male priests. No convincing evidence has proved any of the rationalizing explanations for her trancelike state.

It may seem surprising to us that the Greeks should have referred decisions about something as important as colonization to the pronouncements of a woman in a trance. But the accuracy of the oracle in predicting the future was remarkable. One explanation is that the ambiguity of the language of the prophecies more or less guaranteed that most of them could be proved correct retrospectively, and this applies particularly to prophecies about the choice of site for a new colony. For example, the colonizers from Chalcis, in Euboea, who founded Rhegium, on the toe of Italy, were told by the Pythia to build a town where they discovered "the male married to the female": What they actually found was a vine (which is gendered masculine in the ancient Greek language) entwined with a wild fig tree (which is grammatically feminine). In another example, the Spartans who founded Taras (now Taranto), in Apulia, southern Italy, were told by the oracle to look for a place where a goat dipped his beard into the sea. Since the word for the "shoot" of a vine sounded similar to the word for "goat," when they found a vine that came into contact with seawater, they decided that the provision of the oracle had been fulfilled, and founded their colony on the spot.

Once a group of colonizers had acquired some advice from the Delphic oracle, they set about organizing their departure from their mother city. The Greeks did not found many colonies on the coast of Africa relative to the coasts of south Italy and the Black Sea, but as it happens the most detailed account of the process concerns the foundation of a colony in Libya. This was colonized by migrants from Thera (Santorini), the central Aegean island between the Cyclades and Crete discussed in chapter 1. The episode also introduces us to a remarkable individual, Battus, a man who must have possessed extraordinary courage. He led a group of Therans to found a Greek settlement farther west in Africa than most Greeks could conceive. The date was 630 BC, and the location of the new colony was Cyrene, on the northeastern coast of Libya (now Shahhat). Herodotus offers two versions of the events leading up to the foundation of Cyrene, as asserted by the mother city and the colony, respectively. The version told by the people of Thera in Herodotus's day (around 440 BC), the descendants of the islanders who had decided to send out the colony two centuries earlier, claimed that the underlying reason why the emigration had become necessary was a seven-year drought. The destination was (ambiguously) ordained by the Delphic oracle. The man chosen to be the new king—Battus—was a young courtier of the king of Thera. The colonizers were chosen from every one of the seven districts of Thera, and the brothers in each family drew lots to decide which one was to go. They sailed from Thera on just two pentecont- ers, ships rowed by fifty men each.

But Herodotus says the people of Cyrene tell a different tale. In their version, Battus was something of an outsider, as the son of an emigré Cretan princess, and he became unpopular with the Therans. They blamed their sufferings on him, and would not allow him to remain on Thera. There are two conflicting accounts, therefore, of the reasons why Cyrene was colonized by Therans in the first place. It is one of the great virtues of Herodotus that when he knew two different versions of the same story, he tended to record them both and allowed his reader to compare them. In the eyes of the people of Thera, the island that sent out the colony, the leader of the expedition, Battus, was a full-blooded Theran who was heroically trying to find a solution to the hunger caused on the home island by drought. To the people of

Cyrene, the colony in Libya, Battus was half-Cretan and driven into exile by the Therans.

The two different versions may both hold a grain of truth. They illustrate the variety of causes of Greek colonization. Some colonies must have been founded because of circumstances like those in the Theran version—the inhabitants of long-established cities were short of resources or afflicted by natural disaster. Other individual colonizers may, on the contrary, have been forced to leave, as the people of Cyrene believed Battus had been forced to leave Thera, either because they were politically unpopular or because they were suspected of criminal offenses. But in many cases, political upheavals will have been caused or exacerbated by shortage of land or food. There was a growth in both population and production from the late ninth century onward. It accelerated in the eighth century and lasted into the fifth century BC. The growth was related to expansion into countryside areas within mainland Greece as well as expansion overseas. Some areas that the Greeks colonized early had reputations for providing rich arable land. Sicily is a case in point. Recent research has shown that the ancient climate and soil quality did indeed provide the rich crops that the literary evidence and the importance of the cult of Demeter on that island have long suggested. But in the case of the enterprising Battus and the foundation of his Libyan colony, we do have another piece of evidence. In the mid-1920s, an extraordinary inscription was found by the excavators at Cyrene, which purported to quote the oath taken by the original colonizers. Despite much scholarly skepticism, the dominant view is now that the information contained in this inscribed stone is authentic. The oath not only supports the outlines of the Therans' story as reported by Herodotus but adds fascinating details.

According to the inscription, the Therans swore to sail as Battus's "comrades"—that is, not his subjects or servants. They swore to "sail on equal terms with one another," not divided into nobility and commoners. One adult son was to be enrolled from each family, and "any free man from the Therans who wishes may also sail." Effort has gone into creating a community of consenting adults committed to the enterprise. Yet there is concern that there may be need for coercion when it comes to the brothers chosen by lot: If anyone refuses to go, or hides someone refusing to go, then he is to suffer the death penalty and have his property confiscated. On the other hand, the oath does take precautionary action against problems that might arise. If the colony is successful, then any new colonist who joins the group can have his share in the citizenship, its privileges, and any areas of land that had not already been assigned to public use or to other colonists. But if it proves impossible for the colony to survive safely and put down firm roots in Libya, and there are problems for five years, then the colonists can return to Thera and reclaim their property and citizenship. The oath was ratified by an unusual ritual involving all the Theraeans, both those leaving and those staying behind, "all of them together, men and women, boys and girls." Wax images were burned while the curses on those who might not uphold the terms of the treaty were pronounced by this entire intergenerational congregation. The melting of the wax images symbolized "the person who does not abide by these oaths, but transgresses," for he "shall melt and flow away just as these images, he and his descendants and his property."

The experience of setting up new communities had an irrevocable impact on Greek myth and thought. Every new community had to forge relationships with the ethnic groups it encountered on arrival, whether they were dominantly hostile or cooperative. The Greeks learned new languages and skills in the process. In some places they became more acculturated to the local way of life than in others—Herodotus describes the *meixoellenes*, "mixed-Greek" tribes of the northern Black Sea. The Greeks became expert at identifying indigenous foreign gods with members of their own pantheon—war gods with Ares and goddesses who looked after animals with Artemis. Every new community also needed a foundation story explaining its origin, the identity of its patron gods, and connections with the labyrinth of narratives that constituted Greek mythology. Colonization created many well-loved myths, and they are often more joyous than those we inherit from Homer and tragedy. Cities are founded because Greek gods fall in love with indigenous maidens (whose distinct personalities were designed to reflect the character of the new colony) or pursue them across the sea from their original haunts in Greece. Arethusa, the wild-haired presiding nymph of the great Sicilian city of Syracuse, who adorns its spectacular coins, was chased there from old Greece by the river god Alpheus.

The most westerly Greek settlement of significance was Massalia, where Greeks from Asia Minor imported the grapevine, thus inaugurating the now world-famous French wine industry. A cluster of appealing legends grew up around its foundation. In about 650 BC, an islander from Samos named Kolaios was blown off course on his way to Egypt. When he returned he was loaded with silver, acquired from lands beyond the Pillars of Heracles and the Phoenician colony at Cadiz. Kolaios had visited what we call Spain. Enterprising mariners from Phocaea, in Asia Minor, took their cue from him, sailed west, and set up trading posts on the coast of Spain. Having noticed en route a natural harbor among fertile plains fed by the streams running into the Rhone estuary, they approached the local barbarian king, Nanus of the Ligurians. He just so happened to be preparing a feast at which his daughter Gyptis would select a husband. Conveniently for the Greeks, she took a shine to one of them, variously named Protis and Euxenes, and the wedding of the brave Greek sailor to the French princess thus symbolized the happy union of Greek and indigenous cultures.

Our best source for colonization myths is often Pindar, a Theban commissioned by rich ruling-class Greeks to write praise poems. They were performed on festive occasions, often the return home of a victor in an athletics or musical competition. Beautiful legends about the foundation of Cyrene are narrated in the lavish Epinician (Victory) Odes that Pindar composed to hail the victories of Greek Libyans. One, named Telesicrates, won the event known as the "hoplite race" at Olympia in 476 BC. This was a race in which the runners wore the bronze metal helmet and shin guards of the hoplite soldier (an infantryman armed with shield and spear) and carried a round shield. Pindar's song in praise of Telesicrates recounts how Apollo fell in love with Cyrene, a Thessalian maiden. A tomboy, she preferred hunting to weaving. When Apollo first saw her, she was wrestling with a lion. The persuasive god enticed her into his golden chariot and took her to

Libya, where he made her mistress of the land named after her, "rich in flocks and abounding in fruits . . . on the root of the third continent." The athletes of Cyrene are thus given Apollo as divine progenitor and a feisty foremother renowned for her physical valor. When King Arcesilas of Cyrene won the chariot race at the Pythian games a few years later, Pindar elaborated the story of the foundation of Cyrene by Battus, the version known to Herodotus. But Pindar binds the story to the journey of the Argonauts. Battus's ancestor Euphemus was an Argonaut; Euphemus had visited North Africa before originating the bloodline at Thera that would one day found Cyrene.

Arcesilas IV of Cyrene was a constitutional monarch, the direct eighth-generation descendant of Battus I, the founding father of his city. The Cyrenean colonists may originally have cherished an egalitarian ethos, but the royal family soon acquired special status. By the fifth century, Arcesilas's situation was exceptional in the Greek world. Most of Pindar's customers were much more parvenu, the sons or grandsons of the newly rich tyrants who had replaced hereditary kings in the seventh and sixth centuries BC. The term *tyrannos* always carried some negative connotations, but its basic meaning was a ruler who had seized power, usually with popular support, rather than having inherited it. The philosopher Aristotle later developed a credible theory that these tyrants were "degenerate monarchs," dictators who rode the wave of poorer people's unhappiness with their kings during the economic turmoil at the end of what has been called, as we saw earlier, the Dark Age. When the masses needed an articulate leader to champion their cause and remove the kings, rival aristocrats and newly rich tradesmen exploited the instability of the political situation. Another factor was the rise of hoplite warfare, in which the *demos* ("people," or mass of non-aristocrats) was increasingly a direct participant. Free adult males in the city were now expected to form a hoplite army and be ready to fight with shield and spear against any common enemy. This fostered a new sense of entitlement among ordinary men, who were not yet confident or organized enough to lay claim to sovereign power themselves. The picture was complicated by the economic shifts that ultimately led to the introduction of coinage; some historians argue that a new class of successful traders and manufacturers challenged the landowning aristocracy and that the tyrants resulted from this power struggle. The rising commercial "middle class" needed a single ruler whom they could bulldoze into supporting their interests against kings or oligarchic groups of hereditary landowners. It is also possible that some tyrants, especially those in Ionian cities, emphasized their tribal identity, thus exploiting ethnic tensions between different city-states in ways that may have facilitated the dethroning of aristocratic dynasties, often by bloody and sensational coups d'etat.

Colonization itself was sometimes a result of the factional infighting that afflicted the Greek city-states in the seventh and sixth centuries. But it may also have been a cause. It had created new sources of wealth and movement between cities and their colonies, with concomitant disruptions in balances of power. The shiploads of Greeks on the move around the Mediterranean and the Black Sea often included aristocrats in flight from their ancestral homelands as well as the hungry or disgruntled lower classes. But the tyrants were not just representatives of newly empowered citizen groups. They were flamboyant, ostentatious, egotistical, and materialistic individuals who competed with each other in displays of power and wealth. They had few of the traditional reservations about excess and self-promotion that had sometimes restrained the more pious of the hereditary kings and landowning aristocrats. The tyrants thus exerted a massive influence on the cultural and social life of the Greeks. They loved to be honored and to have their prestige celebrated—their motive was universally understood to be *philotimia*, or love of honor. In particular, they wanted to win personal renown at the festival competitions.

The flamboyant tyrants of Corinth, for example, took power in 655 BC when the first of them, Cypselus, orchestrated a violent coup and overthrew the Bacchiad family. It is possible that Cypselus was himself a poor relation of the royal family, but more likely that this genealogy was concocted to conceal his humble (possibly non-Corinthian) origins. Cypselus was said to have worked for the Bacchiads as a military captain, a *polemarch*, and by winning the allegiance of the militia achieved total power. Once he had become tyrant, he was protected by his own personal bodyguard. Indeed, the personal bodyguard, and the paranoia that made implementing it necessary, were to become characteristic marks of this category of ruler in Greek thought and theater. The tendency of successful militiamen to attempt tyranny is also evinced a little northwest, at Sicyon, where it was another *polemarch*, Orthagoras, who ousted the hereditary dynasts. These two Peloponnesian tyrants, Cypselus and Orthagoras, were followed by Theagenes in Megara in 640, who then supported Cylon, his son-in-law, in an unsuccessful attempt to become tyrant of Athens. Cylon was himself actually an Olympic victor, which gave him the public profile helpful in the acquisition of a tyranny. But Cylon's coup failed. While he personally escaped the Athenians, his supporters were executed.

Tyranny was the least appealing of the practices that the Greeks picked up from non-Greeks. Cypselus and the other tyrants seem to have been consciously following an example set by the enterprising ruler of their closest eastern neighbors, the near-legendary Gyges of Lydia. In about 685 BC this unknown (and possibly less than aristocratic) individual had usurped the hereditary monarch, Candaules, and conquered much of Asia Minor. Gyges acquired wealth as well as international renown, which he fostered by welcoming foreign guests in Lydia and sending gifts overseas. Many far-fetched stories circulated about his coup, including the famous tale that King Candaules had forced him to look at his queen with no clothes on, and that she had subsequently demanded that Gyges kill the king or die himself. The term *tyrannos* came from the language spoken by the Lydians or a people farther south on the Asiatic seaboard, the Lycians or the Carians, and Gyges was one of the first rulers to be called a *tyrant* by the Greeks. They were impressed by his fabulous wealth, displayed in the sumptuous gold and silver artworks he donated to the sanctuary at Delphi, with inscriptions naming the gods to which they were dedicated.

Even among the brutal and high-handed tyrants of ancient Greece, it is the tyrants of the Greek cities of Sicily who were most notorious. The island's tendency toward rule by powerful individuals manifested itself early. In 734 the Corinthians drove out the indigenous Sicels from the island of Ortygia. This small island lies just off the east coast of Sicily, at the point where the colonists subsequently spilled over to build the great city of Syracuse. But a few decades later the family known as the Myletidae was expelled, only to play an important role in the foundation of Himera on the north coast of the island. Leontini, south of Syracuse, was taken over by a tyrant in 610 BC. Farther around the coast to the south and west, Akragas was tyrannized in the first half of the sixth century by Phalaris, the most reviled despot in ancient Greek history. He was said to have roasted his enemies alive in an enormous oven, made for the purpose of executing them, in the form of a huge bronze bull. He enjoyed pretending that their shrieks of pain were the animal bellowing. Phalaris was followed by two more tyrants before the people of Akragas finally established a democracy in the mid-fifth century.

At Selinus, the most westerly Greek city on the island, a tyrant called Peithagoras took power in about 510 BC, only to be ousted by a Spartan named Euryleon. The apparent tolerance of tyrants by Greeks in Sicily has been explained as a response to the permanent threat from the Carthaginians (who never lost possession of Sardinia), from bellicose indigenous tribes, and from the Etruscans, who controlled Corsica and put pressure on the Greeks in southwest Italy. But it was to these political strongmen that we owe the stunning Greek architecture that can still be seen in Sicily and south Italy. The tyrants of Akragas began building the extraordinary temples bestriding the ridge between the city and the sea. The beautiful early sixth-century temples of Hera and probably Poseidon were financed by rich Greeks at Posidonia (Paestum), as well as those of Zeus, Apollo, and Athena at Syracuse.

A more enticing name for the period of the tyrants in the seventh to sixth centuries is the "lyric age of Greece," for it is in these centuries that the foundational poets of Western personal and occasional poetry produced their songs. They were sung to the accompaniment of the lyre (usually smaller than the epic *cithara*) or in some cases pipes. Shorter than the epics of Homer, and in a variety of rhythms suited to dance, song, or both, the poems are astounding in their variety and sophistication. Although most of their authors used writing to perfect their pieces, these songs retain strong marks of their genesis in an oral culture, where people sang to mark every occasion—weddings, funerals, harvests. Each Greek must have known more than a hundred songs by heart. Although the poets shared a vocabulary steeped in Homer, they composed in different dialects of Greek according to their own heritage. The independence of the western Greeks in Magna Graecia is demonstrated by the lyric poet of Himera, Stesichorus, who around 600 BC took to new heights the Dorian genre of lyric mythical narrative for performance by dancing choirs. Stesichorus also composed a notorious poem in which he archly claimed that Helen never went to Troy at all—and this pugnacious tone is not atypical of the poems of the era. Many of them revel in portraying the individuality of their author, and the attitude is often self-assertive, indeed willful.

The poems of the seventh and sixth centuries BC are the preeminent ancient Greek texts for the assertion of joie de vivre, for celebrating love and pleasure, laughter and luxury. Many explore the physical and emotional effects of wine and of sexual desire, and are suitable for symposia; some are elevated in tone, reflecting on how transitory life is, while others are far more earthy. Satirical tirades attack personal enemies and sneer at men in power. There are songs for maidens before they are married. There are dirges to perform at funerals and hymns to be sung in the temples of the gods. Greek lyric poetry is a fast-evolving field. Over the last hundred years, many previously unknown poems have been deciphered from papyri, texts that were once copied out by Greeks in Roman Egypt and preserved by accident. The largest number of papyri come from an ancient rubbish tip in Oxyrhynchus, a Greek city on a tributary of the Nile named after its totemic fish, a sharp-nosed pike.

Many poets of the archaic era were Aegean islanders. The earliest and perhaps the best was Archilochus, the trenchant soldier of Paros, who described himself as both a comrade of Ares and a savant of the Muses. Far from sentimental about his home island, in a famous line he derides "Paros and its fig sheds, surrounded by marine life." He was just as rude about Thasos, where he was involved in establishing a colony and fighting Thracian tribes. He preferred a life on the move, in "a good ship with three sails and a smart steersman." He declares himself uninterested in acquiring either riches or power: "Not for me the wealth of Gyges . . . I have no desire for a great tyranny." But Archilochus knew how to lead a drinking session with a song for Dionysus, his "wits blasted out with wine as if by thunder." He also possessed candor, baldly stating his philosophy, to do as he had been done by: "One big thing I understand: if someone does me wrong, to pay him back with terrible suffering." A recently published fragment reveals his sardonic approach to epic myth: He says that his army recently had to retreat, but that he feels no shame. Look at the Greeks who made a mistake when they attacked Mysia in Asia Minor instead of Troy, says Archilochus, and found themselves having to retreat. In a famous short poem, Archilochus asserts that he doesn't care if he had to abandon his shield on the battlefield, and some barbarian now gloats over it. At least he has escaped with his life.

Archilochus changed the course of poetic history by putting his own irreverent subjectivity at the heart of his songs. In an iambic poem, of which astonishing fragments came to light in the late twentieth century, he lambastes an enemy named Lycambes. Lycambes has broken a promise, perhaps to allow Archilochus to marry his daughter Neoboule. Archilochus therefore attacks Neoboule, deriding her attractiveness and accusing her of promiscuity. He persuades another woman, a virgin, perhaps Neoboule's sister, to let him have nonpenetrative sex with her. He reports that he achieved some kind of intimacy with his new lover; by staying within her "grassy garden plot," he ejaculated white semen on her golden hair. This is the most explicit discussion of sexual activity in archaic literature. The ancient Greeks said that Lycambes's whole family, as a result of Archilochus's vituperation, committed suicide.

In early sixth-century Lesbos, another soldier-poet, Alcaeus, sang with passion and menace about local tyrants, drinking, and life on the battlefield and at sea. A famous hymn honors Castor and Polydeuces, patron divinities of mariners. Another poem celebrated competitions in female beauty held on his home island. Rivalry in female attractiveness is reminiscent of Sappho, these days the most famous of the Greek lyric poets, who, like Alcaeus, was associated with Mytilene on Lesbos. Her poems reflect the island's proximity to the rich bar-barian culture of Lydia, only ten nautical miles away: Her child, she tells us, is a lovely girl named Cleis, whom she would not exchange for the whole of Lydia. The fragmentary poems in Sappho's name include exquisite hymns to Aphrodite, wedding songs, and some per-sonal poems of uncertain genre but stunning emotional directness and sensory appeal. When she watches the woman she loves laughing with a man, she analyzes her own physical responses: "I can't speak, my tongue won't work, a sudden fire darts under my skin, I can't see anymore, there is a roaring in my ears, I run with sweat and shake all over." When forced to part from a lover, she is cast into despair: "Honestly, I wish I were dead." Her thoughts are full of erotic memo-ries: "For beside me you donned many crowns of roses and garlands of flowers around your soft neck; you anointed yourself with costly royal fragrance and satisfied your desire on soft couches." In a recently dis-covered poem, she plays with the gender of lover and beloved by never revealing whether the speaker is male or female, while remembering the beauty of the young Tithonus, carried to the world's end by the lovelorn goddess of the dawn.

Although Sappho is unusual since she is a female poet, the homo-eroticism of some of her works is unremarkable. It is elsewhere found in women's songs related to the cults of goddesses, especially those who oversaw the biological and sexual aspects of their lives—Artemis and Aphrodite, for example, in the Spartan songs for choruses of maid-ens by Alcman. But homoeroticism is a feature of symposium poetry written by men, and the age of tyrants and lyric poetry was the period when the fashion for symposia, probably in imitation of Eastern pal-ace practice, swept across the Greek world. Women held banquets at festivals from which men were excluded, and there is no reason to sup-pose that Sappho's songs were not sung at them as at other parties. The typical symposium, however, was a ritualized male drinking ses-sion, from which respectable women were excluded, although female musicians and sex workers were not. By inviting other men as guests to a symposium, a host could indicate that he shared with them a lei-sured and elegant lifestyle. The wealthy began to build special rooms designed to hold up to twenty men, paired, perfumed, garlanded with flowers and facing each other on couches. They would discuss current affairs, sing, listen to the music of pipe and lyre, and tell stories.

There was also lighthearted and eroticized intergenerational mentoring: One symposium song by Alcaeus begins simply, "Wine, my dear boy, and truth!" The collective excitement and physical intimacy were enhanced by the steady intake of wine. The younger men were schooled in candor, humor, and the behavior appropriate to a leisure-class clique. It is in this context that we need to understand the reason why many symposium poems are addressed, in the voice of an older male lover or admirer, to a much younger man. Hundreds of ancient Greek vase paintings depict such drinking parties, as do cups and jugs created for use at them. The best visual representation is in the Tomb of the Diver at Paestum (Posidonia)—the guests are singing to a pipe, embracing their partners affectionately, and playing *kottabos*, a boisterous party game in which they competed in aiming the dregs of their wine at targets. The playful atmosphere of the symposium is best expressed in the erotic songs of Anacreon, an eastern Greek poet patronized by the tyrant Polycrates of Samos, and resident court poet on that island. The sexual desire he expressed is sometimes heterosexual: He tells a "Thracian filly" that she needs a man to "break her in" and ride her. But it was with beautiful youths that Anacreon was primarily associated. His poems speak of handsome boys who frolic in hyacinth fields, of a "boy with the glance of a girl" who "holds the reins" of his soul. He tells us that he is "crazy" with love for Cleoboulos; Megistes, we hear, is garlanded with willow and has been on a ten-month drinking binge.

In poems like these, the flirtatious homoeroticism has a political aspect. Admiration for physical beauty, and the adornment of the self with fine clothes and flowers, are both channeled into nonreproductive sexual relationships and private recreation, the privileges of an elite leisured class. Homoeroticism is connected with the cult of beauty and bodily excellence central to athletics competitions; indeed, formal competitions in male beauty took place at the Panathenaic games. Consumption of luxury goods in the private and selective environment of a symposium suggests a shared refinement of taste and sensibility. The symposium first took hold in Greek cities as an institution of aristocratic life; it offered rich families a way to affirm private relationships with other households that transcended the boundaries of their own city-states, thus offering an alternative set of alliances in the face of the civic struggles over resources and power that had resulted in the rise of the tyrants. In the poetry of Megarian Theognis, addressed to his lover Cyrnus, we hear the cynical voice of a disgruntled sixth-century aristocrat who has lost land in social upheavals and fears the collapse of what his conservative instincts regard as traditional morality. But the symposium did not remain an exclusively aristocratic phenomenon. The tenor of the poetry of Archilochus and some other symposium poets, especially the invective verses of Hipponax or Semonides, often resembles that of the sullen peasant Hesiod. Their emphasis is not on homoerotic liaisons but on the temporary relief from war, or the daily grind of life, offered by a drinking session. The variety of attitudes expressed in the symposium poetry of the age of the tyrants thus reflects the underlying class struggle.

The importance of the symposium in newly founded colonies is apparent from the large number of cups and jugs for wine that have been found by archaeologists excavating far-flung Greek settlements. In Posidonia, where the Tomb of the Diver portrays an elegant symposium in full swing, potters began making distinctive local symposium pottery instead of importing it. The presiding god of the symposium, Dionysus, is portrayed on many, along with his retinues of reveling satyrs and maenads. In myth, Dionysus is the god of epiphany. He arrives on land from the sea. Sometimes he arrives in a ship accompanied by dolphins, as on a gorgeous black-figure cup proudly signed by the incomparable potter Exekias, where his white-sailed ship, surrounded by glossy black dolphins, glides across the smooth coral-red surface; in some sources Dionysus rides on a dolphin himself. In the archaic *Hymn to Dionysus*, he is captured by Tyrrhenian (Etruscan) pirates and only escapes by changing them into dolphins. The strange image of men-dolphins, or men in the process of metamorphosing into dolphins, which also appears in vase painting, suggests that when Greeks were thinking about Dionysus in a maritime context, they imagined themselves as dolphins of his retinue rather than land-based satyrs; after all, they created a visual link between dolphin and satyr by nicknaming and painting them both as *simos*, "snub-nosed." The very experience of the symposium itself suggested the analogy of the sea voyage, and the link here had something to do with the music of the *aulos*, a reeded instrument more like our modern oboe than the flute.

Plato compared the inhabitants of the cities around the Mediterranean and the Black Sea with communities of frogs or ants round a pond, but the animal that universally symbolized the experience of colonizers was the dolphin. At Taras, the foundation hero Phalanthos was saved from drowning by a dolphin, and he is depicted as such on the coins of the town, along with the eponymous hero Taras, a son of Poseidon. Dolphin-riders appear on the coins of numerous cities both on mainland Greece and on the islands, as well as in the colonies. The most famous was Arion, a poet who played the cithara (Apollo's instrument) but who invented the dithyramb, the hymn to Dionysus. In a story featuring all the core elements of the age of tyrants, lyric poetry, and colonization, Herodotus relates that Arion was a musician from the island of Lesbos. He worked at the court of the Corinthian tyrant Periander. Arion sailed to Taras in Italy to take part in a musical contest. After winning, he was thrown overboard, en route back to Corinth, by crewmen. But a dolphin, in acknowledgment of the beauty of Arion's singing, carried him to shore at Taenarum in the Peloponnese, where there was a sanctuary of Poseidon.

The psychological connection between poetry and the dolphin is stressed by the lyric poet Pindar. He praises the work of another poet—a Sicilian—because it has made him feel "like a dolphin of the sea, which the lovely melody of pipes has excited in the expanse of a waveless sea." The ancient Greek sailors employed musicians to help them keep time as they rowed, and preferred for this purpose the penetrating, plangent music of the *aulos*. The pipe music used to attract dolphins to leap in schools alongside ancient ships was beautifully described by a chorus in a tragedy by Euripides, his *Electra*. Dolphins were therefore associated with the dancing choruses in the cult of Dionysus, who were set in motion both by wine drinking and by the *aulos*, the instrument central to his rites.

The ancient Greek metaphor of the symposium as a voyage in a seagoing ship was produced by the cultural connection between the symposium and colonization. How better to cement the esprit de corps of a new community, who have together braved the perils of the open sea, than by a constructive drinking session? The frenzy of a storm at sea as experienced by a crew is used as a metaphor for the collective psychological experience of fellow symposiasts. Euripides' bibulous Heracles in *Alcestis*, a favorite hero of colonization myth, sees a connection between rhythmically raising and lowering a wine cup to drink and the steady rhythm of rowing. The metaphor became near-reality when a house in the Sicilian city of Akragas was actually renamed the Trireme after a carousal. The young symposiasts became so inebriated that they imagined they were being battered by a storm while out at sea:

> Finally, they completely lost their senses and tossed all the furniture and bedding out of the house as though upon the waters, convinced that the pilot directed them to lighten the ship because of the raging storm. Well, a great crowd gathered and began to carry off the jetsam, but even then the youngsters did not cease from their mad actions.

When the drunkards were called to account, they explained that they had been temporarily deluded. They were pardoned on condition that they never drank excessively again. The implication is that they needed some older men at the symposium to train them in "responsible" drinking.

In the temporary madness of the symposium, the Greek sailor-colonists of the lyric age drank in the presence of the seagoing wine god, with his leaping entourage of music-loving dolphins, until they became "half seas over" and their collective "ship came in." The dolphin was associated with two other senior Olympian gods important during the Greek migrations. Poseidon, frequently portrayed in art with a dolphin, was the grandfather of Theseus, and dolphins helped Theseus come back from the seabed on an adventure on his way to Crete. Poseidon was tied to a dolphin story also involving Dionysus on the Greek mainland at Megara and Corinth, two cities heavily involved in colonization. A Greek princess named Ino hurled herself and her son off the Molurian cliff. Dionysus transformed Ino into an important sea goddess named Leukothea, while a dolphin appeared to transport the body of her son to the Isthmus, where an altar to him was built beside a sacred pine tree. At nearby Corinth, Leukothea and her son were worshipped in conjunction with Poseidon. Here we catch a rare glimpse of a Phoenician element in this seaside tale of a hero and a dolphin (not unlikely given the history of trading between the Phoenicians and Corinth). In some versions of the story, Ino's son is named Palaemon, but in others he is named Melicertes, a straightforward Hellenization of the Phoenician hero Melquart's name.

Greeks were terrified of hideous monsters lurking in the ocean to devour hapless seamen. They felt an affinity with dolphins and imagined them to be victims of the same leviathans. In the *Odyssey*, the monstrous six-headed, twelve-footed Scylla plucks men from ships, but it is dolphins on which she normally preys. Dolphins, like humans, are intelligent mammals with strong social and kinship ties. They evince what appears, to human eyes, to be joy when they cavort in the water. They do not predate on humans. These are some of the reasons why many seagoing human societies have formed psychological and ritual bonds with the dolphin. None have been as intense as the Greeks'. They painted dolphins on their walls, emblazoned them on their shields, and carved them on their gemstones. No fewer than forty Greek cities portrayed a dolphin on their coins. Dolphins appear abundantly in ancient Mediterranean art and literature, from the frescoes of Thera and Knossos to the Byzantine Christian story that the martyred corpse of St. Lucian of Antioch was recovered for his disciples by a dolphin. The Greeks believed that the feeling was reciprocal: A fable by Aesop tells how a dolphin gave a monkey a lift on his back, mistaking him for a human, but, by testing his intelligence with questions, discovered that he was too ignorant to be human and therefore abandoned him to be drowned.

The perceived connection of the dolphin with colonization transcended tribal identities. The cult of Apollo as Delphinios, Apollo of the Dolphin, was originally Ionian, and Ionian men were sometimes given the personal name Delphinios. But the cult and the name were adopted by Dorians as well, for example at Sparta and on Aegina. The myth the Greeks used to explain this title interlaced the themes of seafaring, colonization, poetry, and prophecy at Apollo's Delphic seat. An archaic hymn to Apollo explains that when the god was looking for priests to serve in the sanctuary, he spotted a Cretan ship from Knossos sailing toward Pylos to trade. Apollo turned himself into a dolphin, leaped onto the Cretans' ship, and prevented them from throwing him overboard. A swift wind provided by Apollo propelled them all the way around the Peloponnese to the coast at Crisa, near Delphi. After lighting the fire in his shrine and turning back into anthropomorphic form, Apollo told the Cretans that they were destined to serve his oracular shrine. He ordered them to build an altar on the beach, light a fire, make an offering, and pray to him as Apollo of the Dolphin, because it was in the form of a dolphin that he had led them there. They were to proceed to his oracle singing the paean, the special hymn to Apollo. The Cretan leader raised the issue of earning a livelihood; like any sensible colonist, he had assessed the terrain and seen that it would be hospitable neither to vines nor to livestock. But Apollo promised that their needs would be met, and the Cretan immigrants, brought over the sea by Apollo of the Dolphin, became forefathers of the priests of Pythian Apollo.

Apollo of the Dolphin was worshipped in temples overlooking harbors at the extremities of the Greek colonial world. In the far west, at Massalia, where the Ionian leader from Phocaea had married the local princess, twin temples of Apollo Delphinios and his sister Artemis stood on the rocky headland. When the Greeks took stories about male gods and dolphins on their colonial adventures, they sometimes imported physical statues of Artemis with them as well. These were often bound up with another Apolline myth, the story that Orestes and his sister Iphigenia had stolen the ancient cult image of Artemis from the Taurians of the northern Black Sea in order to bring it to a new home in a temple where Greeks worshipped. Several south Italian Greek communities were traditionally the recipients of the sacred image of the Taurian Artemis, especially around the straits dividing the mainland from Sicily. But at Massalia, Artemis was specifically said to be the Ephesian Artemis; when the Phocaeans set sail for the west, they were told by an oracle to put in at Ephesus (another glamorous Ionian town on the Asiatic seaboard) on the way.

A local woman named Aristarcha dreamed that Artemis ordered her to join the Phocaeans' ship, taking one of the goddess's carved wooden images from Ephesus. Aristarcha obeyed, becoming the first priestess of Artemis in the new colony, presiding over the temple beside her dolphin-brother who shows colonists the way to their new homes across the sea.

At Miletus, indeed, a guild of sacred singers, the Molpoi, were dedicated to Apollo Delphinios. The dolphin's connection with music and poetry thus transcended the difference between the gods Dionysus (in charge of the dithyramb, the pipes, and sympotic poetry) and Apollo (associated with epic poetry, the cithara, and the Muses). There was a connection between the rites of initiation into manhood and the singing of paeans to Apollo in his guise as Apollo Delphinios. His worship may also have involved young men being sent on ritualized return voyages to and from distant locations in order to mark their integration into the adult community. When the Milesians founded colonies across the sea, they intuitively felt that Apollo of the Dolphin had helped them to sail there, and they founded new shrines in his honor. Apollo Delphinios was worshipped in the Milesians' Black Sea colonies of Olbia, Sinope, Gorgippia, and Olbia. At Olbia, Apollo Delphinios was served by a choir given the same name (Molpoi) as their counterparts in Olbia's mother city of Miletus. One of the peculiarities of Olbia was its coins, which did not just depict dolphins, as did the coins of many cities, but were actually minted in the three-dimensional shape of dolphins, with curving backs.

Among the hundreds of Greek colonies established during this period, it is Olbia that best demonstrates the Greeks' ability to adapt to new environments. Olbia was founded by the Milesians at the mouth of the River Hypanis (now Bug) on the northern coast of the Black Sea, to the west of the Crimean peninsula. In the seventh century, Milesians were already trading on the island of Berezan, off the Ukrainian coast; in the early sixth century they began living on the mainland and dividing up parcels of land as fields. The construction of an area sacred to Apollo Delphinios shows their commitment to the construction of a permanent colony. Soon afterward, a marketplace appeared, as well as sanctuaries, a space for the political assembly to meet, a theater, and a system of water pipes furnishing fountains in the civic center with continuous water. But there was one problem. The Olbians were unable to grow any vines. It was not until the later part of the Hellenistic period that they developed a system of viticulture that in the inclement local climate could produce any wine. Indeed, they faced a challenge developing an agrarian economy at all, since they could not simply transfer skills in the production of oil, grains, fruit, and vegetables honed in Aegean conditions.

Undaunted, they imported their wine and founded an unusually enthusiastic cult of Dionysus, as if to ensure his continued approval in their vineless backwater. The local Scythians around them did not drink wine, which no doubt made the Olbians even more convinced that, as a Greek community, they must make Dionysus central. The pottery found at Olbia proves that they enjoyed symposia as much as any other Greek colony. One beautiful fragment of an Athenian red-figured wine jar, adorned with masked actors, performers, and musicians, celebrates the power not just of Dionysus but of theater. Proper names connected with Dionysus were popular—Gift of Dionysus, or Dionysodoros, is named in a dedication to the Olbian Apollo Delphinios in about 450 BC. Perhaps the people of Olbia liked the strand of the myth of Dionysus that depicted him as a sailor, arriving loaded with tasty goods from overseas, even though we know that they were often critical of the quality of such imports.

We leave the age of colonization with the Olbians, complaining about the taste of their imported wine while worshipping Dionysus, and individuals like Dionysodorus, proudly inscribing his personal name on a gift he dedicated to Apollo of the Dolphin. The age of colonization, of tyrants, of the creation of Magna Graecia and the mysterious new world of the Hellenized Black Sea, was also the age of lyric poetry, of the distinctive voices of the islands, and of the symposium.

It is the age symbolized by the dolphin, so closely tied to Poseidon, Apollo, and Dionysus, the gods of the sea, of colonial voyages, and of the drinking parties enjoyed by sailors, traders, and migrants. The literature and art of the Greeks of this era displays all their core traits in unusual abundance—joy, wit, verbal acuity, independence of mind, competitiveness, and especially individuality. The mental resourcefulness born of constant sea voyages and creating that diaspora was about to produce something even more remarkable: Greek science and philosophy.

Democritus discovers Protagoras in Abdera.
Print of a nineteenth-century mezzotint
reproduction of an oil painting by Salvator
Rosa (1663). (*Author's personal collection*)

4

Inquiring Ionians

I f we are to imagine the birth of Greek natural science and philosophy in the Asiatic city of Miletus in the sixth century BC, we
need first to imagine a dramatic change in the physical appearance
of the environment. A large chunk of what we now call western Turkey, approximately the whole middle third, stretching inland from the
modern coast for a minimum of forty miles, had not yet been created.
Miletus in the sixth century BC was a harbor town still surrounded
on three sides—west, north, east—by seawater. But the dusty ruins of
Miletus now stand near a small modern town of Balat, miles from the
sea in any direction at all.

The Milesian thinkers who began discussing the unseen causes of
the world were watching that world change almost every day. In about
1000 BC, their harbor began to silt up as the winding (meandering)
River Maeander disgorged itself into the sea far to the northwest, and
the particles of rock and soil, alluvium, sank to the bottom of the estuary. Every year that passed, the alluvium extended the shore toward
Miletus. By the Christian era, Miletus itself was landlocked. The process must have been about half completed when the first philosophers
were alive. They will have mourned the inexorable annexation of their
beloved sea by the stones of the Asiatic continent. They had ships in
their blood, and a foundational voyage in their history, since their own
town had been settled by colonizers from the Peloponnese. Since, as
Greeks, they were insatiably curious—the third of the ten defining

features I identified in the introduction—they inevitably inquired into the reason. They were watching fresh water and stones meet salt water and sand, producing new land on a daily basis, and they became the first people in recorded history to inquire into the origins of the world exclusively in terms of natural causes.

Where earlier Greeks saw the universe as arising first from Chaos and then from gods who resembled humans, the first scientists of western Asia, these Ionians, proposed that the primary constituents of the universe were material substances. The first of them, Thales, who was born in the 620s, thought that the first cosmic principle, or element—the one being pushed back by new land—was water. The argument he used to support this view is that inanimate things lose water and dry out. His student Anaximander drew a map of all the physical world the Milesians knew and suggested that everything they could perceive—both land and sea, which visibly limited each other—must be surrounded by something else that was limitless and immeasurable—*apeiron*. The third Milesian thinker of the time, Anaximenes, watched land expand and sea shrink, and argued that *all* the constituents of the world man could see—fire, wind, cloud, water, earth, stones—are created out of air by processes of condensation or sublimation: The differences between them are to be explained in terms of their relative density. In Ephesus, another city not far from Miletus that also became steadily cut off from the sea, a fourth thinker, Heraclitus, asserted the principle that the physical universe was constantly changing because of the action of a cosmic fire: *Panta rhei*, he said—"Everything is in flux." It is not possible for one river to be entered twice by the same man, according to Heraclitus, because the water that constitutes the river is constantly changing, and men never remain in exactly same state, either.

The intellectual revolution that started in the Maeander estuary in the early sixth century migrated with men from that part of the Greek world first to its colonies in southern Italy and, in the fifth century, after the exponential rise of the Persian Empire, to classical Athens. Many of the ideas the Ionians had set in motion were consummated in the experimental foundation, by Greeks led by Athenians, of a brand-new city with new laws in the 440s BC. In this chapter we shall ask how and why Thales's intellectual descendants in Ionia, Italy, and then Athens harnessed his spirit of nonreligious inquiry to the investigation of the unseen structures and causes of change not only in land, sea, and sky but also in human experience and human activities. They asked about the invisible inner workings of our bodies; they probed the relationship between the worlds we see in our mind's eye and those our senses tell us are physically there, how we make decisions about right and wrong, how we collect information, why different peoples speak different languages and worship diverse gods, why we fight one another or come together in cities, and how the past became the present—how the world's empires came into existence. Because they now had the phonetic alphabet, they were able, for the first time, to write the results of their inquiries down.

These intellectuals included men with names still famous today—Hippocrates, Pythagoras, Herodotus—and equally seminal figures whose names are now less well known: As we shall see, Xenophanes of Colophon was one of the most influential thinkers of all time. They had used the revolutionary technology of writing they had adapted from the Phoenicians not only to invent physical science and write about it in both poetry and prose; they also developed rational medicine, philosophy, mathematics, political theory, ethnography, geography, and the writing of history. Before analyzing in detail these awe-inspiring achievements and the men responsible for them, it is essential to inquire into the complicated set of circumstances on the Maeander estuary that made them possible in the first place.

The two most important factors here—the Greeks' seagoing lifestyle and their openness to non-Greek skills—are both hinted at in the traditions concerning Thales and his successors. The Roman thinker Seneca attests to the fact that Thales said that earthquakes were "rockings of the boat." Thales suggested that the world we inhabit rests on top of water, as a ship rests on the sea. His student Anaximander continued the use of maritime imagery, arguing that the limitless, imperishable phenomenon surrounding the perceptible world also "steered it" (the verb is *kubernan*, which means "steer a ship"). Thales was also believed to have written a treatise on navigation by use of the heavens, a skill the Greeks developed as colonists, and which helped them to see that there were forces at work moving objects in the universe that did not require the arbitrary whims of gods to explain them.

Ancient tradition made Thales either actually a native Phoenician or the son of Phoenicians living in Miletus. The tradition may not be true in a literal sense. But its existence reflects an ancient intuition that Greek science and philosophy owed much to other ancient Near Eastern cultures. It is not out of the question that a mariner-astronomer living in Miletus had Phoenician blood, nor that a Phoenician prior to Thales and Anaximander had suggested that the perceptible world was an enormous seagoing vessel. Yet the Phoenicians were far from the only non-Greeks with whom the Milesians were in intense interaction. In the seventh century, toward the end of which Thales was born, Miletus had formed an alliance, the Ionian League, with other Anatolian Greek city-states. Under a controversial tyrant named Thrasyboulos, they had also fought a lengthy war with Lydia and preserved their independence from that rich land. The peaceful relationship that emerged from the war meant incessant cross-fertilization between the neighboring barbarian and Greek Anatolian cultures. The Milesians had also become the richest Greeks in the region and perhaps in the world. They had a powerful navy and built a maritime empire; they sent out more colonies than any other polis, founding dozens of settlements, especially in the Black Sea, where they had learned more than scholars like to admit from the northern kingdoms of Scythia. In the middle of the sixth century the Milesians then came under the sway of the Persians when Cyrus conquered Croesus's Lydia. For several decades, however, Miletus, bordered by the old barbarian kingdoms of Asia, had been a formidable force in the culture of the Greek-speaking world.

Thales's reported expertise in navigation by the stars may have been connected with the ancestral cults of Miletus as well as with his inborn talent for natural science. New archaeological evidence has come to light over the last three decades that has illuminated the Milesians' cult of Aphrodite, whom they worshipped in an archaic temple outside the city walls. Many seventh- and sixth-century terra-cotta figurines of the goddess have been found, as well as graffiti testifying to the valuable objects and works of art that Milesians bestowed on her temple. Miletus exported its Ionian cults and calendars to its fifty or more northern and Black Sea colonies and entrepôts, in which Aphrodite was an important goddess, for example at Istria and Olbia, where she had the cult title *Euploia* (Fair Voyage). At Panticapaion she was called *Naukratis*, or Ship Power, and at Cyzicus her epithet was *Pontike*, Of the High Seas. At Miletus she was also worshipped as *Aphrogeneia*, or Foam-Born, in line with the Hesiodic story of her generation. But at both Phanagoria and Miletus she had an additional title, *Ourania*, or Celestial, a form in which the goddess was conceived as overseeing navigation by the stars. Thales may have found the leap from Olympian theology to his water-based cosmic theory less abrupt than we do. ·

In chapter 3, we noted the importance of the cult of Apollo Delphinios to all the Ionian Greeks during their colonial expansion. The historical importance of the Ionian identity is indicated by the derivation of the word for "Greek" and "Greece"—*Yavan*—even in modern Arabic, Hebrew, Turkish, and several Indian languages, from the ancient term *Ionian*, via the ancient Persians who pronounced *Ionian* as *Yauna*. The majority of Greeks in contact with the non-Greeks who stretched into the Asiatic continent—infinitely, or so it must have felt—were indeed Ionian. They intuitively looked eastward and felt themselves distinct from members of the other Greek tribes, especially the warlike Dorians, who dominated the southerly Aegean islands and the southern Peloponnese, including Sparta. The Ionians believed that one of their tribal ancestors was Ion, himself a son of the god Apollo. In the *Iliad* Apollo, despite his indisputably Greek credentials, is associated with Troy, an advanced civilization in Asia Minor. Apollo was from earliest times associated with prophecy, with the quest to understand the unseen and the unknowable, with music and the Muses, wisdom poetry and healing. It is little wonder that his human descendants, the Ionians, invented rational philosophy, science, history, and medicine.

So physical changes in the Maeander estuary, maritime skills including navigation by the stars, intensive contact with older civilizations, and the nature of at least two of their cults were all factors in the Ionian intellectual revolution, and so was the medical science overseen by the god Apollo. Medical professionals still take the oath attributed to the ancient Greek doctor Hippocrates, and preserved along with a group of the seventy or so treatises that have been transmitted under his name. Some of these were certainly written as early as the mid-fifth century BC, including *On the Diseases of Women*. Hippocrates himself was probably a native of the island of Cos. His works crystallized a long-standing tradition of medical inquiry. His guild of medical experts was associated with others on the mainland at Knidos, which also boasted a distinguished school of medicine. Hippocrates' brilliance needs to be understood as a consummation of many decades, even centuries, of medical practice and accumulated lore.

Cos was actually not tribally Ionian, but one of the Dorian colonies sent out from the Peloponnese, indeed from Epidaurus. In historical times, and perhaps earlier, Epidaurus was the site of an important cult of the healing hero Asclepius. Some scholars, both in antiquity and today, have believed that Hippocrates was a member of a hereditary priestly clan, the Asclepiadae, who devoted themselves to the temple cult of this hero. Cos was one of the group of six Dorian city-states established on or near the southwestern corner of Turkey. The other two on the mainland were Halicarnassus and Knidos; three were on Rhodes. Although these Dorian eastern Greeks had tribal loyalties to one another, their geographical location in "Ionia" meant that they also shared the cultural milieu of the cities of the Ionian League. Their choice of the Ionic dialect for their medical treatises, despite being themselves Doric speakers, implies that they felt their professional findings belonged to an Ionian intellectual tradition. There was certainly an established school of thought called "Hippocratic medicine" by the time Plato wrote his *Phaedrus* in the early fourth century, for he reports that Hippocrates said that the nature of the body can't be understood without thinking about the nature of "the whole"— perhaps the whole natural universe.

The methods of the doctors and of the Milesian natural scientists were similar. They all sought to find physical rather than supernatural explanations for natural phenomena, whether related to geology, weather, disease, or injury. The Greeks' rational medicine is all the more impressive if we compare it with, for example, the Babylonians' conviction that disease was caused by angry gods and invasive demons, and the spells and incantations that alternate with prescriptions for drugs in most Egyptian medical papyri. Yet the Greeks learned so much from other cultures that the picture is complicated. One Egyptian papyrus of the fifteenth century BC, named the Edwin Smith Papyrus after the American who bought it in Luxor in 1862, displays a systematic approach to injuries, and includes descriptions of the presentation of each type of wound, along with the appropriate examination procedures, treatments, and prognoses. But the issue is injuries, whose external cause will usually have been witnessed, rather than the more mysterious diseases that appeared to arise from inside and might be felt to require a more religious explanation.

Scholars are conflicted about the degree to which the Greeks owed their advanced medical knowledge to the Egyptians. Greek doctors admired Egyptian pharmaceutical skills, knew that the Persian kings hired physicians from Egypt, and adopted one of their central medical practices from Egypt, namely incubation, or "sleeping over" in the sanctuary of a healing god. But this important source of experience was synthesized with the Greeks' inquiring, human-centered approach to life's problems, producing the rational, scientific tone and method of Hippocrates and his school. One of the concepts developed by medical practitioners was that of likelihood. Given a set of symptoms, they could offer a diagnosis, saying that it was *probable* that a patient had a particular known condition. Moreover, they could predict what was *likely* to happen to the patient in the future, which meant delivering a *prognosis*. Hippocrates believed that this was actually a doctor's duty. It was at about this same time that the Greeks began to use arguments from probability in other contexts, such as legal trials. Characters in the *Iliad* and the *Odyssey* do not argue from probability. The earliest example is in the *Hymn to Hermes*, which probably dates from the sixth century BC. Hermes is still a newborn baby, but he has stolen a herd of cattle belonging to his elder brother Apollo. Hermes is brought to trial before his father, Zeus. He mendaciously defends himself against the charge that he has stolen the cattle of Apollo (which he has), on the ground that as a baby he would be *unlikely* to have sufficient physical strength to drive cattle. Hippocrates used probabilistic logic more constructively—

it was a doctor's duty to use evidence acquired from empirical experience to know what was *likely* to happen to a patient, "to be able to tell the antecedents, know the present and foretell the future" in order to be able "to benefit and not to damage"; "those who are constitutionally obese are *more likely* to die quickly than those who are slender."

The relationship between the Hippocratics and the other intellectuals of Ionia flowed both ways. New archaeological evidence has shown that advanced head surgery was performed on a thirty-year-old woman's injured cranium at Abdera, a colony of Clazomenae, one of the cities of the original Ionian League, by the middle of the seventh century BC. The procedure was successful—she lived for another twenty years. The discovery of the remains of this patient during the excavations at Abdera shows that complicated surgical procedure on bones of the skull, including trepanation (the removal of a disc of bone to allow the removal of damaging bone splinters) was already in use more than two centuries before the sophisticated Hippocratic treatise *On Head Wounds* was written (around 400). This means that, even before Thales and the other Ionian philosophers, the science and practice of medicine was more advanced than we had hitherto realized. Aristotle, both scientist and philosopher, was himself the son of a prominent doctor, and he was in no doubt about the cross-fertilization between the two fields:

> Concerning health and disease, it is the business not only of the physician but also of the natural philosopher to discuss their causes up to a point... for such physicians as have subtle and inquiring minds have something to say about natural science and claim to derive their principles from it. The most accomplished of those who deal with natural science tend to end up investigating medical principles.

The Hippocratic treatises are practical manuals dealing with everyday reality, not works of abstract speculation. Scholars have come to accept that, because of their focus on inference, evidence, and cause and effect, and because of their lack of recourse to supernatural explanation, they must be acknowledged as having played a vital role in the Ionian intellectual revolution.

But how did the interests of the early physicians and physicists become transformed into something resembling what we call "philosophy"? The first ancient Greek to use the term *philosophos*, "wisdom-loving," was Heraclitus, the late sixth-century Greek obsessed with change, a resident of the silting-up city of Ephesus. As we have seen, he said no river stayed the same. He placed fire at the center of the cosmic order and decreed that everything was in flux. Like Thales, later Greeks assumed that Heraclitus had learned from "the barbarian philosophy." Perhaps he had been stimulated by the sanctity of fire in the Persians' religion, Zoroastrianism. But regardless of the source of his ideas, he deserves to be called the first philosopher in the modern sense, because along with proposing that fire was the central principle of the physical world, he considered abstract forces beyond the physical (the metaphysical), aspects of perception, and principles of human behavior. The challenge he faced in finding language to express his novel ideas meant that his books were far from easy reads. This first philosopher immediately gave philosophy its reputation for being abstruse and confusing. His fragments are sometimes maddeningly obscure, to the extent that the Greeks told a story in which the tragedian Euripides gave a copy of Heraclitus's book—written several decades earlier—to Socrates to read; when asked his opinion of the book, Socrates replied, "The part I understand is excellent, and so too is, I dare say, the part I do not understand; but it needs a Delian diver to get to the bottom of it." But Heraclitus, arcane or not, was the first man who thought hard about what philosophy entailed—a self-conscious process of inquiry into the nature of existence.

The increasing breadth of his interests stemmed from his theory of permanent change, which helped him to explain the confusing tension between sameness and otherness in the universe and society. Things that are opposites at one time can become unities at other times or in other circumstances: "As the same things in us are living and dead, waking and sleeping, young and old. For these things having changed around are those, and those in turn having changed around are these." Moreover, constant flux has implications for the attributes of things and for how different agents perceive those attributes: The sea contains water that is at the same time pure and polluted. For fish it is drinkable and promotes health, but for men it is undrinkable and causes harm. Heraclitus argued that all matter was transformed by being turned incessantly into fire and back again. But in a momentous fragment containing another crucial clue about the reasons why the Greeks could invent philosophy, he compares this process with the ceaseless "exchange" of gold into goods and vice versa. The universe was in flux. It could be measured, but only by the equivalent of cosmic money.

The Milesians and Ephesians lived adjacent to Lydia, where, in the seventh century BC, the first coins in human history were minted. Blank discs of metal (flans) of the required weight were heated and placed between two dies. These were the bronze concave molds that had the designs for the coin's sculptures carved in reverse. The smith would place the dies flat and strike the top one hard with a hammer to stamp the carved images onto the flan, producing the coin. This momentous technological advance was one impetus behind Ionian innovative thinking, and especially behind Anaximander's abstract conception of the Unlimited, that things in the universe might be infinite and contained by no boundaries at all. Coins made the ancient Greeks think. Their fable of the Phrygian king Midas, who starved to death because everything he touched turned into gold, dates from this period and region, since Phrygia also bordered on Lydia. Or take the myth of Charon the ferryman. In Aristophanes' comedy *Frogs*, first performed in 405 BC, the god Dionysus and his slave go on an escapade to the underworld. They meet a corpse traveling down, and plead with him to take their luggage on his bier. But he demands two drachmas, the equivalent of four days' pay for a laborer. The amount was also twelve times as much as the single coin that the Greeks placed in the mouths of the dead to pay the ferryman—the obol. The corpse's bartering couldn't help him, since money could buy nothing in Hades. An ancient popular drinking song ran, "Midas was blessed, but what man ever took with him to Hades more than a one-obol coin?" Aristophanes' dialogue on the road to the underworld therefore asks whether money can get the better of death. Is there a form of value that can last beyond the grave? Can you take it with you when you die? Can it make you immortal? At Rome, the god credited with the invention of coinage should have been Vulcan, the god of metalworkers and blacksmiths. But instead it was Janus, the two-faced god who inaugurates new years and looks backward and forward through infinity.

Coins represent timeless value, which can be divided into fractions of tiny denomination but can also be accumulated limitlessly. Coins make it possible to imagine an amount of money too huge to be spent in a lifetime. This underlies money's connection with philosophy. Coins are different from portable chunks of bullion. The value they represent need not be the same as the value of the metal as a commodity. In extreme cases the coins may be counterfeit. In many ancient cities, coins of small denominations were issued in bronze. Their face value bore little relation to their intrinsic worth. But the slippage between the two values—the nominal and the actual—began the minute the first coin was struck in archaic Lydia. Karl Marx described this in the first volume of *Das Kapital*. The circulation of coins always reduces them to a semblance of the value they symbolize. What starts out as actually being made of gold, and worth the numerical weight stamped upon it, always ends up being replaced by coins or banknotes that symbolize a numerical value but are themselves physically worthless. Marx calls this process the transformation of money from "actually being gold," *Goldsein*, to "appearing to be gold," *Goldschein*. Coins are concrete. They are made out of matter. But they signify a quantity in the self-contained world of purely *abstract* symbolic value. All human labor and real-world objects can be measured by money and converted into it. This new, self-contained abstract world, existing only in the mind, suddenly allowed the Greeks neighboring the Lydian realm to reason and to argue intangible ideas conceptually. Abstract notions of value, time, and existence were for the first time in intellectual history divorced from the real world of work, bodily needs, and the physical environment.

The most undervalued of all ancient philosophers was the brilliant Xenophanes, who had seen the Lydian kingdom in action firsthand, and regarded its invention of coinage as momentous. Like

Heraclitus, he was interested in change and in the relationship between sameness and difference, but he focused on how change was manifested in human communities rather than the physical constitution of the universe, thus laying the groundwork for the invention of political theory. His city, Colophon, a little north of Ephesus, was a member of the Ionian League. Founded by Athens, it had been subdued by Gyges in the mid-seventh century but had maintained friendly relations with the later Lydian king Alyattes between 613 and 560 BC. There was a tradition that Alyattes had brought the Colophonians to heel by disbanding their cavalry.

Xenophanes criticized his compatriots for flaunting the extreme aspects of the Lydians' plush lifestyle, especially their sumptuous purple robes, perfumes, and ostentatious hairstyles. This "delicate" or "refined" way of life, learned from the eastern barbarians, was popular in many Ionian cities as well as Colophon. Xenophanes called this affected lifestyle "useless" because it did not help the civic community. His rejection of the lifestyle was connected with his notorious objection to the extravagant prizes (cash rewards and free meals) bestowed on athletes by their hometowns after they had won victories at the Olympic Games. He objects that the benefit athletes confer on communities is short-lived and does not improve the city's government or prosperity. Xenophanes is staking a claim to deserving rewards himself, as a skilled and enlightening poet. He was no ascetic, since he also composed a song about how to drink at a symposium. But since athletics were the prerogative of the elite, there is an edgy, proto-democratic political undertone to his critique.

Disenchanted politically, Xenophanes moved from Colophon to southern Italy and is therefore the transitional figure between the eastern Greek inventors of rational thought and the second group of early philosophers, who worked in the far west of the Greek world. Xenophanes was a foundational figure. He was the first philosopher to use ridicule as a formal device for critiquing other thinkers' positions. He was also the first ancient Greek author who clearly espoused a relativist position. That is, he denied that any proposition could be absolutely true, since whether it was regarded as true or false depended on the subjective outlook of the individual assessing it—an important principle that holders of dogmatic opinions today still find hard to accept. Xenophanes is so sure of the difficulties involved in acquiring true knowledge that he has been called the first Skeptic. He was the first to argue systematically that there is a difference between belief and knowledge. He proposed that aiming for certain knowledge in the case of matters that were not evident was hazardous—indeed, even if humans do accidentally hit on the truth about such matters, they have no way of knowing for certain that it is true. He does not, however, deny that it is worth *trying*, by persistent inquiry, to increase human knowledge.

Xenophanes used poetry to criticize the poems constituting the repository of Greek wisdom, those of Homer and Hesiod. He targeted the stories that these poets related about the gods doing things that men regard as disgraceful—adultery, theft, and deceit. With Xenophanes we can see a radical advance to a more remote and disinterested deity. These new deities had little in common with the spiteful, childish Olympians. Xenophanes also learned, as a Greek living at close quarters with many ethnic groups, that humans tend to make gods in *exactly* their own image: "The Ethiopians make their gods black and blunt-nosed; the Thracians say theirs have blue eyes and red hair." We see Xenophanes using absurdist humor to make profound intellectual points in his reference to the animal kingdom: If cattle and horses and lions could create images of gods, they would portray them in the form of cattle and horses and lions, respectively.

It is not that Xenophanes did not have a god, or rather God. His supreme God was to be identified with the entire universe, a single, motionless entity. This God has neither human form nor a mind like a human's. He does not speak to humans directly and does not make appearances in their circles. This leads to one of Xenophanes' most profound inferences—profound since many subsequent Greeks who doubted the existence of the Olympians nevertheless participated in all the rituals of their cities. Xenophanes despised a ritual in which houses were decorated with pine branches because they were supposed to have a numinous power. He derided prophets and miracle workers. He did not believe that divination worked. This thoroughgoing skepticism about religious practice resulted from his understanding of the physical properties of the universe. Some spectacular events that occurred in nature, popularly believed to be signs from the gods, were, he scoffed, no such thing. The rainbow, which the Greeks knew as the goddess Iris, was just a cloud with colorful streaks. When sailors saw purple lights flashing from the top of their masts (St. Elmo's fire, caused by freak electrical charges, often after thunder), it was not the Dioscuri pledging their protection but clouds generating light as they moved. God did not communicate with man.

Apparent physical miracles, insisted Xenophanes, must be caused by non-miraculous causes invisible to the naked eye. The other philosopher who took a ship sailing west from Ionia to Italy, Pythagoras, inquired into the secrets that the pure science of invisible numbers could reveal about the structure of the discernible world. Pythagoras was born on the Ionian island of Samos but abandoned it, perhaps fleeing the tyranny of Polycrates, and settled in Croton on the ball of the foot of south Italy. Like so many ancient philosophers he was associated with "barbarian wisdom." Indeed, Pythagoras was held by some in antiquity to have studied "at Babylon" with Zoroaster himself; others said his teacher was a Delphic priestess. His doctrines were more mystical than those of the other Ionians, and the sect he ran was esoteric, practicing vegetarianism and other austerities. He was attracted by the ideas of metempsychosis and reincarnation. He made important advances in the relationship between music and mathematics; harmony was conceptually important in his cosmic theories. He is of course best known for the theorem that goes under his name: In a right-angled triangle, the area of the square of the side opposite the right angle is the same as the sum of the areas of the two squares made from the other side of the triangle. But in this case, there is no doubt that the Greek thinker was drawing on "barbarian lore," for the Babylonians had cracked the fundamental relationship of the "Pythagorean" triples as early as 1800 BC.

Once Xenophanes and Pythagoras brought philosophy westward, Italy and Sicily soon produced their own thinkers. Pythagoras influenced Empedocles of Akragas, perhaps the most famous Sicilian of antiquity and a colorful character. Like Pythagoras, he believed in reincarnation and was said to have hurled himself into the volcano of

Mount Etna in order to persuade the world by disappearing that he had turned into God (unfortunately, his sandal was spewed back out, thus undermining his claim). Where the Milesians had argued about which substance was primary, Empedocles identified all four classical elements—water, earth, fire, and air—as *jointly* constituting the universe. These elements were perpetually brought together and drawn apart by the competing forces of Love and Strife, which explains the changing nature of the world, plants and animals, in the course of evolution.

Over on the Italian mainland, the chief philosophers were the Eleatics, who took their name from their town of Elea (now Velia) on the western side of the boot's "ankle." With them the study of philosophy went up a notch in terms of abstraction. Their leader was Parmenides, born in Elea as a native Italian Greek in about 510 BC. The fragments of his poem *Way of Truth* are some of the most contested in the history of philosophy. Yet they do show his significance as the founder of the study of the nature of existence itself, of Being (ontology) as a defined and separate topic for serious debate. Parmenides rejected the Heraclitan idea that everything was in flux. He insisted that existence was unchanging and formed a single whole. It was therefore knowable. Things cannot come into being from nothing and cannot pass away. There is no change or plurality, which means that motion is illusory. Existence has no past and no future. It just *is*. Modern philosophers sometimes claim that Parmenides was the father of Western philosophy in the *technical* sense, because he argued systematically. His thesis was general and offered a coherent explanation for how everything in the universe worked as a totality. It identified and built on some of the central planks of rational thought—concepts such as truth and continuity. Parmenides also used argumentative methods that Socrates later developed at length, such as the identification of contradiction.

Parmenides' argument that motion is illusory was defended by a younger Eleatic, Zeno, in a series of colorful paradoxes. These are fascinating because they show the classroom training that a young philosopher might have experienced in Parmenides' school. Even today, they are often the first philosophical bones that undergraduates are given to chew on. The term *paradox* technically means "demonstrations that absurd consequences can follow from seemingly reasonable assumptions." The most famous is known as "Achilles and the tortoise." The majority of people assume that because Achilles can run faster than the tortoise, he will overtake it if he chases it. But Zeno said that every time Achilles is just about to catch up with the tortoise, the tortoise has a chance to progress forward very slightly. If taken to infinity, this means that Achilles can never actually get to the place the tortoise is in before the tortoise leaves it. A second notorious paradox argued that a flying arrow is not in motion, even though most people believe it is, because at any single instant it is in a particular place, and therefore still. These and Zeno's other paradoxes are actually harder to disprove than it might appear.

By the fifth century, the inquiring Greeks of Ionia and Italy had essentially formulated the great questions that underpin ancient and much modern science and philosophy: What is the nature of the world and of existence? How do we learn things and know them for certain? How do we explain human behavior? They had questioned the existence of the Olympian gods, at least as Homer and Hesiod portrayed them, and the effectiveness of traditional ritual; they had invented natural science and advanced the understanding of mathematics. A fascinating combination of circumstances made sixth-century Ionian culture produce men who articulated these questions head-on, without waiting for a god to tell them the answers: their observations of change in the landscape; the advances made in medicine in nearby cities and islands; their sense of affiliation with the cerebral god Apollo; the confidence and intellectual equipment they had acquired as mariners; their eastern-facing outlook; their intensive contact and cultural exchange with other peoples, especially the Phoenicians, Lydians, and Persians; and their response to the invention of abstract value in the form of minted coins.

The third and last act of the drama of the Ionian Enlightenment, which ultimately brought the center of intellectual endeavor to classical Athens to produce the political theory of Protagoras and the *Histories* of Herodotus, coincided with the astonishing rise of the Persian Empire. Until the seventh century BC, the ancient Near Eastern superpowers were the Neo-Assyrians, based at Babylon, and the Egyptians. But in the late seventh century, after the Mermnad dynasty had expanded the Lydian empire to cover much of the western seaboard of Asia, one of the inland Iranian peoples, the Medes, began to accumulate land and power. By around 600 the Medes occupied territory encompassing much of modern Iran, Afghanistan, and eastern Turkey. But their Iranian rivals, the Persians, who were previously a vassal kingdom of the Medes, gained the upper hand under Cyrus II the Great in 549 BC. This Cyrus was (and is) therefore regarded as the founder of the Achaemenid Medo-Persian empire, which was to prove central to the ancient Greeks' history and self-image for centuries.

It must have been terrifying for Greeks in Asia Minor to watch the sheer speed at which the Achaemenids gobbled up the world. During Cyrus's lifetime alone, the Achaemenids took Lydia, Lycia, the Greek cities of Anatolia, Phoenicia, Cilicia, and Babylonia, creating an enormous empire extending from modern India to western Turkey and the eastern Balkans. Cyrus's son, Cambyses II, only ruled for eight years, 530–522, but conquered Egypt. Darius I then achieved the consolidation of the empire symbolized by the building of massive royal edifices at Susa and Persepolis. In 499 BC, many of the Greek cities of Ionia revolted against Persian rule, which in their communities was mostly maintained in the name of the Persian king by carefully chosen Greek tyrants. The rebels against Persia were supported by ships and troops sent from Athens and Eretria, Ionian cities in mainland Greece. But the Persian Empire successfully crushed the revolt. The rebellion finally ended when the Persians devastated the Ionian Greek city of Miletus in 494, killing and enslaving its inhabitants. But Darius's annoyance at Greek insouciance lay behind his decision to invade Greece itself four years later, in the first of the two momentous Persian Wars won triumphantly by the Greeks. His army was defeated at the battle of Marathon and retreated. His son Xerxes tried again ten years later, only to be defeated at the battles of Salamis and Plataea.

After the retreat of the Persians from mainland Greece in 479, the center of intellectual innovation shifted westward to Athens (itself an Ionian city), which had emphatically put itself on the map as one of the two leading city-states of the free Greek world. But in the figures of Anaxagoras, Democritus, and Protagoras, who visited or migrated to Athens, we can see the link with the older Ionian tradition being maintained. Anaxagoras of Clazomenae, an Asiatic city of the Ionian League, was regarded as having introduced philosophy to Athens after the Persian Wars. Like the Milesians before him, Anaxagoras maintained that the world consisted of a material substance, consisting in his case of infinite and indestructible primary elements, which could not multiply or vanish but only mingle and separate. Anaxagoras's material universe was, however, governed by the principle of Mind, or divine Reason, which he called *Nous* (Intelligence).

Democritus had connections with Miletus but came from a fascinating colony of Clazomenae—Abdera, in the far northern Aegean on the Thracian coast, where we earlier encountered the patient who had undergone skull surgery. Democritus's ideas were of incalculable importance to ancient science and to the philosophical school of Epicureanism. Unlike Anaxagoras, he dispensed with the idea that the universe had any purpose or governing principle to which its material constituents were subordinated. He was the first known scientist to argue that everything is constituted by tiny indivisible and indestructible material bodies (atoms) that move around in an infinite void. The changes humans can see are caused by atoms eternally combining, separating, colliding, and relocating. The movements are all caused mechanically by previous movements and are unavoidable and random. All worlds, including the world humans experience, are created by atoms whirling around each other and forming clusters. Worlds are destroyed when the clusters in due course inevitably separate.

Before he left Abdera for Athens, Democritus is said to have encountered a man working as a porter. Amazed at the geometric perfection with which the porter had bound up the pieces of wood in the bundle he was carrying, Democritus announced that he was a genius at mathematics. He invited him to join his household and taught him philosophy. The laborer's name was Protagoras and he soon followed Democritus to Athens, where he became the most important political thinker in the democracy, as befits a workingman who rose to eminence on the strength of his intellectual prowess. There are many lost ancient texts that classicists would like to recover, but Protagoras's complete works would be at the top of my personal list. Protagoras's two most famous sayings were that "man is the measure of all things" and that the existence of gods is an unverifiable assumption. He developed a concept of civic "concord," an early form of "social contract" theory. His ideas are relevant today. The problem is the difficulty of accessing them. They are discussed in the *Protagoras* and *Theaetetus* of Plato, who himself profoundly disagreed with the gifted Abderite—and took issue with the idea of democracy. Since Protagoras, who was born in about 490 BC, was much older than Socrates, Plato had a relatively free hand in the degree to which he could distort or even misrepresent Protagoras. On the other hand, he treats Protagoras with much more respect than he shows toward most of Socrates' sophistic interlocutors.

The wise democratic theorist held the relativist view that there is no absolute right or wrong, but that each community needs to work out for itself what to deem right or wrong. This view of laws as contingently created during human progress, and therefore relative, was grounded in Protagoras's historical vision of the progress made by humans as they traveled from cave dwelling to the city-state. In addition to Plato, another probable source to which we can turn for Protagoras's ideas are some tragedies produced during the period when he was active at Athens. In the *Prometheus Bound* attributed to Aeschylus, humans were taught not only the use of fire but all their fundamental arts and crafts by the philanthropic Titan, as he proudly states himself. To the sympathetic chorus of daughters of Ocean, Prometheus describes his work:

> They did not know how to use bricks to build houses facing the sun, nor anything of carpentry, but lived in sunless caves underground, like swarming ants. They had no way in which they could rely on marking winter, or flowery springtime, or fruitful summer, but handled everything unscientifically, until I taught them the difficult art of detecting the rising and settings of the stars.

Prometheus subsequently adds arithmetic, writing, medicine, augury, and metallurgy, as well as the use of beasts of burden and sailing, to this impressive list of gifts he has bestowed on humankind. The Greeks had several "technology" heroes, and elsewhere attribute the invention of writing to Palamedes, one of the Greeks at Troy. But in Prometheus's speeches in this tragedy, the Protagorean vision of human progress receives its grandest articulation.

The repeated experience of setting up new communities accelerated the Greek development of political theory. Thousands of new groups of Greeks founded hundreds of new towns in the centuries when Ionians were pioneering the new ways of thought. As we have seen, several philosophers themselves moved to a newer city from an older one at least once in their lives, often because their cities were under pressure from barbarian kingdoms of the east. Some of the most brilliant Greeks who ever lived were involved in the foundation of Thurii in 444 BC. It was an unusual colony, designed to be a Panhellenic project. It was an attempt to create a model democratic Greek polis in which migrants from several cities participated under the leadership of Athens. One of the unusual things about the foundation of Thurii was that Ionian and Doric Greeks were both involved. The impetus behind the project is not altogether clear, although the Athenians, led by the statesman Pericles, wanted to strengthen their foothold in the west. They were also attracted by the plentiful timber supplies in the area. But there was a serious intellectual idealism underlying the enterprise, a view supported by the ancient belief that the man charged with drawing up the laws of Thurii was Protagoras and that the Sicilian Empedocles paid a visit.

The extraordinary experiment being conducted at the new model city of Thurii also attracted no less a figure than Herodotus, the father of a revolutionary form of inquiry—history. Indeed, the very word derives from the Greek word for "inquiry," *historie*. The form of super-inquiry that Herodotus invented sought for the first time to explain how the entirety of the contemporary world resulted from past circumstances and real events, in his case the events of the Persian Wars, which he felt passionately deserved to be written down and remembered by future generations. We have to thank Herodotus for creating the idea that to understand the present we need to understand our past and that of all the other nations in the world as well. He set out his path-breaking manifesto in his opening sentence: He has conducted his inquiry (*historie*) "to prevent the deeds of mankind being forgotten over the course of time, and the great and marvellous works produced by both Greeks and barbarians losing their renown, especially the reason why they waged war on one another." He influenced every historian whom antiquity subsequently produced. Since he first began to be read again in the mid-fifteenth century, he has been the world's main source for classical Greek and Persian history and for much information about the Egyptians and the Balkan and Black Sea barbarians of Thrace and Scythia as well.

The work of Herodotus shows the extent to which the Greeks before and contemporary with him, especially those who, like him, were born and raised in Asia, were in dialogue with "barbarian" cultures. One important predecessor of Herodotus, Hecataeus of Miletus, had already engaged in the systematic study of the lifestyles of different peoples. Hecataeus had extended Anaximander's map by adding the lands that comprised the Persian Empire by the end of the sixth century, especially Egypt. He also included detail about Scythia and the western Mediterranean, which colonization had opened up to the Greeks and which had stimulated the curiosity of their thinkers. Part of his achievement was cartographic, but what absorbed him was the study of the individual character of different ethnic groups—ethnology. To put it another way, Hecataeus pioneered comparative anthropology. To understand a people—say, the Libyans—it was of course necessary to know something about their past and their physical environment as well as their customs, and so both historical and geographical material contributed to his great work, *Journey Round the Earth*. This read like a mariner's handbook, detailing different places and their inhabitants in the order in which a ship would pass them as it sailed along the coastline.

Herodotus continued Hecataeus's interest in anthropology, but also traveled, gathered eyewitness evidence and oral histories, and consulted records kept by the barbarians he was studying. His account of Egyptian religion was dependent on Egyptian versions of their own temple history; the Achaemenid Persians used Greek intermediaries to learn about aspects of Greek myth and tradition, which they then incorporated into their own versions of history and which Herodotus, in turn, records. Herodotus never lets us forget that Greek writing about the Orient needs to be seen as just one component in a dynamic and unceasing exchange between the two, rather than as a view from one side of a conceptual wall; Greek elites in and around the northwest regions of the Persian Empire cultivated warm relationships with the courts of the king and his satraps. There were large numbers of individuals living in ethnically complicated civic communities, above all in the Black Sea region and Asia Minor. The diverse Aegean and Near Eastern spheres need to be visualized "as a mosaic of highly individual and distinctive cultures, which had overlapped and interacted more and less intensely over several thousand years."

Like several of the other enlightened eastern Greeks we have encountered in this chapter, Herodotus migrated westward from an Asiatic Greek city, first to Athens (where he perhaps wrote much of his *Histories*) and then to the new model colony at Thurii, which is where he may have polished his seminal work and in due course have died. Although he was himself a native of Halicarnassus, one of the Dorian cities of southern Anatolia, he wrote his *Histories* in the Ionic dialect, thus revealing, like the Hippocratic writers, the intellectual tradition to which he belongs. For all the originality of his project, Herodotus could not have invented the genre of history writing without the output of the eastern intellectuals who had preceded him—without Anaximander's map, Xenophanes' skeptical relativism, Hecataeus's anthropology, and the systems of hypothesis, evidence, and proof and probabilistic logic that were refined for medical purposes. But he indeed discovered a new genre—history—which could accommodate every branch of thought developed by Thales and his successors: Herodotus is as happy to inquire into the physical behavior of the River Nile, or the reasons why different tribes worship different gods, as the causes of the expansion of the Persian Empire. Herodotus also enjoyed the precedent set by those Ionian poets who had reflected on the history of their own communities, such as Mimnermus of Colophon, whose poems had recounted the wars of the Ionians with Gyges. But Herodotus's greatest poetic debt is undoubtedly to the *Iliad*, which is omnipresent in his *Histories*. It serves both as his model (since he sees it as a precedent in the endeavor to narrate a great war between Europe and Asia) and as an earlier authority, the historical truth of which he often questions. He insists, for example, that Homer really knew what Herodotus regards as the historical truth about Helen of Troy—that she had never been to Troy but had spent the war years in Egypt. Herodotus thinks that Homer had simply ignored the truth because it did not suit his own goals, which were poetic.

Herodotus perhaps began with an ethnographic project similar to that of his predecessor Hecataeus. His book contains long sections where he describes the peoples inhabiting particular regions—the Egyptians in book 2, and the Scythians in book 4, for example. But at some point he incorporated the ethnographic passages into an account of the Persian Wars possessing a broad chronological as well as spatial sweep: It entailed tracing the rise of the Persian Empire. It is this framing element of narrative across time in Herodotus's *Histories* that has given its name both to the genre of history writing and the academic discipline of history. Herodotus deserves his title, Father of History. His reputation suffered in the early modern period and in the eighteenth century, when he was compared by serious thinkers like David Hume with Thucydides, the father of "real" history, and judged inferior. The eventual rehabilitation of Herodotus as a serious thinker in the late nineteenth century was related to the rise of anthropology in tandem with imperial ethnography. In the twentieth century, the combined efforts of Arnaldo Momigliano and Isaiah Berlin illustrated the incomparable role played by Herodotus in the philosophy as well as the practice of history, while the reinstatement of oral sources at the heart of the historical discipline did much to revive interest in the way he wrote about the past.

Yet the arguments over Herodotus's status as history writer have obscured his monumental *literary* achievement. His writing is a sheer joy: Although ancient writers routinely attacked him for his perceived tendency to confuse myth with reality and his tendency to say unpatriotically positive things about barbarians, he was universally admired for his literary qualities. Herodotus was the Father of European Prose. He almost singlehandedly took writing, without the aid of meter, from plodding strings of simple phrases to high art; his genius at word order and variation in sentence length has never been surpassed. He was immersed in poetry and seems to have realized that prose was a medium of equivalent potential. There are sentences in Herodotus of heart-stopping beauty, created by surprising word order (*hyperbaton*), the mirroring of the content in the aural effect (as when the Nile rises), and the use of abstract nouns to denote the onset of an emotion, as in "fear falling" on someone. There are narratives so colorful that they have allowed the ancient Persians and Greeks to remain living presences in our culture—Xerxes ordering the waters of the Hellespont to be flogged, or the Spartans' last stand at Thermopylae. Herodotus himself moved from Halicarnassus to Athens and also traveled in the Black Sea region and probably Egypt before joining the project at Thurii. His outlook allows us unique access to the "great and marvellous works produced by both Greeks and barbarians." For anyone interested in classical Greece, Herodotus, the consummation of the whole Ionian intellectual revolution, is the ideal escort.

Nineteenth-century engraving of the interior of the Athenian Parthenon. (*Author's personal collection*)

5

The Open Society of Athens

In democratic Athens of the fifth and fourth centuries BC, Greek civilization reached the apex of creativity. Perhaps alone among the Greek communities studied in this book, the classical Athenians demonstrated their ample endowment with every one of the ten characteristics that defined the ancient Greek mind-set. They were superb sailors, insatiably curious, and unusually suspicious of individuals with any kind of power. They were deeply competitive, masters of the spoken word, enjoyed laughing so much that they institutionalized comic theater, and were addicted to pleasurable pastimes. Yet the feature of the Athenian character that underlies every aspect of their collective achievement is undoubtedly their *openness*—to innovation, to adopting ideas from outside, and to self-expression.

The Athenian democracy, for which the statesman Solon had prepared the constitutional ground in the early sixth century, but which was not established until 507 BC, was itself a polity of a novel kind. "The Athenians are addicted to innovation, and their plans are characterized by speed both in their conception and execution," said a Corinthian diplomat, according to the Athenian soldier and historian Thucydides. They also took pride in their cultural openness—in a speech in praise of the Athenian soldiers who had died in battle during the summer of 431 BC, the statesman Pericles praised his fellow citizens thus: "we throw open our city to the world, and never expel a foreigner or prevent him from seeing or learning anything."

This crucial sentence shows that Athenian openness was no simple one-way process. Athenians certainly welcomed non-Athenians in their city, and were consistently receptive to new ideas from outside. But they were also fearless about allowing others to scrutinize their way of life from within, and this social and psychological honesty was in turn intimately related to their genius for the honest examination of emotions and human behavior in the theater and in philosophy.

Athenians' openness to new ideas meant that they became outstanding mariners suddenly, and relatively late, when threatened by the Persian Empire. They acquired a new revenue stream from silver mines at Laurion in south Attica (the territory constituting their whole city-state), and their inspired general Themistocles persuaded them to build and man a two-hundred-trireme navy worthy of an Aegean superpower. But since they lived on a peninsula with excellent harbors, and coasts facing in most compass directions, their exposure to other cultures was incessant. Even Athens's staunchest critics were impressed by its cosmopolitan atmosphere: One anti-democratic pamphleteer, known as the Old Oligarch, made the observation that Athenian *naval* prowess made many luxury items available in Athens, whether from Sicily, Cyprus, Egypt, Lydia, or the Black Sea. The Athenian instinct to "mingle with various peoples," he notes, has made even their speech a potpourri of elements: "hearing every kind of dialect, they have taken something from each; other Greeks rather tend to use their own dialect, way of life, and type of dress, but the Athenians use a mixture from all the Greeks and barbarians."

The Athenians positively welcomed immigrants. The Archaeological Museum at Athens houses a bilingual gravestone with inscriptions in both Greek and Phoenician dating from the fourth century and found in the Kerameikos quarter of Athens, a thriving commercial district to the northwest of the Acropolis. The dead man's father was named from the Phoenician goddess Astarte (Abdashtart), but in Greek this became Aphrodisios, after the Greek goddess Aphrodite. The gravestone sculpture shows men fighting a lion and the prow of a ship, more Phoenician than Greek in symbolism. But the inscribed Greek poem, which explains the picture to Greeks, proves that the original mourners constituted a truly bicultural community.

Athenian citizens took pride in being supreme transnational "minglers." They encouraged other peoples to learn, in turn, from them. Athenian ceramics merchants flooded the Etruscan pottery market in Italy with Athenian vases combining images from Greek mythology and shapes appealing to indigenous Etruscan taste. Athenian initiates in the Attic Mysteries at Eleusis worshipped there alongside their slaves, who were welcome to attend provided they had learned how to speak Greek. Critics of the democracy even complained that slaves at Athens were treated so liberally and behaved so boldly that it was difficult to tell the difference between slaves and free in the street.

The Athenians wrestled with the question of how far they should extend the rights of citizens to outsiders and even to deserving slaves. In 404, after readmitting known opponents of the democracy to citizenship, they ended up losing the democracy and enduring the terrifying regime of the Thirty Tyrants for over a year. Five years later, the restored democracy put Socrates to death for asking too many questions about the conduct of the city's affairs and exploring philosophical ideas that they found too challenging. The question raised by Athenian democracy, with its principle that every citizen had the right to express his opinion, was where to draw the limits to either membership of the citizen body or the subversive potential of opinions allowed to be expressed. The story of the rise and fall of the Athenian Empire in the fifth century BC is also the story of the Athenian struggle with the ideal of openness.

Yet it is also a story of almost incredible feats. A population of perhaps thirty or forty thousand free citizen males could produce, within three generations, the pioneering tragedian Sophocles (born in 496 BC), the statesman Pericles (495), the tragedian Euripides and the sculptor Pheidias (both c. 480), the philosopher Socrates (c. 469), the historian Thucydides (c. 460), the comic dramatist Aristophanes (c. 448), the historian and moralist Xenophon (c. 430), and the philosopher Plato (c. 427). As if these intellects were not enough, Athens welcomed resident foreigners, to whom it gave the status of *metic*, and attracted from overseas such seminal figures as the historian Herodotus, the rhetorician Gorgias, the scientist Anaxagoras, the political theorist Protagoras, the mathematician Theodorus from Cyrene, and the orator

Lysias (a permanent resident whose family came from Sicily). Their conversations were among the most dynamic the world has witnessed. It is hardly surprising that the Theban poet Pindar called Athens "the noisy city," a city of ceaseless talk.

This chapter sets the achievements of the classical Athenians, as they wrestled with their ideal of openness, in the context of their democratic revolution of 507 and the two wars in which they were engaged at the height of their power. The first was with the Persians in 490 and 480, and the second with the Spartans, the Athenians' rivals for domination of the Greek world, during the long Peloponnesian War of 431–404. The best witness to the earlier period is the dramatist Aeschylus, who fought the Persians himself and wrote the earliest surviving play, his *Persians* of 472, to celebrate the Greek victory. He died in the 450s, at the zenith of Athenian power, when the core political institutions of the democracy (the Assembly, Council, and law courts) were brought to full development. For the first two decades of the Peloponnesian War, however, Thucydides and the Athenian festivals provide our contemporary window on the Athenian mind. The chapter concludes with the enigmatic philosopher Socrates. He was closely associated with all three of the Athenians whose voices record the disastrous path taken by their city in the last years of the war, between 413 and 404, and its partial recovery thereafter: the soldier Xenophon, the comic poet Aristophanes, and the philosopher Plato.

The foundations of the cosmopolitan, innovative culture that nourished the Athenians' open minds were laid with the revolution of 507 BC, followed by their successful resistance against imperialism in 490 and 480–79. Besides the *Histories* of Herodotus, the best source for these wars is Aeschylus's tragedy *Persians* of 472 BC, the earliest surviving dramatic text in the world. Aeschylus, who was born in 525 BCE, was an impressionable youth of eighteen at the time of the democratic revolution. His was an aristocratic family that lived thirteen miles to the city's west in the coastal district of Eleusis, renowned for its ancient cult of Demeter. Aeschylus was born two years after the death of the Athenian tyrant Peisistratus, during the rule of his despotic sons, Hippias and Hipparchus. When Aeschylus was about eleven years old, in 514 BC, Hipparchus was assassinated—an event that, in Athenian democratic propaganda, came to symbolize the liberation of the people from tyranny; the tyrannicides, Harmodius and Aristogeiton, were commemorated in democratic drinking songs and a famous statue group, set up prominently in the agora (marketplace). But there were seven more years of tension between the Peisistratids and the Athenian people.

The leading opponents of the sons of Peisistratus were the Alcmaeonids, a family that traditionally supported lower-class citizens and with whom Aeschylus became politically allied. They traced their descent from one Alcmaeon, a great-grandson, they said, of Nestor of Pylos. The foremost Alcmaeonid of his generation was Cleisthenes. He was fathered in around 570 by the Alcmaeonid statesman Megacles, but his maternal lineage was even more significant. Cleisthenes' grandfather on his mother's side had been Cleisthenes of Sicyon, a prominent tyrant. The young man therefore had ancestral credentials as a leader as well as a friend of the people.

The teenaged Aeschylus would have watched with bated breath as Cleisthenes orchestrated the deposition of Hippias in 510, before engaging in a protracted struggle with his main rival, another Athenian aristocrat named Isagoras. Cleisthenes had more support with the lower classes, but Isagoras had one strong card. The members of the Alcmaeonid family were widely believed to be polluted—they were thought to be untouchable and it was believed that they could pass on their contagion. They had supposedly incurred this pollution when they had broken sacred law by killing some enemies who were supplicants, having sought religious asylum at an altar. Cleisthenes went into exile, and Isagoras called on the Spartan king Cleomenes, a family friend, to help him establish an oligarchic government of only three hundred men. In an unforgettable series of events, the Athenian Council, backed by the people, opposed Isagoras's coup. Isagoras and his Spartan allies took refuge on the Acropolis, where the people besieged them for two days. On the third they allowed the Spartans to leave, and invited Cleisthenes back to Athens as their popular leader. It was only with this overwhelming mandate, after such an intense struggle at the heart of the city, that Cleisthenes could introduce the reforms that created Athenian democracy. To denote it he perhaps used the term *isonomia*, or "equality for all citizens under the law."

Aeschylus's fellow citizens loved to remember the momentous day when Cleomenes climbed their Acropolis and one of the Athenian women stood up to him. Herodotus reports that when the Spartan tried to enter the temple of Athena, the priestess rose from her chair to prevent him from doing so, and declared, "Spartan stranger, go back! Do not enter the holy place. No Dorian is permitted to go in!" The openness of the Athenians' most sacred temple had its limits. In the event, Cleomenes was forced to depart. The priesthood of Athena Polias—Athena in her role as protector of the city—was a revered public office, held for life, and the incumbent was supplied by an ancient family, the Eteoboutadai. The priestess, who could not be married, was the most powerful woman in Athens. But this particular priestess, at the time of the democratic revolution, was also outstandingly brave. Athena's own mouthpiece in Athens had said no to the anti-democrats.

The difference Aeschylus would have noticed most quickly in public life was the reorganization of group loyalties effected by Cleisthenes' reforms throughout all Attica. Before Cleisthenes, the aristocratic families (including Aeschylus's own) had maintained power through membership of one of the four ancient tribes or clans (*phylai*) of Attica. Cleisthenes swept these kinship allegiances away and replaced them with group identities based on region of residence, or deme. There were 139 demes. But this left the problem of creating a civic identity to unite citizens of Attica living in the different environments of the city, the coast, and the inland villages. So in a far-reaching change, Cleisthenes grouped the demes into three unions called thirds (*trittyes*), but each included coastal, inland, and city demes. The brand-new tribes he brought in, of which there were ten, took their shape from the tripartite division, ensuring that identities could not be limited to place or type of residence.

Aeschylus's deme was Eleusis, which was coastal. But it was teamed up with the agricultural deme of Decelea, and—crucially—with the urban harbor deme of Piraeus. All three demes belonged to the new tribe named after the hero Hippothoon, a son of Poseidon and the legendary king of Eleusis. Aeschylus's family needed to build relationships, consolidated by regular meetings, with the working-class seamen and small traders of the docks. Moreover, lottery, rather than bloodline, was now used to select the members of the legislative Council, and which was to have five hundred members at any one time, fifty from each of the new transregional tribes. The patrician Aeschylus was often represented in the Council by peasants and dockworkers. These measures must have been disorienting. But they constituted a masterstroke. They created a sense of Attic identity, shared by men of all classes and livelihoods, which offered them, for the first time, equality under the law.

Within nine years of the revolution, the Persian threat loomed as large in any young Athenian's consciousness as the reorganization of demes. Aeschylus's fellow citizens had been involved in military operations against the Persians from 498 BC, when they had sent ships to Ionia to aid in the revolt that ended catastrophically in the Persians' subjugation of Miletus, an event that must have terrified them. The poet was in his physical prime—about thirty-five—when Darius finally invaded mainland Greece. Aeschylus fought alongside his brother in the battle of Marathon, an Athenian deme, in 490 BC; his brother died of a fatal injury sustained in action. The decade between the Persian invasions was marked by turbulent internal politics at Athens, in which the citizens often used their right to exile one of their number, chosen by the voting system known as ostracism, against aristocrats suspected of pro-Persian leanings. When the fresh Persian offensive came in 480, Aeschylus, now forty-five, was witness to the crumbling of the Greek defense in Boeotia, the horrifying march of Xerxes on Athens, the evacuation of the city, and its subsequent sacking. The Persians looted and burned with abandon. Terror was converted to triumph with the Greek victories at the sea battle of Salamis (an island near Athens) and the final infantry showdown a day's march northwest at the battle of Plataea. Aeschylus had then lived among the ruins of his city, and conceived his plan for a play that would immortalize the victory over the barbarians. When it was finally produced in 472 BC, *Persians* was sponsored by the young Pericles, an ambitious Alcmaeonid, great-nephew of Cleisthenes himself.

At the play's climax, the ghost of the dead Persian king Darius rises from his tomb and warns his war-traumatized countrymen to "remember Athens!" This awe-inspiring scene is imagined to have taken place on the day that King Xerxes arrived home, disgraced, from the Persians' humiliating defeat by the Athenian navy at the battle of Salamis in 480 BC. It is typical of the flexible, open Athenian mind-set that Aeschylus did not write a tub-thumping patriotic eulogy featuring Athenian war heroes, but creatively imagined what the Persian Wars might have looked like from the Persians' perspective.

He probably overstates their despair. The Persians would have been annoyed by failing to seize mainland Greece, but the failure did not jeopardize the security of their vast Asiatic empire. The people who really wanted to "remember Athens" and the battles of the Persian Wars were the Athenians and their allies themselves. In *Persians*, the Athenians were given a theatrical experience, and an instantly canonical text, which gave expression to the fundamental building blocks of their identity. They were proud to have secured the fledgling democratic constitution, since Darius had intended to reinstate Hippias, the surviving son of the tyrant Peisistratus, and even brought him on the campaign of 490 BC. The original audience would have approved warmly when the Persian queen in the play, who has asked for the name of the Athenians' ruler, is astonished to hear that the Athenians "are the slaves and subjects of no single man."

The second constituent of Athenian democratic identity that Aeschylus's *Persians* affirms is that it was a sea power whose well-being was dependent on its rowers. The oarsmen were from the lowest of the citizen classes (they were *thetes*) and thus had the most at stake in defending the democracy: Many of them lived in Piraeus, the city deme that been teamed with Aeschylus's home deme. He probably knew many personally. The play creates a (not strictly accurate) version of recent history in which the defense of Greece depended less on the land battle of Plataea in 479, in which the Spartans had excelled, than on the sea battle of Salamis. In Aeschylus's play, Athenian democracy and the freedom of Greece are portrayed as depending on Athenian naval expertise, strategic thinking, and dauntless courage. Had they not defeated the most powerful man in the world, the king of Persia, who himself had the command over an unparalleled land force and the magnificent warships of Phoenicia? *Persians* suggests that the Persians failed because they tried to assert mastery over the sea, an element in which the Athenians now felt supremely confident.

The Athenians' identity as democrats who had secured freedom with their hands on their oars was intertwined with their aspiration to be leaders of other Greeks and soon to become their imperial masters. Their defeat of the Persians allowed them to increase their own power across the Aegean. The Athenians built up the alliance of city-states, ostensibly in "defense" of Greece, which evolved into a mighty sea-based empire of their own. Any pretense that the "alliance" was not an empire could no longer be sustained after the islanders of Naxos seceded in 468. Athens crushed them violently and Naxos lost her independence. The defeat of the Persians at Marathon and Salamis became the foundational narrative of the classical Athenian *imperial* democracy. Legends were reinterpreted in its light: The battles the Athenians had fought against the Amazons, for example, became a staple in art, identified as a forerunner of the Persian Wars; in vase painting and sculpture, Amazons begin to wear Persian clothes and bear Persian weapons. Theseus, mythical king of Athens, is painted in poses reminiscent of the famous statue of the tyrannicides. Aeschylus's *Persians* was part of a program of cultural production stimulated by the new "story" of the Persian Wars. Crucial in the new narrative were the generals and war heroes Themistocles (born about 524), and Cimon (a little younger, born about 510).

The magnificence of Aeschylus's patriotic *Persians* is appropriate to the enormity of the events that took place during his lifetime. Such was the case with all his plays. He was a pioneering innovator who had effected a crucial transformation in the genre; his ancient biography records that he was the first tragedian "to make tragedy grander by means of nobler emotions. He decked out the stage and stunned his audience with brilliant visual effects, with paintings and machines, with stage props such as altars and tombs, with trumpets, ghosts, and Furies." The historical encounter with the Persians' vast armies profoundly affected his work, not only in his vision of the Persian court or members of the Egyptian royal family (in another play, *Suppliants*) but in the "other country" that is constituted by the past. The grandeur of Aeschylus's archaic and aristocratic Argos in his cycle of plays entitled the *Oresteia* is informed by the fifth-century Athenians' encounter with barbarian monarchies. Aeschylus's language is also crammed with newly coined compound words, and experimental; the comic dramatist Aristophanes later alleged that this poet's diction could stun listeners into unconsciousness!

The scale of Aeschylus's theatrical effects and poetry is reflected in the magnitude of his conception of history and of the universe. The underlying philosophy of all his plays is that the progress of civilization, although god-ordained, necessary, and magnificent, is bought at the cost of terrible suffering. The suffering may be the bereavement of the entire Persian people as a result of Xerxes' imperial strategy, or the dark emotional deadlock afflicting successive generations of the family of Atreus in the *Oresteia*. But it is always underpinned by a sense of inevitability, and a hope that the divine reason for the suffering will eventually be revealed: In the *Oresteia*, civilization develops from archaic monarchy, blighted by vendettas, to the bright new dawn of democracy at Athens, where the rule of law prevails. In the first play of the *Oresteia*, Agamemnon returns home from Troy to be punished by his wife, Clytemnestra, because he sacrificed their daughter before the expedition. Because law courts had not yet been invented, Clytemnestra had no alternative if Agamemnon was to be called to account. In the second play, Clytemnestra and her lover run Argos as tyrants, with an iron fist, but Clytemnestra's son Orestes returns to Argos to assassinate them and claim his throne. In the third play, Orestes, as a murderer, is pursued by the Furies. It is the ghost of his mother that has aroused them against him. Only after he is put on trial at Athens by the world's first democratic jury, and acquitted by the casting vote of Athena herself, can his family—and, it is implied, the world—be released from the endless cycle of reciprocal vengeance killings.

When the *Oresteia* was performed in 458 BC, Athens was recovering from devastating violence in a primal class struggle ultimately caused by the opening up of rights to the lowest class of citizens by Cleisthenes' reforms. Thetes were excluded from access to the substantial powers exercised by the ancient Council of the Areopagus. The aristocratic Areopagites met on the Rock of Ares from which they took their name. But a radical democrat named Ephialtes had campaigned to divide the aristocratic old body's powers among the three core institutions of the city that *were* open to all male citizens: the Assembly, the Council that advised it, and the law courts. These measures produced bloodshed in the streets and an oligarchic plot to destabilize the democracy. Ephialtes the revolutionary was assassinated in 461 BC. But the powers of the Areopagus were indeed now restricted to jurisdiction in certain cases of homicide and sacrilege. Orestes' trial for the murder of his mother is presented in *Eumenides*, the last tragedy of the *Oresteia*, as the institution's foundational first trial. The death of Ephialtes and others lent relevance to Athena's ban on factional violence at the end of the *Oresteia* just three years later.

The reform of the Areopagus finally put the entire sovereign power (*kratos*) in the hands of the whole citizenry (*demos*). The nine city magistrates (*archons*) were selected annually by lot, from the citizen body, as a precaution against corruption; the ten generals were elected annually but could be repeatedly reelected. All officials were subjected to scrutiny at the end of their term of office. The generals had responsibility for more than just military affairs, although since all citizens and some metics were liable for military service, and the Athenians were almost always fighting somewhere in their empire, military matters featured large in all Athenians' lives.

The democracy at its height gave even the least prosperous citizen an enviable set of rights and standard of living. Until 451, these privileges could be passed down by a citizen father to his legitimate sons, regardless of his wife's provenance. It was common practice to introduce a wife from a non-Athenian family. Pericles foresaw that the citizen body might grow too quickly to keep its privileges, and in 451 BC he saw a law through the Assembly that restricted citizenship to those whose parents both came from citizen families. The openness of Athens created by the democracy, he had seen, threatened to destabilize the democracy itself. It is one of the ironies of Athenian history that Pericles himself suffered on account of this legislation. His wife bore him two legitimate sons, but around the time that he obtained a divorce from her in the mid-440s, he had a third son, also named Pericles, by his beloved mistress Aspasia. Unfortunately, Aspasia was from Miletus, and so the boy was ineligible for citizen rights.

When Pericles and his legitimate sons died during the plague less than two decades later, the Athenians took the unusual step of awarding his surviving son citizenship.

All adult male citizens had the right to attend and vote directly on state policy in the Assembly, the executive body of the city. Voting required that a quorum of six thousand men be present. The Assembly met about forty times a year and voted on all major issues—treatment of allies, administration of the empire, and declaration of war. It also elected magistrates and the ten generals, who in the fifth century had substantial domestic power. All members of the Assembly had the right to speak, provided they had performed two years of military service, although in practice the body was dominated by elite men and professional politicians. It was thought inappropriate for young men to talk for long. Citizens congregated in the marketplace and moved toward the Pnyx Hill, west of the Acropolis, where Assemblies convened, but they required a battalion of state slaves, archers from Scythia, to steer them there with ropes and keep order during proceedings—for example, they removed men who were drunk or brawling or who displeased people with their speeches. Contemporary sources emphasize the deafening noise: Speakers required massive vocal volume, and claques of supporters and opponents competed to drown out the opposition. In one comedy by Aristophanes, *Knights*, the parody of two politicians competing for the people's support in an Assembly debate consists of two rival streams of obscenities, slogans, bribes, and threats, screamed at the top of the actors' voices.

The agenda for the Assembly was usually determined by the Council, which seems remarkably democratic when viewed from the perspective of our own much-diluted representative system. The Council was called the *boule*, which means the "place for deliberation." Its importance is underlined by the speed with which the oligarchs who seized power in 411 ousted the democratically elected councillors and took over their building, the *bouleuterion*, to serve as their own center of power. The *boule* required no fewer than five hundred citizens to serve, proportionately selected from each deme, and they were replaced every year, by lot (at least from the mid-fifth century): It "could thus have contained a fair cross-section of the citizen body." Since no man could serve more than twice in his life, the chances that any particular citizen would serve at some point in his life were high, especially after pay was instituted in the later fifth century, apparently to encourage poorer citizens to serve. Originally only the top three property classes could serve, to the exclusion of the *thetes*, but this qualification for eligibility was dropped or not enforced. The Council met almost every day, and it considered matters relating not only to the state's finances and the scrutiny of magistrates, but the Athenian festivals, navy, building program, and care for the sick, disabled, and orphaned. To serve as a councillor required accumulating information, assessing past actions, and deliberating about future ones virtually all day, every day. The quality of attention required by service on the Council seems breathtaking compared with what is required of politicians, let alone ordinary citizens, today.

The third institution in which all citizens were eligible to participate was the system of Athenian *dikasteria*, or popular courts of law. The venues for most of these were buildings around the agora; different categories of crime were allotted to specialist courts. The Athenians constituted their own state prosecution service: Individuals introduced prosecutions for both private criminal and political offenses, and individuals presented in person the arguments for both the prosecution and the defense. They might hire speechwriters with expertise in rhetoric to put together a plausible case, but they had to present it themselves. The surviving legal speeches, which come from trials ranging from disputes over drainage of agricultural land to homicide and plotting to subvert the democracy, show that speechwriters took their customers' vocal abilities into consideration: Those written for less confident speakers use shorter sentences. The jury consisted of large numbers of citizens, often elderly and from the lowest social class, especially after payment for service was introduced mid-century. Six thousand volunteer citizens a year formed a pool from which jurors could be drawn, perhaps six hundred from each of the ten Cleisthenic tribes. The underlying principle was that large juries offered the safest guarantee of fairness and deterred bribery; juries hearing cases that involved minor offenses consisted of "only" 201 jurors, while cases important to the city consisted of at least 501.

The Old Oligarch thinks it unfortunate that the Athenians could only conduct public business on some days a year because "they have to hold more festivals than any other Greek city, and when these are going on it is even less possible for any of the city's affairs to be transacted." He explains that the Athenian people, however poor many are as individuals, have been clever in discovering "how to have sacrifices, shrines, banquets, and temples. The city sacrifices at public expense many victims, but it is the people who enjoy the feasts and to whom the victims are allotted." Festival culture functioned as a series of public parties, parts of which—especially the lavish street processions—were open to anyone in town. In trying to understand how a city could produce so many great men in so few generations, it is illuminating to consider their collective experience of growing up as participants in such a rich festival calendar. We can see the importance of festivals in creating the Athenians' identity from an important passage in Xenophon. In the late fifth century BC, Athens was enduring the reign of terror of the Thirty Tyrants at the end of the Peloponnesian War, and the prominent democrats of Athens were in exile. They raised an army and won a victory, after which their spokesman, Cleocritus, addressed the defeated aristocrats in an inspirational speech:

> Fellow citizens, why are you keeping us out of Athens? Why do you seek our deaths? For we have never done you any harm. We have taken part alongside you in the most hallowed rituals and sacrifices, and in the finest festivals. We have been your co-dancers in choruses and co-students, as well as your co-soldiers.

The identity nurtured by festivals and choral dancing created bonds that Cleocritus implies were of greater intensity even than those engendered by studying or fighting together.

So how did it feel as a young Athenian to experience the crammed calendar of festivals as well as regular preparation for warfare? Besides the important trips farther afield to the Panhellenic festivals, at Athens there were significant festivals in every month, for every one of the twelve Olympian gods except Ares. Even he was worshipped in a local cult in the largest Attic deme, Acharnae. Other gods and heroes—

Cronos and Rhea, Gaia, Heracles, Theseus, and Adonis—also were worshipped at festivals or were honored within festivals to the major gods. The most important gods had several festivals under different titles: Apollo was worshipped as Delphinios in the spring, at the start of the sailing season, and in the late summer at the Boedromia, the "festival of running to help when called," which was associated with military training. Some festivals excluded men (the Thesmophoria, a festival of Demeter and Persephone), and others excluded women (those associated with Heracles). They almost all featured choral dances that nurtured peer group identity. Some were held in city center sanctuaries; others involved processions to distant Attic sanctuaries. Two of the latter were the festival of Artemis at Brauron, which celebrated young girls' arrival at biological womanhood, and the Mysteries at Eleusis, eleven miles northwest of the city shrine of Demeter, called the Eleusinion, underneath the Acropolis.

The greatest Athenian festival was the Panathenaea, held at the end of the first month of the new year, equivalent to July. Nine months beforehand, two high-born teenage girls were selected to live on the Acropolis. Under the direction of the priestess of Athena, they wove a new gown for the statue of Athena Polias—a wonderful textile portraying the goddess performing her most famous feats. Eleven younger girls helped. The climax of the festival was based on the ancient nucleus of core rituals, and began on the evening of the twenty-eighth of the month, with a torch race to light up the summer sky and introduce the ritual songs and dances of the priestesses of Athena. These lasted throughout the night and, in the early morning, complemented by choruses of men and boys, culminated in the magnificent procession and sacrifices.

The procession displayed a range of groups constituting Athenian imperial identity and showed the relationships among them. Participants included the victors in the competitions, the generals, respected elders carrying olive branches, cavalry, and probably some of the young soldiers in training (*ephebes*). Athenian women bearing baskets made up a large section. The Athenians celebrated their open, multi-ethnic community by including non-Athenians in the procession, not only metics bearing trays of bread and cakes, with their wives and daughters following them with portable stools, but representatives from the allied states and colonies. The mass of Athenians brought up the rear, organized into contingents by deme. The highlight of the procession was the new gown for the ancient statue, which was hung from poles, like a sail from a mast, on a float perhaps designed to resemble a ship. After mustering at the city walls, the procession wound through the agora to the Acropolis. A hundred head of cattle were sacrificed on the public altar of Athena Polias, and the roasted meat shared out evenly among representatives of every deme.

Every four years the Panathenaea was turned into a larger event, thrown open to visitors from all over the Greek world. It lasted for twelve long days and included musical and gymnastic contests and boat races held on the coast. But there was a Panathenaea on a smaller scale, lasting perhaps only two days, in all the intervening years. The Lesser Panathenaea, more focused on the Athenians, did include some competitions, including those in the heavily armed war dance known as the Pyrrhic, horse races, and the curious contests in male beauty that we know were only open to Athenians.

The experience of the Panathenaea was changed by the transformation of the Acropolis under the Periclean building program. Pericles, as we have seen, was the Alcmaeonid great-nephew of Cleisthenes. He had made his name when he subsidized the first production of Aeschylus's *Persians* in 472. From 461 onward he had dominated the Athenian political scene and was reelected to a generalship repeatedly. He had consistently supported policies allowing Athens to benefit strategically from her "allies," increasingly treated as taxable subject states. He had overseen the transference of the treasury of the Athenians' allies from the island of Delos to the city itself. He had led successful campaigns in northern Greece and established colonies in Thrace. He had conducted delicate negotiations with the Spartans, despite the increasing inevitability that the two Greek superpowers would again come into conflict. He had quelled revolts against Athens in Samos and Byzantium and advanced Athenian interests in the Black Sea. But his most enduring achievement was his plan, initiated in 447 BC, to use some of the wealth the Athenians had acquired from their empire to finance the architectural transformation of the Acropolis, where the city's gods and its treasury were housed. The Persians had razed the temples of the Acropolis to the ground during the 480 invasion. Until Pericles, they had not been rebuilt.

In 432 BC, the dazzling new Parthenon, temple of Athena, with its Doric columns, friezes, and pediment sculptures, was completed under the supervision of Pheidias, who had also created the massive new gold-and-ivory statue of Athena Parthenos herself. Standing more than forty feet high, helmeted, breast-plated, and holding a shield and a statue of Nike (Victory), encrusted with over a thousand kilos of gold plate, Pheidias's Athena Parthenos was one of the most imposing statues the Greeks had ever seen. The Parthenon frieze, which runs around the outside surface of the inner building of the temple, represents scenes suggestive of a procession in honor of the goddess housed inside—horses and riders, chariots, men bearing musical instruments, water jars and trays, sacrificial animals, a group of ten important men (perhaps heroes), seated gods and a scene involving a male and female official, three children, and a folded textile. To the Athenians the frieze can only have suggested the Panathenaic procession.

The Dionysia was the only Athenian festival on a scale comparable with the Panathenaea. It was held in the spring month of Elaphebolion, when it was safe to resume sailing after the winter weather. Athens reopened to the seagoing world, becoming packed with visitors. Many months before the festival, dramatic authors submitted proposals to the senior city magistrate, the eponymous archon. Each tragedian had to propose a group of four plays (a tetralogy), three tragedies and a rambunctious satyr drama, to be performed consecutively on a single day of the festival. In 458 BC, for example, Aeschylus submitted his tetralogy the *Oresteia*, consisting of *Agamemnon*, *Libation-Bearers*, *Eumenides*, and a satyr drama called *Proteus*. We know little about the process by which the archon decided which three tragedians were to compete at the next festival and be allocated their principal actors, their chorus, and also their *choregos*. This was a wealthy funder of the maintenance, costuming, and training of the citizen chorus who would be made available to each of the tragedians, as Pericles had sponsored Aeschylus in 472. Sponsoring a chorus was costly, and since there was pressure to win, the spending by the three tragic *choregoi* became competitive in itself.

The drama competitions at the City Dionysia were inaugurated at an event called the *Proagon* ("preliminary to the competition"). After about 440 BC this was held in Pericles' new *odeon* (song hall). The competing dramatists ascended a rostrum, along with their unmasked actors and chorus-men, and gave an account of their compositions. On the next day, the religious rituals began, with the procession called the Introduction (*Eisagoge*), which annually reenacted the introduction of Dionysus to his theater in the city sanctuary. According to myth, this commemorated his original journey from Eleutherae on the border with Boeotia into Attica. The entire journey was not re-created; rather, the icon of Dionysus, which consisted of a wooden pole with a mask at one end, was adorned with a costume and ivy and was carried from his city sanctuary to an olive grove sacred to Athena outside the city called the Academy, on the road toward Eleutherae. A day or two later, after hymns and sacrifices, Dionysus was brought by torchlight back to the theater in his sanctuary.

The festival opened officially the next morning with the *Pompe*, "procession." All the city was now excited: The Assembly could not be held, nor legal proceedings initiated, and even prisoners could be released temporarily on bail. The Dionysiac procession, which began at the city walls, would stop at several shrines on its way to the sanctuary to sing and dance for gods. At the same time, it defined, by symbolical enactment, the relationships between the groups that made up Athenian society. It was led by a virginal young woman from an aristocratic family, who carried the ceremonial golden basket that would contain the choicest pieces of meat from the sacrifice. The *choregoi* who had funded the productions wore expensive costumes, sometimes made of gold. Provision was made for the public feast, and the thousands of festival participants needed a great deal to eat: The bull chosen to be the principal sacrificial animal, as "worthy of the god," was accompanied by younger citizens in military training. There were, in addition, hundreds of lesser sacrifices; the sanctuary of Dionysus must have resembled a massive sunlit abattoir attached to a barbecue. It resounded with the bellowing and bleating of frightened animals, was awash with their blood, and reeked of carcasses and roasting meat.

To accompany the meal, enormous loaves of bread on spits and wine in leather skins were carried by citizens, while the metics brought bowls for mixing the wine with water, borne in pitchers by their daughters. More men brought up the rear, carrying the ritual phalluses of Dionysus. There were competitions in choral singing by fifty-strong choruses of citizens. The theater itself was prepared for the culmination of the festival, the performance of the plays, by ceremonies beginning with a purification rite. The ten generals then poured out libations of wine to the gods. A public herald proclaimed benefactors of the city. When the theater was full, there was a display of rows of silver money bars (talents), the revenue Athens had accrued that year as tribute. The imperial flavor was heightened by the public presentation of a suit of armor to all those sons of Athenian war dead who had achieved military age.

A herald with a trumpet announced each of the dramatic productions. Although the festival program was altered over the fifth century, especially in terms of the performances of the comedies, the program for tragedy remained constant: Each of the three competing poets had his tetralogy performed in one go on a single day, probably starting early in the morning. At the end of the competition, the results were decided by the judges, who were ordinary citizens selected at the last minute from a cross-section of all the tribes, rather than elected, in order to avoid corruption. The judges were under pressure, however, to vote in accordance with public opinion, apparent from the applause. The victorious tragedian was crowned with ivy, and led in a procession, like a victorious athlete returning from the Olympics, to a wealthy friend's house. The general atmosphere of the party, with drinking competitions, a sexual undercurrent, pipe girls, and carousing outside in the streets into the small hours, is well conveyed by the post-performance party dramatized in Plato's *Symposium*.

In 431 BC, there was an amazing competition between tragic playwrights, even by Athenian standards. It featured all three great dynasties of tragedians the city had produced. The first prize was won by Aeschylus's son Euphorion, perhaps with a revival of some of his father's famous plays. In third place and last place came the controversial Euripides, with the group that included his most shocking and still most familiar play, *Medea*. We do not know for which of his plays Sophocles was awarded second place, but the group may have included his undated masterpiece *Oedipus the Tyrant*, which we know was a runner-up. This would mean that not one but *two* masterpieces of the world theatrical repertoire were first performed—and not fully appreciated—within the space of a couple of days in the spring of the fateful year of 431 BC, just as the Peloponnesian War broke out.

It is not difficult to see why a classical Athenian male might have found *Medea* challenging. Medea is the Athenian husband's worst nightmare realized: She is a non-citizen mother of Jason's children, and she is jeopardizing his political ambitions in Corinth. When he abandons her to marry the king's daughter instead, Medea kills the princess and the king, subsequently massacring her own children. At the climax it is revealed that she is not fully mortal, for she flies off to a safe refuge in the aerial chariot lent to her by her grandfather, the Sun (Helios). The problem for the Athenian audience may have been that her destination was Athens. She has managed to extract a promise of asylum from King Aegeus in exchange for advice on curing his infertility. It would be understandable if Athenian citizens may not have enjoyed watching one of their own favorite mythical ancestors being duped by a barbarian sorceress living in Corinth who is also an infanticide. Yet the Greeks being Greeks, *Medea*, despite failing to win at its debut, almost instantly became a classic, precisely because it offered such an honest and searing approach to a perennial problem—it is not just a play about marital breakdown and parenthood but an intense psychological examination of how humans, regardless of their sex, can work themselves up to the point where they can kill people they love.

The problems posed by Corinthians were on the minds of audiences at the 431 Dionysia. Athens had infuriated some other Greek states, including the Corinthians, during controversial military operations. In 432 BC the Spartans summoned a meeting of the Peloponnesian League in order to hear grievances against Athens. As a result, the Spartans in effect declared war by voting in support of the motion that the Athenians had broken the terms of the fragile peace between them. In fact, substantial numbers of Athenian hoplites and rowers were already engaged in the long-standing siege of the Corinthian colony of Potidaea, in northern Greece, where Socrates, fighting for his city, rescued his disciple Alcibiades. Yet life in Athens was about to change for the worse. Soon after the Dionysia, the Thebans invaded the city of Plataea, only eight miles from Thebes but allied to Athens. The affair ended in a Plataean victory of sorts, but the Plataeans summarily put to death 180 men, thus setting the tone for the atrocities and savage reprisals that were to blight the whole Peloponnesian War.

Shortly afterward, the Spartan king Archidamus II began invading Attica and occupying farmland. Although the Spartans only stayed for a few weeks at a time, the threat they posed was sufficient to persuade many of the rural Athenians to follow the policy advocated by Pericles, and move themselves, their families, and even their wooden furniture from their ancestral farmsteads to within the long walls that stretched from the city to the harbors at Piraeus. They sent their livestock to friendly islands. But being torn from their ancient roots and penned in by the city walls caused severe emotional problems to the freedom-loving Athenians, who had for centuries farmed the open plains of Attica. Many had to make temporary cramped homes in the turrets of the walls.

By midsummer the Spartans were ravaging land at Acharnae, a few miles from Athens. The young men became impatient at Pericles' policy of keeping the Athenians safe within the walls. The Athenians also sent out fleets to cruise the waters around the Peloponnese and to guard Euboea. They made or secured alliances with the rulers of Thrace and Macedonia. In the late summer, after the Spartans had returned home for the winter, Pericles finally led a whole force into Megarian territory, and Athenian self-confidence had never been so high. Thucydides reports:

> This was indeed the largest Athenian army ever amassed, for the city was still in her prime and had not yet been afflicted by the plague. There were no fewer than ten thousand heavily armed infantrymen, all of them Athenian citizens, in addition to the three thousand who were then at Potidaea. There were also at least three thousand heavily armed soldiers drawn from the resident foreigners on the campaign, besides all the many lightly armed troops.

This was to be the last winter of Pericles' glory. He was chosen to deliver the oration at the annual public funeral for the war dead. In a special tent, friends and relatives paid their last respects to the bones of their loved ones for three days. The funeral procession consisted of mourners, including women, who accompanied the cypress coffins, one for each of the tribes, with an additional empty bier to represent those missing in action. The cortege wound its way to the public tomb in the Kerameikos, where Pericles mounted a platform and delivered the most influential speech in Western history: Its praise of the democratic values and love of liberty for which that year's crop of war dead had laid down their lives has informed countless significant orations since, including Abraham Lincoln's address at Gettysburg.

"Our government," said Pericles to the bereaved of all classes, "is called a democracy because it functions on behalf of the many and not on behalf of the few. Under our laws, everyone has the same entitlement as everyone else in private disputes. When it comes to social standing, we evaluate men according to their reputation, and their class background is less important than merit. Poverty is not a barrier, either, since a man who can do something to benefit the city is not prevented from doing so by coming from insignificant circumstances."

Yet the Athenians' pride in themselves, their city, and their empire was about to face its greatest challenge in history. By the next spring, when the Spartans began to invade Attica again, the Athenians began to die from a fearsome plague that they caught from their water supplies, exacerbated by the close quarters in which they were confined behind the city walls. Neither doctors nor prayers to the gods could alleviate it. It was during this plague that Pericles and his legitimate sons died. Thucydides, who was one of the few to contract the plague and yet survive it, offers a chilling description of the symptoms:

People who were healthy were suddenly afflicted by powerful waves of heat in their heads, and their eyes became red and inflamed. The insides of their mouths, the throat and tongue, became instantly covered in blood, and their breath smelled unnatural and foul. These symptoms were followed by sneezing and hoarseness, and then the pain descended into the chest, with a hacking cough. When the disease settled in the gut, it caused a serious upset, with discharges of every type of bile to which doctors have given a name, and acute misery. Most victims retched unproductively, with violent spasms, some for a short period and some for much longer. The surface of the body was not particularly hot, nor pale, but very red and livid, with eruptions of small boils and ulcers. But internally the sense of burning meant that patients could not tolerate clothing or linen even of the very lightest description, but could only bear being stark naked. What they really wanted to do most was to hurl themselves into cold water, and some of those who were ill but not being looked after actually did so, throwing themselves into the rain tanks, beset by a thirst they could not quench, although however much or little they drank it made no difference. In addition, they were afflicted by the desperation caused by being unable to get either rest or sleep.

Thucydides' scientific description is transformed by the information that he had himself experienced these agonies, but that does not make it any less dispassionate. We know what Pericles said to the Athenians at the funeral of the first to die in the Peloponnesian War, and we know what it felt like to suffer from the plague in the heat of the next Athenian summer, because Thucydides covered the events in the second great work of history in ancient Greek, his analytical *History of the Peloponnesian War*. He was aware of the example set by Herodotus in writing a unified history of a war, but his attitude to history is different. He was himself involved in the war as a general several years after the plague and must have written much of his book in the home he retired to, in Thrace, after he was exiled in 424 BC. Something happened to him in the year 411, the year in which his narrative breaks off.

Thucydides looks for causes and consequences in history. But his greatest legacy is the tragic tenor of his work. He is frank about the atrocities that humans on both sides in the war were capable of committing, and about Realpolitik: He candidly assumes that Greek city-states were always motivated by expediency and self-interest. He knows that rich and powerful states want to stay rich and powerful. This is why Nietzsche so admired him:

> From the despicable beautification and idealization of the Greeks which the classically educated youth carries away into real life as reward for his high school training, there is no cure so fundamental as Thucydides. . . . Thucydides is the great culmination and last manifestation of that strong, severe, hard realism which was instinctive in the more ancient Greeks.

But the pragmatic realist Thucydides could also portray suffering better than any poet. What makes the work so tragic and sound so eerily modern is his dogged insistence that human action must be explained from human psychology and human nature, from "the human thing," the principle he calls *to anthropinon*, and not from supernatural causes. Humans in Thucydides are sometimes motivated by fear or love of gods, or faith in divination, but Thucydides only accepts rational explanations for historical events. He is careful to produce evidence, and subjects it to thorough examination. People do terrible things to each other when competition over scant resources becomes unbearable. In Thucydides, the Greek Enlightenment of the sixth and fifth centuries found its culmination and historically most influential mouthpiece.

After the death of Pericles, the Athenians were afflicted by catastrophes during the whole last quarter of the fifth century. They led to their defeat by the Spartans, the temporary loss of their democracy, and the permanent loss of most of their empire. As we shall see, they also resulted in terrible waste of human resources, since between 411 and Socrates' execution in 399, hundreds of the most able Athenians were put to death in their prime by their fellow citizens. Once the Athenians had recovered from the plague, they rallied and gained the upper hand at the battle of Sphacteria in 425 BC under the popular leader Cleon. But the Spartans gave them a hard time in Thrace and seven years later won a brilliant victory over Athens and her Peloponnesian allies, mostly Argives, at the major battle of Mantinea, in the central

Peloponnese. The Spartans lost three hundred men; those fighting with Athens more than a thousand. It was the end of their ambitions in the Peloponnese that lay behind the Athenians' decision to turn their eyes farther westward and attempt to conquer Sicily. Sicily would have been an extraordinary coup: The Athenians had always coveted it, partly because it was dominantly Dorian and therefore inclined to support Sparta. But rich farmlands and the cultural life of Sicily, especially in its largest city, Syracuse, made it even more appealing.

Tragically for the Athenians, their plan to hegemonize Sicily ended in total defeat in 413 BC. Alcibiades was supposed to lead the expedition, but after a scandalous incident involving vandalism against statues representing Hermes, he defected to Sparta. The Athenian commanders then made several fatal errors. Tens of thousands of Athenian and allied hoplites and oarsmen were killed in Sicily. Their commanders were executed. The last seven thousand captives went mad with thirst in stone quarries near Syracuse, and almost all died of hunger and disease. As Thucydides put it,

> Of all the events of this war, this was the most momentous, and indeed I think it was the most momentous of any event ever reported to have happened in the Greek world. It brought the most glory to the winners, and the greatest misfortune to the losers. For the losers were absolutely wiped out in every respect and their sufferings were too awful for words. Total destruction was the fate of both army and navy. Everything was obliterated. Of the many who had gone to war few returned home again.

The annihilation of almost its entire population of men of fighting age sent Athens reeling. Two years later, the democracy was overthrown in a violent oligarchic coup, producing a government of only four hundred. It was soon deposed and a larger number, five thousand, given the reins of power, before the democracy was reintroduced, amid much bitterness, litigation, and executions, in 410.

The Athenians then commenced the dance of death that culminated in their surrender to the Spartans in 404 BC. The focus of the war shifted to the eastern Aegean, and in a series of naval battles, the

Athenians suffered humiliating defeats; even their unexpected victory at the battle of Arginusae in 406 was ruined by the heavy fatalities. The crews of the many damaged Athenian triremes had not been rescued and had drowned. The Athenians summarily executed six of the eight generals, but were in desperate straits: The executions were of at best questionable legality, and demoralized even ardent democrats while providing their opponents with evidence that democracy was simply rule by the rabble. This perception was sharpened further by the changing face of the Athenian citizens: They were now so short of manpower that, ever resourceful and open to radical solutions, they conferred citizenship on all the slaves who had rowed in the battle. In 405 BC the Athenians were defeated in a further sea battle, and the Peloponnesian War came to an end. The regime of the Thirty Tyrants amenable to Sparta, who included the ferocious and willful Critias, lasted for just over a year before exiled Athenians succeeded in returning and restoring the democracy in 403. Athens remained independent until 338 BC but never recovered the wealth and imperial power she had enjoyed under Pericles.

Thucydides' account of the Peloponnesian War peters out in 411. The three most significant Athenians who lived through the last decade of the fifth century and the first few decades of the fourth, and who supply our knowledge of events in those years, are all connected with the philosopher Socrates. One is the comic dramatist Aristophanes, who was intrigued by Socrates' ideas and a member of the same social circle; the other two, Plato and the soldier and historian Xenophon, were both Socrates' students. Socrates' experiences between 411 and his death in 399 reveal the serial emergencies into which the Athenians plunged themselves during those years. His responses to the crisis show how his presence, his conduct, and his probing of public affairs tested the very limits of the Athenian democrats' ideals of openness and freedom of opinion and its expression.

Socrates was a middle-class son of a stonemason, born in the heyday of the expanding Athenian Empire. He was a loyal citizen of Athens and an excellent soldier, distinguishing himself for valor in several battles during the 430s and 420s. By this time he had also become a natural scientist and philosopher, although he gave up his interest in physics and cosmology in favor of philosophy midcareer. He did not take money in exchange for teaching. Aristophanes, more than twenty years Socrates' junior, was fascinated by his ideas, writing an entire comedy about them, *Clouds*, first produced in 423 BC. Although Socrates later claimed that attacks on him in comedy had been instrumental in creating the Athenians' prejudice against him, Aristophanes' criticism of the philosopher is mild in comparison with Aristophanes' attacks on politicians and generals. Aristophanes also features as a guest in Plato's *Symposium*, in which he gives a delightful speech and is one of the last two drinkers to stay awake while Socrates talks. This implies that Plato recognized Aristophanes' intellectual ability; after all, they both used humorous literature in forms of dialogue to encourage intellectual reflection. Aristophanes certainly shared Socrates' objections to the extreme positions taken by arch-democrats. In his most beautiful drama, *Birds* (414), he satirizes the idea that salvation can be found by establishing new communities in far-distant colonies, perhaps a critique of the entire Sicilian expedition, which had by then been launched. The fatalities in the Syracusan disaster of 413 is the background to the women's sex strike and occupation of the Acropolis in *Lysistrata* (411), although *Women Celebrating the Thesmophoria*, produced the same year, avoids political subject matter, perhaps reflecting the tension in the city. Aristophanes' interest in Socrates lingered after the philosopher's death. In his *Assemblywomen*, composed around 392 BC, Aristophanes satirizes ideas discussed in Plato's Academy but originating with Socrates, including communistic sharing of property and empowering at least educated women.

Socrates inevitably irritated many public men. Some of his students were upper-class youths known to hold anti-democratic views. As an open-minded political theorist he did not assume that democracy was self-evidently the best form of government, and he had many positive things to say about different systems operative in Sparta, Crete, and even barbarian lands. To be perceived as criticizing democracy even indirectly was to sail close to the wind in democratic Athens, for all her supposed tolerance of the free exchange of opinions. But Socrates was in no more danger than other prominent Athenians until 406, when he was serving on the Council. This was the year of the sea battle of

Arginusae, when hundreds of Athenians died in the sea after being abandoned by the generals who claimed the weather made it impossible to rescue them. Socrates happened to be chairing the committee to which it was proposed—unconstitutionally—that six generals be prosecuted en masse. He refused on principle to allow the proposal to be passed, and faced threats. When he was no longer in charge, the generals were tried and summarily executed.

The fallout from Arginusae is reflected in Aristophanes' *Frogs*, produced the following year. The Athenians had become so short of manpower that they required slaves to row at Arginusae, on the promise that this would earn them their freedom. A large number of newly freed slaves joined the Athenian citizen body as a result, and in *Frogs* Aristophanes praises this measure. But he also protests that the democracy had still not reenfranchised many of the men who had been associated with the oligarchic coup in 411. He puts into the mouth of the chorus of the play the plea to the audience of citizens that all the exiled oligarchs be allowed to return. The audience heard him, and in reality did readmit the exiles. But the result—predictably enough—was the pro-Spartan regime of the Thirty Tyrants. Athenian inclusiveness, pushed too far, wiped the democracy out altogether. Aristophanes, who depended on the constitution being democratic for his right to make biting political satire, should have known better.

Socrates was suspected of being on too friendly terms with the Thirty, although it is known that he refused to hand a man called Leon over to them for execution. After the restoration of the democracy, he was targeted by political enemies. It did not help that he was associated with the deeply unpopular tyrant Critias, who was also a relative of his star student Plato. Nor did Socrates help himself by his unapologetic insistence on asking his fellow citizens awkward questions, often humiliating ambitious statesmen in public. This resulted in his prosecution for "introducing new gods" and subverting the youth of Athens. He was condemned to death by drinking hemlock. A more robust democracy might have been able to tolerate him.

Among Socrates' keenest supporters were several young men from the Athenian upper class who were opposed to the democracy. Some of them were actually involved in the coups by which it was temporarily overturned in both 411 and 404. One member of this group of Socrates' students was Xenophon, whose political views were anti-democratic. He was lucky to survive. His *Hellenica* picks up the narrative of the Peloponnesian War in 411, at the point where Thucydides' text breaks off. Like Plato, Xenophon left Socratic dialogues that are set in Socrates' lifetime, but they focus on practical and ethical issues rather than more abstruse philosophy. As we shall see in the next chapter, like Critias and some other Athenian anti-democrats, Xenophon was an admirer of the Spartan constitution. When forced to leave Athens because of his political associations, he defected to Sparta.

Socrates' other brilliant student, Plato, also left Athens at the time that his teacher was executed. But as the open-mindedness of the democracy reasserted itself, he soon returned to found his Academy, and all the different strands constituting the innovative, hybrid, colorful city of democratic Athens are woven together in Plato's dialogues. Since Socrates left no words of his own for us to read, we can never know how much the Platonic Socrates, any more than Xenophon's Socrates, owes to the pupil rather than to Socrates himself.

Plato was born into a rich family, which assured him the leisure to focus on training his mind and body. Before he joined Socrates' circle, he had studied with Cratylus, a philosopher of the Heraclitan school. Plato had distinguished forebears on both sides of his family tree and pays respect to some of his relatives by introducing them into his dialogues—his brothers Glaucus and Adeimantus in the *Republic*, in others his anti-democratic maternal uncle Charmides and great-uncle Critias the tyrant. Although Plato never portrays himself as a speaker in any of the dialogues, he is named as one of Socrates' devoted adherents and was involved in trying to raise money to offer a fine in lieu of Socrates' life. Many of the questions Plato asks had previously been put by thinkers before or contemporary with Socrates. Some of the thinkers whose ideas are debated and explored by speakers within the dialogues are Athenians (for example, the mathematician Theaetetus of Sounion), but he repeatedly represents the cosmopolitan Socrates talking to intellectuals from elsewhere—the rhetorician Gorgias from Leontini in Sicily, and the sensational political theorist Protagoras from Abdera.

By devoting particular dialogues to specific questions about a broad range of fields of inquiry, Plato provided us with the canonical textual foundations for the main branches of philosophical inquiry. In his *Theaetetus*, for example, he investigates the nature of knowledge, and in the metaphysics of the *Phaedo*, he defines the ideal "forms" that he believed constituted the ultimate reality. More than thirty of Plato's dialogues have survived. They face head-on the question of what philosophy actually is. They also fearlessly address the big questions asked by the Greeks, which underlie the main branches of Western philosophy even today—ontology and metaphysics, epistemology, ethics, and political theory. Other fields than these three core branches of philosophy were also given their foundational texts by Plato—literary criticism and Aesthetics, for example, in his *Ion* and *Republic*, books 2, 3, and 10.

Yet in their broad outlines, Plato's core doctrines would find few advocates today. Platonic philosophy is idealist in that it denied the primacy of the material world, physically apprehensible by the senses, and asserted that true reality existed in an immaterial realm that he called the world of the "forms" or of "ideas." Materialists such as Democritus and the Epicureans disagreed, arguing that the material world is a *prerequisite* of thought. Today we question the legitimacy of such a harsh division between the world of the body and the world of the mind, let alone the idea that the world of ideas is superior. Plato's study of the basis of knowledge, although it brilliantly displays the way that truth becomes mangled by rhetoric, is also compromised by his assumption that reality can't be understood by what we would call scientific observation. This may well not even have been the view of Socrates: Aristotle implies in his *Metaphysics* that Socrates' forms can indeed be discovered through investigating the natural world, whereas Plato *differed* from Socrates in saying that the forms are entirely beyond the ability of a human to understand. Plato's political philosophy, moreover, despite the egalitarian principles that he thinks should be adopted within the exclusive community of "guardians" in his ideal republic, is relentlessly elitist. Platonic ideas about art and literature lead inevitably to strict state censorship by enlightened oligarchs.

So why is Plato still so important? One, his dialogues are set in the esoteric world of elite conversations that took place mostly in privileged private houses during a period when democracy was on the defensive. Two, he provides fascinating portraits of towering intellectual figures, including Protagoras, whose works are otherwise almost completely lost. Three, he was a brilliant and innovative writer whose output constitutes a literary tour de force even if the reader has little interest in philosophy. Although, once again, he was sometimes recycling ideas that had been framed before, Plato's beautiful texts have provided our collective imagination with some of its most exquisite furniture. His *Timaeus* and *Critias* have given us Poseidon's fabled lost city of Atlantis, submerged many fathoms deep near the Pillars of Heracles. His *Phaedrus* has given us the image of the soul as a charioteer trying to steer his two winged horses toward enlightenment, while one of them, the irrational one, resists all control. Plato's *Republic* has given us the allegory of the cave to illustrate how difficult it is for humans to understand the world around them. The limitations of human sense-perception are such that we are like prisoners chained up in a cavern, able to see only the shadows projected onto a blank wall by a fire behind us rather than the entities that produce those shadows.

Yet the most important legacy left by Plato is the composition of philosophical reasoning in an open-ended dialogue form. It forces readers to react, to agree or disagree with Socrates, to think the issues through for themselves. Plato's texts demonstrate in practice how thinking and argument is a dialectical process: People who disagree can make progress toward understanding each other's positions if they continue their dialogue indefinitely and do not close it down. The Socratic dialogue, as recorded by the Athenian Plato, has had an incalculable influence, not only on methods of teaching but on the theory and practice of democracy.

Nineteenth-century engraving of the Spartan infantry in combat with the Persian army at the battle of Plataea. (*Author's personal collection*)

6

Spartan Inscrutability

The self-sacrificial death of King Leonidas and his three hundred warriors at the battle of Thermopylae, the "Hot Gates," is the enduring image of Sparta that has come down to us. In late summer 480 BC Xerxes, king of Persia, marched with his enormous army southward through the country, having hitherto met little opposition. According to Herodotus, who was writing within living memory, Leonidas had decided to meet Xerxes at Thermopylae because he was stung by allegations that the Spartans were secretly siding with the Persians and because he wanted to test the resolution of the other Greek states. He may also have expected reinforcements from Sparta to arrive before he joined battle. Although his three hundred Spartans were actually supported by nearly seven thousand other Greeks, they were still vastly outnumbered. Leonidas had nerves of steel and played a waiting game for days, hoping to unnerve the invaders. His bravest hoplite, Dieneces, used biting Spartan humor to keep up Greek morale: A rumor spread that the Persians had so many archers that their arrows would block out the sun, so Dieneces responded, simply, "Then we shall fight our battle in the shade!" It took thirty-six hours of violent combat for the Persians to wipe out Leonidas and Dieneces, along with almost their entire rear guard, the hard core of Spartan hoplites.

The image of warriors of Sparta cracking acerbic jokes in the face of death encapsulates the paradox this strange city-state presents. The most military and brutal of ancient Greeks, the Spartans were also the most famously witty. One of the names for their home territory in the Peloponnese was Laconia, or Lacedaemon—which is why their shields bore the letter *L* (*lambda*) rather than the letter *S*. This explains our resonant word "Laconic," first adopted into the English language in the late sixteenth century. Plutarch (AD 46–120) assembled *Laconic Sayings* and *Sayings of Laconian Women*, which circulated in modern-language translations. They are still studied by speechwriters and stand-up comics as the foundational examples of the one-line putdown that silences wordier interlocutors: "With it or on it!," as the Spartan mother commanded, pointing at her son's shield as he left for war. "Come and get them!" replied Leonidas, when the Persians demanded that his Spartans hand over their arms. In the *Iliad*, Menelaus's way of talking is described by a Trojan who has met him: "he did not say much, for he was a man of few words, but he spoke very clearly and to the point." Spartan kings were already regarded as economical with words when the *Iliad* was composed in the eighth century.

Yet no amount of grim gallows humor can explain why Leonidas led the Spartans to near-certain defeat at Thermopylae, a narrow pass on the east coast of central Greece with impenetrable mountains on its inland side. Herodotus thinks that Leonidas desired to win immortal glory for the Spartans but that he was also responding to the oracle given to the Spartans by Delphi. The Pythian priestess had warned that either the barbarians would conquer Sparta or a king would have to die. Leonidas was already over fifty years old. He took with him only Spartans who had fathered living sons. This looks like the decision of a man who did not have great expectations that they would return. Why Leonidas chose to embrace near-certain death is a question that has been much debated, but one factor has been overlooked. Leonidas, like all the Spartans, genuinely believed he was a direct descendant of Heracles. One of the Spartans' own patriotic marching songs stressed this ancestry: "You are the race of Heracles the Invincible, so take courage!" The mountain that towers above the pass of Thermopylae is Mount Oeta, on the summit of which Heracles himself violently expired, joining the gods. When Leonidas and the other senior Spartan hoplites took on the Persian army, they were spiritually joining their most illustrious progenitor. They could not have chosen a more auspicious place to die.

Admired by Machiavelli, Samuel Adams, and Adolf Hitler, screened lucratively in Hollywood's blockbuster *300*, the sardonic, authoritarian but egalitarian men of the Spartan ruling class have exerted more influence than most Greeks. Yet they are the ones about whom the least is known. Or rather, they are the ones about whom the least is *directly* known. While Athenian playwrights, historians, and philosophers address us candidly in their own writings, the Spartan voices that speak to us unmediated are few. The influence has been exerted less by the actual, historical Spartans than by the near-mythical *image* of Spartans as insuperable soldiers of brutal habits, few words, and pungent humor. This picture was already in circulation throughout classical Greece.

The swiftest way for a modern reader to grasp the contours of the Spartan myth as it circulated in antiquity, and informed the Renaissance, is to read Plutarch's engaging *Life* of Lycurgus, the original Spartan lawgiver. But this exercise, alas, will not reveal how much of Plutarch's colorful mirage is based on fact. Plutarch, who was not even from the Peloponnese, worked centuries after Sparta's ascendancy, at a more peaceful time, when classical Sparta had become a nostalgic theme park for Roman tourists. Plutarch admits that nothing is actually known about Lycurgus. So how much did the Spartans themselves contribute to their own mirage, whether deliberately or unconsciously? And if we dissect the mirage carefully, can it bring us anywhere near the truth?

The most serious problem, besides the Spartans' own near-silence, is that by the late fifth century, Sparta was being used by non-Spartan philosophers in discussions of the ideal political system. This is certainly the case with Socrates' disciple Xenophon. The Athenian aristocrat defected to the Spartans after fighting alongside them in the Asiatic expedition (and retreat up-country) of the Ten Thousand, which he recorded in his *Anabasis*. Xenophon's account of the stability of the Spartan system in his *Constitution of the Spartans* is adulatory but nevertheless may derive from their own self-image and therefore contain accurate information:

This city has never been motivated by envy of the privileges granted to her kings to deprive them of their right to rule. Nor have her kings ever tried to acquire greater privileges than those that originally set limits to their kingship. This explains why the Spartan kingship is the only form of government that has survived continuously, whereas it is quite clear that no other constitution anywhere, whether democratic, oligarchic, tyrannical, or monarchical, has ever endured unbroken.

Even more evident than Xenophon's pro-Spartan bias is that of Socrates' anti-democratic interlocutor Critias, the callous Athenian whom the Spartans had installed as one of the Thirty Tyrants at the end of the Peloponnesian War. Sparta recurred as a philosophical example of a state in utopian thinking, a type of discourse in which the goal is not accurate *description* but political *prescription*. The utopian image of Sparta was enthusiastically adopted by the early Stoic philosophers and, by the third century BC, may have influenced Spartan self-governance. It was then that the Black Sea Stoic Sphaerus arrived in Sparta as advisor to King Cleomenes III.

Among our sources, Herodotus and Thucydides both maintain that there was something distinctive about the character of the warlike, mordantly witty Spartans. Yet Thucydides consistently uses Sparta in the Athenians' *self*-definition, and so may well impose exaggeration or binary contrast that distorts the true picture. Fortunately, there is one fourth-century source who may be reasonably objective, and that is Aristotle. Although he lived for many years in Athens, he was from a northern Greek city in the orbit of Macedon, and his own city-state identity was not built in direct antithesis to the stereotype of Sparta. Equally, although he was a student of Plato's, he was at no point beguiled by the utopianism that marks the responses to Sparta of Xenophon and Critias. As a scholar with a strong sense of admissible evidence, his information is more reliable. In his *Politics* he finds fault with several laws relating to the Spartans' helots (slave class), women, and property and its inheritance. In particular, he says that the five annually elected officials called *ephors* were prone to corruption, which jeopardized the whole community.

The stark outlines of the history of Sparta in relation to the rest of the Greeks and to the non-Greek world are in fact clear enough. During the eighth century, the Spartans invaded what was to become their territory of Laconia. They in due course subjugated all the local peoples, including the Messenians to their west, and in the seventh century Sparta became the most prominent land-based military power in Greece. By the time of the Persian Wars it dominated the Peloponnese and was the acknowledged leader of the defense of Greece against the invading Persian armies.

Sparta's claim to leadership was legitimized by the magnificent performances of its army, especially at the battle that was really instrumental in removing the Persian threat to the Greek mainland for good, the battle of Plataea in 479 BC. Hundreds of years later, Plutarch still grew excited as he described the feats of the Spartan phalanx at Plataea, its unbroken front rank of shields and spears "bristling like a wild animal at bay." But Sparta became vulnerable afterward, with the revolt of Tegea, supported by Argos, destabilizing its power in the Peloponnese. Then it endured a terrible earthquake in 464, followed by a mass rebellion of the helots. Athens, meanwhile, was building her empire, and tensions between the two Greek superpowers erupted in the Peloponnesian War. After victory over Athens, thanks to Persian financial support, the Spartans enjoyed a brief period of virtually unquestioned ascendancy in the Greek world under Agesilaus II, until their defeat by Thebes in 371 BC. By midcentury, the greatest military state in Greece had been "reduced to the status of a mere Peloponnesian squabbler." In hindsight, it is clear that Agesilaus's reign marked the beginning of the end of the Spartans' prominence, although they managed to stay officially independent, even of Macedon, until the second century BC.

Agesilaus is the subject of the second oldest literary biography in existence (the earliest is the *Evagoras*, by another Athenian author, approximately coeval with Xenophon, named Isocrates). Designed as a tribute to Agesilaus after his death, Xenophon's *Agesilaus* does not offer the objective critical assessment of his achievements that we might appreciate in a biography. Yet he does provide an account of Agesilaus's successful campaigns in Asia in the 390s, when he amassed a great deal of wealth. He also outmaneuvered, by battle and diplomacy, two of the most able men in the Persian Empire, the satraps Tissaphernes and Pharnabazus. Agesilaus's original aim had been to liberate the Asiatic Greek cities from the Persians, and although problems nearer home meant that he had to abandon this policy, he strengthened the power and wealth of Sparta during his raiding expeditions in the satrapies of Hellespontine Phrygia and Lydia. Xenophon's vivid prose, the work of an eyewitness, conveys the sheer excitement that the Spartan army felt before battle as they made their preparations at Ephesus under Agesilaus's supervision.

> What a spectacle was then offered by the soldiers exercising in the gymnasiums, the cavalrymen training on horseback in the racecourse, and the spearmen and archers at target practice! In fact, the whole city was a sight to behold. The marketplace brimmed with weapons and arms and horses of all kinds up for sale. There were bronze smiths and carpenters and iron casters and cobblers and painters—all of them making the equipment needed for war. The result was that you might have thought that the entire city was a factory. Anybody who saw it would have felt the excitement when, led by Agesilaus, all the soldiers marched with garlands on their heads out of the gymnasiums to the statue of Artemis and dedicated the garlands to her.

Artemis was the patron god of Ephesus, but she was also, along with her twin brother, Apollo, prominent in Spartan religion.

The spaces between the problematic sources and the bare chronological outline are only partially filled in by the scanty material evidence. Laconia was nearly three times as big as Attica, although much of the land was too mountainous to be productively farmed. It consists of a large horseshoe-shaped chunk of the southeastern Peloponnese, the western prong being the Mani peninsula and the eastern projection running down to Cape Malea. But the bend of the horseshoe extends northward inland to the mountains of the central Peloponnese, to Arcadia, Sparta's neighbor. Sparta itself lies in the fertile Eurotas valley, which has huge mountain ranges on either side, the higher peaks belonging to Taygetos to its west. Bounded as they were on every side by mountains or sea, with only one easily accessible harbor, the Spartans were never tempted to build themselves walls or an acropolis of more than modest height. A fifth-century poet called Ion, from Chios, explained why: "This Laconian city has no walls, but whenever fresh war falls upon her regiments, counsel rules and the hand carries out the act." Their topographical isolation fueled the Spartans' tendencies toward keeping to themselves and social conservatism. Nor did they ever feel the need to build the sort of magnificent city center, with fine architecture, public buildings, and temples, that would impress visitors. Thucydides, who so admired Pericles, the instigator of the Athenian building program, could scarcely disguise his disdain for the architecture of Sparta, which "has no splendid temples or other buildings; it looks more like a collection of villages in the manner of the ancient towns of Greece."

The surviving ruins of Sparta, including the theater, mostly derive from the Roman era. What we know of the classical period suggests that commemorating military victories was the main feature of the Spartans' building policy. There was once an imposing colonnade, built in the fifth century, with spoils taken in the Persian Wars. The sanctuaries of Sparta are archaeologically disappointing; only the foundations survive of their famous Athena of the Bronze House, which the Spartans covered completely with a cladding made of bronze arms taken from defeated enemies on the battlefield. The base of the equally famous temple of Artemis Orthia, on the western bank of the Eurotas, reveals that in Leonidas's day it consisted of a small Doric building with no colonnade, and a sacred space containing the altar over which the young Spartan soldiers were ritually flogged under the scrutiny of the priestess of Artemis.

The temple, like many sanctuaries of Artemis, was built in marshy ground, full of reeds, where the small game sacred to this hunter goddess flourished. Yet the Orthia excavations have uncovered some surprising finds, besides archaic ivory depictions of Artemis with birds and animals. More than six hundred life-size terra-cotta masks, still wearable today if a cord is threaded through the holes bored in the top and sides, force us to question the idea that in the archaic period

Sparta was as inward-looking as the ancient written sources imply. Many of the masks, which are distinctively furrowed and mostly grotesque, belong to a type that shows the certain influence of imagery from Canaanite sources, probably brought to Sparta from Cyprus by Phoenician traders. The epithet of the goddess Artemis at Sparta, Orthia, which may be connected with un-Artemisian phallic imagery, has never been satisfactorily explained and points to an eastern origin.

It was at the temple of Artemis that adolescent girls of Sparta performed what remains of their lyrical *Partheneia*, or Maiden Choruses, composed by the poet Alcman. One substantial text survives, and it makes riveting reading. It opens with a story about the Spartan twin heroes Castor and Polydeuces, but in the main section the chorus describes a ritual they are performing for a goddess associated with the dawn; they are bringing her statue a new garment. Their names give us, uniquely, intimate contact with real Spartan women: Nanno, Areta, Thylacis, Philylla. The two leading celebrants are Hagesichora and Agido, both of whose names, interestingly, mean something like "female leader," for there is not only a homoerotic atmosphere but humorous fighting and competitive banter between two groups involved in the ritual. The girls are also compared in their beauty to racehorses.

Another song by Alcman describes the girls' separation from one of their number, Astumeloisa, "She Who Sings for the City." This beauty has a mane of gorgeous hair and is probably dancing as the maidens sing at her wedding. There may also be echoes of Alcman and other early lyric poets in an exquisite poem by Theocritus, written in the third century BC, which describes the marriage of Menelaus and Helen and their wedding song, performed by a chorus of twelve lovely Spartan maidens. They in turn describe the ritual they will perform in a meadow at sunrise after the wedding night. They will suspend the leaves of wild plants from the branches of a plane tree, along with a dripping silver-lipped vial of olive oil, and carve Helen's name, in the Doric dialect, in the bark of the tree.

The Spartans did have more impressive religious buildings if they traveled a greater distance from their city. The most famous Laconian sanctuary was about three miles south at Amyclae, and some remains of its outer courtyard and wall can be seen in the Spartan Archaeological Museum. Here the Spartans celebrated two important festivals, the Hyacinthia in honor of Apollo and the youthful hero Hyacinthus, and the Gymnopaidiai, at which young trainee Spartiates performed naked war dances. To design and build the temple complex, shaped like an enormous throne, the Spartans, for all their reputation for xenophobia, commissioned a famous architect named Bathycles from faraway Ionia. He brought his own builders, whom he depicted dancing at the top of the stone "throne" that constituted the temple. The artistry of this sanctuary, described in detail by the later travel writer Pausanias, calls into doubt the idea that the Spartans were insensitive to visual art and architecture. The sanctuary contained offerings from as early as the archaic period, tripods and statues, including images of the Graces and Artemis dedicated by Bathycles himself. The temple's pillars were both Ionic and Doric.

The relief sculptures were astonishing. Pausanias's list sounds like a manual of Greek mythology, although certain figures and themes beloved of the Spartans predominated—Menelaus, Heracles' labors, and energetic erotic encounters between gods and mortals. On the throne was placed a pedestal said to contain Hyacinthus's buried body, and on the pedestal there stood the bizarre cult image of Apollo, which was thought to be very ancient. It was an elongated bronze pillar or cone, made to look slightly anthropomorphic only by the addition of a head, feet, and hands. It wore a helmet and carried a spear and a bow. Looking at Apollo in this form resembled staring into the inscrutable helmeted face of the bronze-clad hoplite enemy.

At Amyclae there was also a cult of Agamemnon and Cassandra, worshipped under her alternative name Alexandra. East of Amyclae, in the hills of Therapne rising above the Eurotas, the Spartans worshipped Agamemnon's brother Menelaus in company with Helen. The ruins of the rectangular monument can be seen today. The monument occupies an imposing, elevated position and dates from the fifth century but replaced an older shrine and may have been rebuilt after damage in the earthquake of 464 BC. A small flask, perhaps containing perfume, was dedicated to Helen there by a man named Deinis in the seventh century. In the fifth century, another man named Euthycrenes brought an offering of a bronze meat hook for the hero Menelaus.

Some offerings are figures of soldiers, perhaps suitable for dedication by men or by women hoping for doughty sons. Many are lead or terra-cotta figurines of animals, connected with Helen's role as promoter of fertility. The loom weights and necklaces may have been dedicated by women: Helen in the *Iliad* is represented as an outstanding weaver of richly pictorial textiles. We have important written evidence that women felt a strong psychological connection with Helen of Therapne, embodiment of absolute female erotic allure. Herodotus tells the story of a nurse in charge of an uncommonly plain infant girl. She took remedial action by regularly placing the child before the statue of Helen. One day a mysterious woman—perhaps a manifestation of the cult heroine herself—stroked the unfortunate girl's face and announced that she would become the most beautiful woman in Sparta. Defying all expectations, she did grow up lovely, and married a Spartan king.

Partly as a result of Helen's famed erotic reputation, one of the most discussed aspects of the Spartan system was its women, who were usually said to have been allowed far more freedom than other Greek females. They were as witty as their menfolk, and a collection of their tart sayings has survived. They had more economic independence than women in other Greek cities and held property in their own names. Since many Spartan men lived in the public messes, their wives and daughters were less supervised, on an everyday basis, than their counterparts in other cities. They were said to appear often in public and even engage in physical exercise, revealing their bodies like men. This may reflect an institutionalized cultivation of female beauty, strength, sexual attractiveness, and perhaps independence. They probably engaged in organized contests in wrestling, running, and throwing the javelin and discus, in accordance with the imperative that they should reproduce a maximally vigorous ruling class of Spartiates. Girls in Sparta benefited from being married rather later than in other Greek states, where the customary age was fourteen or even younger, since Lycurgus's prescriptions said that marriages should happen "at the prime of physical development, since this was also conducive to the birth of strong children." Here the Spartans were practicing good sense. The death toll in childbirth among babies and their young mothers soon after menarche was then, and is now, higher than in mothers over the age of twenty.

In *Lysistrata*, first staged in 411 BC, the Athenian stereotype of a Spartan woman charges onto the stage in the form of Lampito (Shining One), so strong she could strangle a bull, and endowed with a beautiful bosom. A Spartan princess, Cynisca, was the first woman to win an Olympic event in her own name, as the owner and perhaps trainer of horses for equestrian events twice in the 390s BC. The inscription in which she describes her victor's statue, set up at Olympia, proudly proclaimed, "My father and brothers are kings of Sparta, but Cynisca, victorious in the chariot race of swift-footed horses, set up this image proclaiming myself the only woman in all Greece to have received the crown."

The witty, athletic women of Sparta were being prepared to become wives and mothers of Spartiates, and one of the more bizarre aspects of Spartan life was the marriage ceremony. Marriage was the business of the state; Spartiate men were penalized for not marrying and for marrying too old or inappropriately. Producing healthy sons was rewarded: A man who fathered three was exempt from military service, and if he fathered four he was relieved even of making financial contributions to the state. The verb used of Spartan bridegrooms acquiring their brides is "seize," and it is not clear whether the abduction of the bride was a ritual or a reality. Bridegrooms under thirty, who lived, as we have seen, in the collective public messes, were only allowed to visit their brides covertly and mate in total darkness. Perhaps this was intended to heighten the sexual tension and produce more babies—certainly Plutarch says that some men had children before they ever discovered what their wives looked like in daylight.

Lycurgus's prescriptions also encouraged a high birth rate by authorizing a young wife of an older man to have children by another man, provided her husband agreed. The older man then adopted the sons she produced, thus enhancing his own status. One source, Polybius, says that women had children by three or four men, and that when a man had fathered a sufficient number, it was regarded as honorable for him to give away his wife to a friend. Needless to say, the patriarchal Greeks of other city-states were outraged at what they saw as a legal authorization of female sexual freedom. Aristotle regarded the Spartan women as wholly self-indulgent and out of control.

Understanding the Spartans' sexual and affective ties is complicated by the inconsistency of the sources on the topic of homosexuality. Plutarch assumes it was widespread, but Xenophon, who had spent time in Sparta, implies that any open physical expression of homosexuality was discouraged. The question would be easier to answer if we knew more about the festival of the Hyacinthia, celebrated in honor of Apollo and Hyacinthus, the Spartan youth beloved of the god. Hyacinthus was killed by accident when training with a discus, and the festival traced in ritual the beautiful youth's life, death, and apotheosis. In the sanctuary of Apollo at Amyclae, the whole citizen class of Sparta, women as well as men, congregated to celebrate this festival with games and sacrifices.

Intense camaraderie between Spartiates is conveyed by the poems of Tyrtaeus, the only authentic voice, besides Alcman's, we can hear well from early Sparta. Like Alcman, Tyrtaeus was probably Spartan, although both men are said to have come from elsewhere in Greece. The idea that Sparta produced poets may have seemed incompatible with its militarism. Tyrtaeus composed patriotic songs in marching meters. They were called *embateria* or *enoplia*, which translate as "songs for the battle charge" or "songs for singing under arms," respectively. He was said to have composed the songs for the Spartans to encourage them in the war against the Messenians they wanted to enslave. Leonidas is supposed to have recommended Tyrtaeus as "a good poet for sharpening the courage of the young." Tyrtaeus's songs celebrate the victory over the Messenians, and the burden of tax that the Spartans imposed upon them, proclaiming that it is "a good thing for a good man to fall and die on the front line for his fatherland." The same poem then exhorts the young Spartiates directly: "Come then, O youths, stand and fight alongside one another! No shameful running away, no feelings of fear! Be stout-hearted and courageous; never shrink from combat with your enemy!" Another Tyrtaean refrain plans a bloodthirsty day when the singers shall together "stand up to men of the spear, with a terrifying din, as the adversaries clash rounded shield against rounded shield; awful will be the screams as they fall on one another, thrusting spears through the breasts of men."

Tyrtaeus's songs prepared Spartan youths emotionally for their military future. One classical source, an Athenian speech, claims that listening to his songs was compulsory for trainee Spartiates. Such a rule would not be inconsistent with the Spartan system of pedagogy, the *agoge*, which the Spartans legitimized by developing an account of their early history to explain it. Unlike the Athenians, who stressed that they had sprung from Attic soil, the Spartans based their claim to their kingdom on a myth of violent invasion. They had been led by Zeus into the Peloponnese and were a permanent army of occupation. They also liked to think that the foundation of Spartan institutions had been the necessary response to chaotic strife and were not to be tampered with in any way. Lycurgus, a descendant of Heracles usually placed in the eighth century BC, was believed to have obtained a Delphic oracle that was called his *rhetra* and contained the basic laws of the Spartans. These were what made them invincible: Herodotus makes Demaratus say to Xerxes that law is the Spartans' master; they are the best soldiers in the world because they unquestioningly obey it.

There were three hereditary classes in Spartan society. The superior or citizen class were the Spartiates. There was no distinction of status within this group—they also called themselves the *homoioi*, meaning "equals." The *homoioi* were, however, subdivided into tribes. They lived together in the "city," which consisted of five villages. The status of Spartiate needed to be inherited, consolidated through participation in the rigorous training of the *agoge* and maintained by membership in a mess and suitable conduct in battle. If these requirements were not met, the Spartiate could lose his status, suffer public humiliation, and have all his contracts with Spartiates annulled. The social system at Sparta, however peculiar, was probably a response to the same kind of crisis over land distribution that led to tyrannies and subsequently democracies in some other Greek cities, but it took a different form: the creation of a sense of solidarity and peer-group similarity among the ruling class.

The group's solidarity was reinforced by a complex system of power distribution within it. There were always supposed to be two kings—

constituting a dyarchy rather than a monarchy. This was intended to prevent either king from accumulating excessive authority. The two Peloponnesian kings Menelaus and Agamemnon may be a mythical reflection of this constitutional peculiarity, although in reality the dyarchs were not brothers. They inherited their position as members of two distinct dynasties, the Agids and the Eurypontids, both of which claimed direct descent from Heracles, son of Zeus. When not at war, the kings' main role was religious; they were both priests of Zeus. They swore reciprocal oaths with the ephors, the five annually elected officers of the Spartan citizen Assembly, vowing to respect each other's authority: The lesson most taken to heart at Sparta, according to numerous sources, was "to rule and likewise to be ruled." The ephors appointed magistrates and scrutinized their performance, although the Assembly voted on whether to go to war.

To outsiders like Herodotus and Xenophon, however, the most remarkable feature of classical Sparta was the power of the older men. It was a gerontocracy. Herodotus is surprised that strong young Spartans always make way in the street for senior citizens, and there may have been a rule that Spartan youths had to give up their seats to their elders. The name of the council at Sparta, *gerousia*, even translates as something like "House of Elders." Only men over sixty were eligible to become one of the twenty-eight *gerontes* (plus the two kings) who formed this body. The *gerontes* were the judges in capital offenses.

According to Plutarch, at least, boys (and probably girls) were inspected at birth by the elders. Weaklings were immediately exposed. Xenophon's *Constitution of Sparta* supplies further details: At seven years old, a Spartiate boy joined the public education system and lived with other boys. He was subjected to an austere lifestyle and arduous training, aimed at creating excellent soldiers with a developed sense of shame and obedience. They were in the control of a *paidonomos*, a Spartiate who could call on selected young men. They carried whips and administered the punishments he ordained. But any Spartiate could punish other men's sons if he saw fit. The boys were also encouraged to steal food, since it was felt to make them resourceful and aggressive, but if they were caught they were punished. Between the ages of twenty and thirty the Spartiates were in an intermediate position. They could grow their hair long but still slept in a state dormitory, were not yet allowed to hold office and probably not to attend meetings of the Assembly. The three hundred best soldiers in each year at the end of this period were selected as the crack troops for the army. Spartiates over thirty were expected to fight until they were sixty and continue to exercise appropriately; gymnastics were compulsory. The penalty for refusing to go to war or for desertion was death. Some rules are so odd that they are likely to be true—for example, that Spartiates were not allowed to carry a light around in the dark, to ensure that they remained on high alert permanently.

In all the other settlements in Laconian land there lived the *perioikoi*, "dwellers-around," who were nominally free but, in ways not well understood, subject to the hereditary Spartiates. The third class were the slaves—helots. They were said originally to have been the free inhabitants of a place called Helos who had been conquered and enslaved. Later, the Spartans also conquered Messenia and added the Messenians to the helots. The helots did all the agricultural labor and had to hand over a sizable portion of the proceeds: Tyrtaeus compares them to donkeys, "oppressed with great burdens, grimly compelled to produce for their masters half of the fruits of their field." They belonged to the state rather than to any individual Spartiate; only the state could emancipate helots, and it occasionally did so, for example as a reward for loyal conduct during war.

The life of the helot was wretched. Each Spartiate warrior was responsible for disciplining the helots who worked the land belonging to him, and this arrangement resulted in humiliating and intimidating practices. Helots had to wear a rough uniform of a dogskin cap and leather tunic, and it was laid down that they "should be beaten a fixed number of strokes annually, besides any offence they committed, so that they would never forget that they were slaves." Moreover, if they started to look too physically strong, they were executed and a fine imposed on their master. The Spartiates even had a ritual whereby the ephors annually reenacted the conquest of Laconia by declaring war on the helots, in order to remove any impiety or illegality from the act of murdering them. According to Plutarch, the

Spartan "secret service" (*krupteia*) often killed helots, especially those who were physically strong.

The Spartans' supremacy as a land-based militia, which allowed them to dominate not only their helots but much of the Greek world from the seventh century to the mid-fourth century, ultimately came down to their highly trained, heavily armed infantry. The violence of the combat between phalanxes of heavily armed hoplites has produced, in the scholarly realm, a corresponding level of violence in argumentation. The method of conflict resolution it represented is indeed unparalleled in other known societies of primitive or peasant agriculturalists, as some historians, shocked by the bloodiness of hoplite warfare, have complained. On the other hand, some hawkish classicists discuss hoplite warfare with open approval, claiming that it was an efficient, stylized form of dueling that resulted in less overall suffering than war waged with the pursuits, sieges, ambushes, protracted campaigns, and mass executions characteristic of other forms of ancient warfare. This line of argument finds glory in the fact that hoplites were fighting in defense of their own autonomy and civic privileges: "A citizen of a Greek city-state understood that the simplicity, clarity and brevity of hoplite battle defined the entire relationship with a man's family and community, the one day of uncertain date that might end his life but surely give significance to his entire existence." Yet even the Greeks were aware that there was something remarkable about hoplite warfare, to the extent that Herodotus makes a Persian general, Mardonius, describe how the Greeks "wage their wars in the most nonsensical way. The minute they declare war on one another, they look for the finest and flattest ground, and go there to do battle. As a result, even the victors suffer extreme fatalities. Needless to say, the losing side is annihilated."

Mardonius was not wrong. One of the few honest accounts of the aftermath of hoplite battle occurs in Xenophon's eyewitness description of the battlefield after clash between Thebes and Sparta in 394: "the earth was stained with gore, with the bodies of friends and enemies strewn alongside one another, shields shattered into pieces, spears smashed in two, swords pulled out of their scabbards—some on the ground, some in cadavers, some still clutched in the hand." Tyrtaeus describes the experience of hoplite warfare in graphic detail: "Everyone must bite his lip and stand firm, his feet firmly planted bestriding the ground, using his broad shield to cover his thighs and shins below, and breast and shoulders above. He must shake his mighty spear in his right hand and wave the crest frighteningly on his head!" Each hoplite went into combat identically equipped with a large, heavy, convex shield, a spear with an iron tip and a spike on the other end, a short sword, a corselet, and a crested helmet. He would line up side by side with his comrades in the rectangular formation known as the phalanx, with the best fighters standing on the front and the back lines. The front line stared the enemy's front line full in their frightening helmeted faces. When the trumpet blared, the phalanxes moved toward and attacked each other with shields and spears. The loud delivery of intimidating traditional battle cries was customary.

A violent shoving competition ensued, each front-line hoplite taking on his opposite number. The whole-body assault was accompanied by brutal upward and downward spear thrusts. Tyrtaeus's hoplite anthem continues: "Let each warrior get up close to one of the enemy, wound him and take him down with long spear or sword. He must fight his opponent placing foot against foot, pressing shield against shield, crest beside crest and helmet beside helmet—fight breast to breast, gripping his sword or long spear."

This went on until one side gave way, which often happened quickly, each soldier's "knee pressed in the dust, and spear splintered in the assault," as a soldier in Aeschylus puts it. If anyone broke ranks through cowardice or recklessness, he put the rest of his line in immediate lethal danger. If the phalanx was forced to turn, exposing one side, everyone on that side was made critically vulnerable. The losing side gave way when too many of the front line fell to be replaced by the men standing in the line behind them, or they were forced into retreat or surrounded. Sometimes there was fighting with swords and even teeth and nails, as in the last stand of Leonidas's Spartans at Thermopylae. Sometimes hardly any of the defeated side was left alive.

Repeated participation in this kind of battle could produce in Spartans something equivalent to what is now diagnosed as post-traumatic stress disorder. In Xenophon's account of the Spartan general Clearchus, it has been argued by Vietnam veteran Larry Tritle that we have "the first known case of PTSD . . . in the western literary tradition." Clearchus, says Xenophon, *chose* to go to war; he could have spent his large fortune on peacetime pursuits but instead waged a war in which he had no personal investment. An adventurer, Clearchus led from the front and only looked happy when he was fighting (otherwise he looked angry and forbidding). He had a harsh voice, was incapable of personal attachments, and practiced brutal discipline. A law unto himself, he could not abide serving under the orders of any other man. On one occasion, after a camp dispute caused by his excessive punishments, he flew off the handle and nearly started an all-out battle between fellow Greeks. It was only on the intervention of the Persian supreme commander, Cyrus, that Clearchus "came to his senses" again. Yet other Spartans, including Leonidas, reached grand old ages apparently without mental damage. In Thucydides' portrait of the brave Spartan Brasidas, we receive the impression of an exceptionally intelligent, committed, and principled leader who died leading his men into battle in 422 BC. A few years later, it was the Spartan Gylippus whose strategic thinking and inspired rhetoric altered the course of the Peloponnesian War by leading to the humiliation of the Athenians at Syracuse.

Sparta's success at hoplite warfare was bound up with its cultivation, through humor, of collective morale, and with its internal civic ethos and skill at organization, which were profoundly egalitarian if you were one of the select free Spartan males. Kings and commanders fought and risked death alongside lower-ranking hoplites. All free male Spartans wore exactly the same quality of clothing, and careful restrictions in consumption of all types of goods were observed. The years of training together, eating and living together as mess-mates, and fighting together in successive battles fostered a spirit of comradeship and collective identity unsurpassed in any other city-state's citizen army. Any man who fought irresponsibly or feebly would be held to account by the entire phalanx afterward.

The solidarity was also fostered by rigorous observance of religious rites. The militaristic Spartans were devout and superstitious to a bewildering degree. These traits can best be explained as functioning to preserve an unquestioning obedience to the ancestral laws.

It is also why, I think, Leonidas may have been spiritually motivated to go to Thermopylae—his ancestor Heracles had died on a nearby mountain. The Spartans reacted to the deaths of all their kings, not just Leonidas, with great solemnity. Anybody who did not attend the funeral, dressed in full mourning, was fined; all matters related to government were suspended for ten days. The Spartans also took augury and divination with meticulous seriousness. They never embarked on an invasion or battle without exhaustive sacrifices and often decided to go home if the animals' entrails provided insufficient reassurance. The only two men from outside Sparta whom they ever made full citizens were a professional seer and his brother.

The Spartans were also zealous in the cultivation of the Delphic oracle. They dedicated a category of official unknown in any other Greek state, the Pythioi, to consult Apollo and look after the oracles he gave them. Most of the great events in their history—for example, Lycurgus's *Rhetra* and Leonidas's decision to go to Thermopylae—were connected with an oracle from Delphi. On the other hand, Leonidas departed for Thermopylae unconstitutionally. He lacked the sanction of the ephors representing the Assembly, who objected to him campaigning during the Carneia, their ten-day festival of Apollo. The Spartans paid such heed to their festivals that even crucial military developments took second place to observing them. It was the Carneia of 490 BC that prevented the Spartans from helping the Athenians win the battle of Marathon. Paradoxically, the festival was itself a carnivalesque enactment of life in a military camp, in which young unmarried men slept in tents and received orders from a herald.

Ambivalence is the only possible response toward the Spartans of the classical period. Their cynical exploitation and mistreatment of the helots are rebarbative. So are several aspects of their brutal upbringing of boys. Yet if the picture painted by the motley sources is at all reliable, it is difficult not to admire their wit and particularly the ethos of equality, mutual loyalty, and solidarity cultivated by their ruling class, and their physical discipline and courage. The freedom of their womenfolk relative to other Greek women is attractive. There is no reason to disbelieve Aristophanes when he says that there was a female Spartan poet named Kleitagora, although the claim of Iamblichos that there were several Spartan women who practiced Pythagoreanism is of too late a date (third or fourth century AD) to be reliable. Both Spartan men and women performed challenging sung-and-danced choruses, in Alcman's case involving the memorization of exquisite lyrics. An advanced aesthetic sensibility is implied by the celebrated beauty of their horses and their women. Life for the free in classical Sparta had its moments of lightheartedness and enchantment; I am convinced that they were far more cultured than their own propaganda implied. The archaeological evidence at the temples of Artemis Orthia and at Amyclae contradicts the conventional view that they were averse to introducing expertise from outside. Spartans created excellent vase paintings and sculptures. There is no reason to doubt Plato when he claims that two of the legendary "seven sages" of Greece came from Sparta. There was nothing inherently incompatible in training for war and enjoying the celebrated works of Greek culture as much as the rest of Greece. It is not at all impossible that King Cleomenes saw the absolute distinction—however cruel—between the Spartiates and the helots in the poetic terms Plutarch attributed to him: "Homer is the poet of the Spartans, and Hesiod of the Helots; for Homer gave the necessary directions for fighting, and Hesiod for farming."

Yet the Spartans were very strange Greeks. With their large fertile inland plain, they were not obsessed by sailing, travel, and trade. Nor were they curiosity-driven; indeed, their culture *discouraged* asking questions to which no answer was provided by the gods or the ancestral laws. Their ascetic lifestyle did not promote the pursuit of sensual pleasure. Although liberty and independence were of inestimable importance to them collectively, the belligerent streak common to most Greeks was channeled in patriotic directions by their training. Yet they shared most of the features that collectively defined the ancient Greek mind-set. Their recognition of naked power structures and Realpolitik implies emotional honesty. They adored competitive sports and honored their athletics victors as well as their warriors. They were also very humorous, in their distinctive, succinct, saturnine way, and as such were skilled craftsmen of the Greek language. Indeed, their humor and military prowess were deeply interconnected, since laughing in the face of danger is one of the most effective ways to maintain collective morale: Many of the famous Spartan jokes are designed to embolden the hearer. King Agis quipped that the Spartans never asked "*how many* are the enemy," but "*where* are they?"

The terse Laconic phrase combines insightfulness and brevity with a pungent wit and often a note of absurdity. When a physician praised King Pausanias for achieving a great age, the king retorted, "That is because I never employed you as my physician!" Perhaps the funniest one-liner ever delivered by a Spartan in literature is a response of Menelaus to Hecuba in Euripides' otherwise bleak tragedy *Trojan Women*. The old Trojan queen wants to see Helen punished; fearing that the incomparable beauty will wheedle her way back into Menelaus's bed, Hecuba begs him not to travel back to Sparta on the same ship as his errant wife. "Why?" he answers grimly. "Has she put on weight?" Hecuba has the ground swept from beneath her through Menelaus's comical image of a now obese Helen of Troy sinking his warship in the mid–Aegean Sea. Euripides realized that Laconian speech was a rhetorical style unto itself rather than the product of a lower level of education in Sparta. Socrates shared his view: The Spartans, he said, deliberately "feign ignorance" and pretend that their superiority rests on their fighting skills and courage. But even the ordinary Spartan, who appears unimpressive at first, "eventually shoots off some noteworthy remark, terse and compressed, like a javelin thrower"; a Laconian quip, says Socrates, can be so profound that it makes the other person feel "as silly as a child."

Alexander Cuts Through the Gordian Knot (Alexander hakt de Gordiaanse knoop door), engraving by Theodor Matham (1627–1691) in the Rijksmuseum, Amsterdam. *(Reproduced with the permission of the museum)*

7

The Rivalrous Macedonians

For a brief period of less than two decades, enormous parts of the world, including the territory we now call Greece, were united under two successive rulers who spoke Greek. They were Philip II of Macedon and his son Alexander III, usually known as Alexander the Great. They were the last in the long line of kings from the same family who had ruled Macedonia for centuries and were known as the Argeads because they said they had originally come from Argos. But before their dynasty disappeared, they taught the Greeks to trade in big ideas. Macedonians went farther east than any Greeks before them. They gave the Greeks the idea of a world empire. They built the best cavalry that Greece had ever produced and developed the technology of siege warfare, psychologically crucial to maintaining imperial power on an international scale. Following Alexander's conquests and his death, his Macedonian generals known as "the Successors" carved up the territories and, after much bloodshed, introduced Greek-speaking monarchies and courts, supported by elaborate protocol and sumptuous palaces, everywhere.

When the Macedonians first enter history, it is in the context of a competition. In around 500 BC, Alexander I applied to compete in the Olympic Games, which meant that his claim to Greek ethnicity needed to be approved by the judges. It was agreed that his descent from inhabitants of Argos in the Peloponnese legitimized his desire to compete against other Greeks in the most famous Panhellenic venue of all. Alexander I's descendant Philip II, over a century and a half later, had conquered the other mainland Greeks not just in the athletics stadium but on the battlefield at Chaeronea in 338 BC. He commissioned a monument at Olympia, which shows that he now saw himself as the rival not of other Greeks but of the gods. The circular building, called the Philippeion, contained statues of himself, his father, Amyntas, and his son Alexander. Alongside them stood icons representing Philip's mother and Alexander's mother, Olympias. But these statues and icons were made, with more than a touch of arrogance, from gold and ivory, the material reserved for cult statues of the gods. The Philippeion was not quite a temple, but Philip was inviting viewers to compare his power, and that of his family, with that of divinities.

The Macedonians took competitiveness (the seventh of the characteristics I believe defined the ancient Greeks) to literally cutthroat levels. This started at home in the family. The Macedonian elite consisted of dominating individuals who understood intuitively how to acquire, maintain, and increase their power. Philip and Alexander, like all Macedonian rulers, never hesitated to use ruthless violence, even against family and associates. The general acceptance of polygamy, with several wives or concubines producing rival claimants to be heirs, heightened the competitive ethos. Macedonian history is a complex saga of internal struggle within dominant clans. Different factions, often supporting half-brothers born to the king, attempted to outmaneuver one another; rival wives and children were regarded as disposable. Alexander's mother, Olympias, may have conspired to kill Philip's "other woman," Eurydice, along with her child or children, after Philip was killed by his own bodyguard. She may even have conspired in her husband's assassination. The internal competition for power in Macedon was deeply entrenched. There was a general consensus that this system ensured the continuing strength of the kingdom on the principle of survival of the fittest.

Raised on rivalry between wives, between siblings and half-siblings, between dynastic families and warlords, it is hardly surprising that Philip and Alexander III competed in power first with the ancient city-states of Greece and then with the Persian king himself. The problem inherent in the Macedonians' love of competition was that—at least from the moment that Philip became king in 359 BC—they were never satisfied with what they had already conquered. With their eyes always on the next rung of the ladder, they often forgot to look after the rungs they had already occupied. This hazard is most clearly seen in the enigmatic figure of Alexander, whose extraordinary conquests and permanent absence destabilized and impoverished both his home district of Macedonia and the rest of mainland Greece. His death left all the Greeks and all the peoples formerly under the Persian Empire in a state of anarchy, vulnerable to the mass destruction caused by the Wars of the Successors. Their descendants continued to murder each other, as well as intermarry, for several centuries, until the Romans annexed each one of their kingdoms in succession in the second and first centuries BC.

This chapter places Alexander's conquests in the context of the distinctive character and lifestyle of these brash, wrangling inhabitants of the far north of Greece, with their wild drinking parties. It asks whether Alexander was motivated by a dream of a peaceful ideal of a global brotherhood of man, supported by a brilliant instinct for the manipulation of public opinion, or by a low boredom threshold, alcohol, and megalomaniac delusions. It inquires into the reasons for his achievements: His personal great gift, inherited from his father, was in military organization, but he also had exceptional support from his tough and ambitious mother. Both Philip and Alexander were able to compete and win hands-down on the world stage because they had the money to fund military campaigns and to import world-class brainpower—not only leading engineers and admirals but the philosopher Aristotle, mentor to Alexander. The last part of the chapter functions as a coda to the achievements of Alexander by showing how the questing, competitive spirit of the Macedonians who succeeded him kept much of the world under the control of Greeks, despite all their infighting, and even expanded Greek horizons further.

Philip always led from the front in battle, and he incurred many injuries, including the loss of his right eye at the siege of Methone in 354 BC. But the Macedonian legend begins in 338 BC, at the battle of Chaeronea. On a plain beneath Mount Parnassus, Philip defeated the venerable city-states of Athens and Thebes, breaking the heart of the

Athenian orator Demosthenes, who had spent years warning his compatriots that the Macedonians were coming. Philip's son Alexander, at
the age of only eighteen, displayed courage and skill in combat.

Every community in mainland Greece, with the exception of
Sparta, now agreed under the terms of a treaty sworn at Corinth to
form a league. Although presented as a group of autonomous states
united by a peace treaty, the league was intended to create a huge
world-conquering new Hellenic army under the absolute control of its
one-eyed Macedonian commander in his capital city of Pella. Every
member-state was to provide troops and military equipment. So who
exactly were these combative new masters of Greece, whom some of
their new subjects found uncouth and strange? Indeed, their Greek
opponents, including Demosthenes, sometimes accused them actually
of being barbarians, exploiting the difficulty many found in understanding the Macedonian dialect, at least as spoken by the uneducated
classes. Macedonian commanders would heighten their regional ver-
nacular when they needed to communicate with the Macedonian rank
and file. But a tombstone found at Vergina (in antiquity Aigai, the
ancient seat of the Macedonian kings before Archelaus I built Pella in
the late fifth century) shows that Macedonian men had predominantly
Greek names. Their dialect was undoubtedly Greek, closer to Doric
than Ionian; it had specific variations that were identified in antiquity,
including their pronunciation and therefore transcription of the letter
phi (f) as beta (b). The popular Macedonian woman's name Berenice,
therefore, was their equivalent of Pherenice, or Bearer of Victory.

Although the Macedonians naturally shared some aspects of their
lifestyle with their Thracian and Illyrian neighbors, they were Greek
in terms of their culture. Their earliest religious hub was called *Dion*,
the etymology of which shows that they were Zeus-worshippers. A
libation bowl found in an early fifth-century northern Macedonian
grave is dedicated to Athena. Dionysus was important in the region.
Women of all age groups participated in rites for Dionysus, dress-
ing as maenads and running down mountainsides, just as they did
elsewhere in Greece. The Macedonians also had an ancestor in the
Greek prehistoric genealogy articulated as early as Hesiod, who named
their forefather Macedon and stated that his descendants inhabited

the mountainous region "around Pieria and Olympus." Archaeological finds confirm that Macedonians were centered there before they expanded across northern Greece. The Macedonians said the expansion began when Philip's ancestors arrived from Argos.

Philip's dynastic origins in the Peloponnese must have been one reason why he decided to conquer Greece, but another was his temperament. Restless and autocratic, he was never going to be content with being master of Macedonia alone. In 336 BC he ordered the invasion of Asia by an advance force of ten thousand, led by his trusted general Parmenion. Philip took advantage of the crisis in the Persian monarchy caused by the murder of the king, Artaxerxes IV, and the surprise accession of his nephew Darius III. Subsequently, Philip was himself murdered at home before he could cross over to Asia and join his army. His twenty-year-old son inherited both the throne and the offensive war against Persia. But before Alexander joined Parmenion, he silenced all rivals by proving that he was as invincible as his father. He quelled an incipient rebellion in Thessaly. He attacked tribes to the north and west of Macedonia in what are now Bulgaria, Albania, and Serbia. When the Athenian Demosthenes fomented rebellion farther south and the Thebans assaulted the Macedonian garrison stationed in their city, Alexander marched south and, with the sterling assistance of his general Perdiccas, succeeded in razing Thebes. He executed or sold into slavery its entire population. The young Macedonian monarch meant business, and the Corinthian League swiftly fell back into line.

Alexander crossed the Hellespont in May 334, visited Troy where Greeks had crushed Priam and his Asiatic allies long before, and defeated one Persian army at the River Granicus. He then "liberated" some the Greek cities on the Asiatic seaboard from Persian rule, took Hellespontine Phrygia and Sardis, and achieved hard-won victories at Miletus and near Halicarnassus. Caria was crucial to his continued progress; this wealthy, Hellenized satrapy had expanded under the rule of Mausolus (377–53 BC), commemorated along with his sister/wife Artemisia in one of the Seven Wonders of the World, the astoundingly sculpted Mausoleum. Alexander obtained the help of Caria by making Mausolus's younger sister Ada sole ruler; she took to the young Macedonian king and adopted him officially as her son. Although she died at around the age of forty, a tomb claimed to be hers has been discovered, and her appearance reconstructed from her skeleton; Ada's life-size mannequin can today be seen impassively gazing down at visitors to the Bodrum Museum of Underwater Archaeology.

The Macedonian army then moved down the coast, systematically taking all port cities to prevent ships from docking. They annexed the entire Persian satrapy of Phrygia, after defeating the Persian army at Gordium in April 333. It was at Gordium that the most telling incident in Alexander's career took place. In the temple of Zeus there was an ancient oxcart, dedicated by a farmer named Gordius, who had been made king after fulfilling an oracle that the new monarch would arrive on such a vehicle. The oxcart was dedicated to Sabazios (the Phrygian god identified with Zeus) and immobilized by a complicated knot made from a cable of bark. The ends of the cable were invisible to the eye. Alexander, correctly perceiving that the cart and the knot could help confer legitimacy on his claim to rule in Asia, either sliced through the knot with his sword or removed the pin holding it together. His prophet declared that Zeus had thus indicated his approval of Alexander, and an oracle was revealed predicting that the man who undid the knot was destined to become king of Asia. The cutting of the Gordian knot shows Alexander's audacity—he must have known that his action might have been perceived as a hubristic assault on a sacred object—but at the same time shows his self-belief, his genius for public relations stunts, and his capacity for lateral thinking.

He then marched on toward Cilicia, taking the Cilician Gates (a mountain pass of the Taurus range) and Tarsus itself. But he was not unopposed. Darius III was preparing a large army in Babylonia and Syria. Darius trapped Alexander, but the Macedonians won through the superb tactics they deployed at the momentous battle of Issus. Alexander's general Parmenion then took Damascus, along with plentiful booty.

With such success behind him, Alexander did indeed begin to call himself king of Asia and to suggest that he was at least semi-divine. He moved along the Orontes and advanced into Phoenicia. After the surrender of Gaza and Egypt in 332, he founded Alexandria in 331, before visiting the oracle of Egyptian Amun and declaring, offensively to traditionally minded Greeks, that he was the son of Zeus. He had to move backward to secure Samaria and faced the Persians again at the battle of Gaugamela in northern Iraq on October 1, 331. Despite winning, the Macedonians still could not take Darius III captive. But Babylon now surrendered to Alexander, making him ruler of Babylonia, the largest satrapy of the Persian Empire. Scarcely pausing for breath, he took Susa in December, Persepolis in January 330, and then Pasargadae. Alexander then finally arranged for the satrap of Bactria to assassinate Darius. The entire Persian Empire became subject to the Macedonian son of Zeus.

His appetite for campaigning inexplicably unsatisfied, Alexander pressed on eastward, taking two years to subdue Bactria and Sogdiana. In 327 he invaded the Punjab, which occupied him for three years. He did return to Susa in 324 and set about unifying the taxation system and coinage. But he died the next year, possibly poisoned, and certainly demoralized by the death of his lifelong companion, Hephaestion. He left uncompleted the organization of the central administration his unprecedentedly large empire desperately needed. The seminal ancient account of Alexander's death occurs in the work of the Sicilian Greek historian Diodorus. Diodorus relates that, although soothsayers were instructing Alexander to perform grand sacrifices, he was distracted by his retinue of official "Friends," an inner circle of trusted lieutenants, and joined a carousal in honor of his ancestor Heracles. Although the Greeks normally diluted their wine with water, that night Alexander drank it undiluted, and (as often) in far too great a quantity.

> Suddenly he let out a loud cry, like someone struck by a violent blow, and was lifted up and taken out in the arms of his friends. His bedroom attendants laid him down and attended him assiduously, but his suffering grew more intense. The doctors were summoned, but none of them could help. He could find no relief from his discomfort and was in considerable pain. When he realized that he would not survive, he took off his ring and gave it to Perdiccas. His friends asked him, "To whom do you bequeath the kingdom?" He answered, "To the strongest."

With these dying words he begot many decades of chaotic competition between his Successors—his generals and their associates.

Alexander did no favors to his homeland in fighting far away for so long. He disastrously depleted Macedonian manpower. His regent Antipater and his indomitable mother, Olympias, conducted an exhausting power struggle that dominated court life. Macedonian rule did not benefit the Greeks of the Corinthian League much, if at all. They simply installed garrisons in most of the city-states they ruled in the Peloponnese, or at least near enough to keep the local inhabitants sufficiently intimidated not to rebel. On many occasions Alexander was wiping out other Greeks, employed by the Persians as mercenaries. The lack of interest in Greece and the Greeks themselves is a factor in questions concerning Alexander's character and motivations, one of the great conundrums of history.

In and since antiquity he has been seen by some as a drunken megalomaniac but by others as a visionary who dreamed of a peaceful, unified family of mankind. Many Macedonians resented his cultivation of Persian friends, allies, and court protocol (especially the encouragement of belief in the divinity of the king), as well as his politically motivated marriage to Roxana, the Bactrian princess. But did he want to rule the Persian Empire as autocratically as the Achaemenids before him? He may have planned a new kind of tolerant, "multicultural" arrangement, an ethnically diverse joint enterprise. Yet overall I am inclined to think that he was too driven a character—always too wrapped up in his immediate situation—to give much thought to the future or to utopian ideals. Moreover, there is no evidence that his attitude differed much from Philip's. Philip had already conceived a project of turning the Macedonian monarchy into something grand by international standards: His conscious imitation of the Persian court can be seen in art and aspects of court ceremonial. Other Greeks put their best architecture and art to the service of the gods, in temples and sanctuaries, but the Macedonians lavished money on the fabric and content of their palaces. The elaborately painted tomb believed to be Philip's, Tomb II at Vergina, was modeled on the tomb of Cyrus the Great at Pasargadae.

It is also easy to forget that Philip had already ordered the invasion

of the Persian Empire—two years before Alexander—as had Agesilaus the Spartan half a century before. The Greeks had never given up
the dream of punishing the Persians for their invasions back in 490
and 480 BC. Our ability to see Alexander's true self is also hampered
by the lateness of the sources—Diodorus Siculus (first century BC),
Quintus Curtius (first century AD), Plutarch (first to second century
AD), Arrian (second century AD), Justin, and the imaginative *Alexander Romance* (third century AD), whose author is unknown. These
writers all drew to an uncertain degree on early sources, including
the eyewitness accounts of Alexander's general Ptolemy, his engineer
Aristoboulos, his admiral Nearchos, and the mysterious Cleitarchos,
whose biography was completed by 301 BC. But even these original
documents are unlikely to have been objective, since they served pro-
pagandist aims during the Wars of the Successors.

Perhaps the most important question is whether Alexander really
did believe that divine blood ran in his veins, or whether he cynically
adopted such propaganda to justify to superstitious subjects what
may actually have been a rational and enlightened project. It is almost
impossible to judge from the available evidence, such as the new
coins he had minted at Damascus when he needed to court Phoenician support. On one side was stamped the head of Heracles, but with
Alexander's facial features. The reverse side depicted Heracles'—and,
allegedly, Alexander's—father Zeus. Heracles and Zeus were carefully
chosen, as the Greek equivalents of the Phoenicians' Melquart and
Ba'al. But did Alexander in any sense believe that he was a spiritual
reiteration, or even reincarnation, of the colonizing hero Heracles?

I suspect that he did at least half believe it. Fourth-century ruling-
class Macedonians were much empowered by their inner, religious
lives, which were dominated by their initiation into an intense mystery cult. This offered them profound psychological sustenance and a
beatific afterlife in the islands of the blessed or the Elysian fields. In
order to be eligible, the deceased individual needed to have lived an
upright life and needed to be prepared to give certain responses to the
judges of the underworld, chaired by Rhadamanthys, when he or she
was led to them by Hermes, escort of dead souls. A scene depicting a
scene of underworld judgment is painted on a Macedonian tomb at

Lefkadia, south of Pella, the largest such tomb to have been found. It probably belonged to one of Alexander's own commanders. Upon initiation into the mystery cult, the initiate had access to arcane writings that held the correct answers, and in 1962 a specimen, known as the Derveni Papyrus, was actually discovered in a Macedonian necropolis near Thessalonica. It dates from the mid-fourth century and is thus the oldest surviving Western book.

Its abstruse, atmospheric fragments offer an amazing window onto the secret religious convictions of the Macedonian elite, which make Alexander's own claim to be the son of Zeus and the equal of Heracles seem less peculiar. It speaks of powerful vengeance spirits and their "kindly" avatars. It claims that paying attention to dream-visions can make the initiate free of the fear of Hades. It talks of mysterious *magoi* who conduct sacrifices of liquids and cakes with many humps. It also provides a long commentary on an earlier text by Orpheus involving riddles, which talked of Zeus ousting his father, of the relationship between fire and the other elements, and of Night as making prophecies. The idea that the Sun can be equated with a genital organ is discussed, as is the Orphic version of the creation of the cosmos, in which Mind (*Nous*), Fate, and Zeus figure large: Zeus is equated with Aphrodite, Persuasion, and Harmony. The secret world of the Orphic initiates of Macedon was vibrant, self-confident, and intriguing. If Alexander was initiated, which is very likely, he would have been convinced that he enjoyed special status in relation to the divine.

Olympias, a northern Greek associated in ancient sources with membership in esoteric cults, was of undoubted importance in Alexander's success. The sexist ancient sources paint pictures of her as an intrigue-addicted harridan, but she was actually fighting in her son's corner from almost the minute he was born. Women in the Macedonian court were undoubtedly powerful, although it is difficult to be sure of the degree to which they had access to official power or whether the political culture of the court simply meant that they exerted even more *unofficial* pressure on affairs of state than elite women in most other Greek states. But fourth-century sources offer glimpses into the queens' and consorts' behavior: A contemporary speech by the Athenian statesman Aeschines shows that Philip II's mother, Eurydice, courted support outside Macedon for her son's claim to the succession. Crate-sipolis, the wife of the Macedonian general Polyperchon, stepped into her husband's shoes when he was assassinated in 314 BC, and with his army quelled a rebellion in the city of Sicyon. Eurydice was responsi-ble for at least two expensive statues at Aigai.

The sort of psychological resources available to Olympias and others was illuminated in 1986 by the discovery at Pella of a tablet inscribed with a curse made by a Macedonian woman and buried with a dead man called Makron between 380 and 350 BC. The woman issuing the curse wants to marry and bear children to a man named Dionysophon, but she is concerned that he will marry a rival named Thetima instead. She consigns all other unmarried women to the spirit of the dead Makron and to demons but is especially concerned to pre-vent Thetima from getting in her way. She says that she is burying the curse tablet and that the demons are to ensure that Dionysophon does not marry until she digs it up again. It looks as though she never did. We will probably never know whether Dionysophon really did marry Thetima.

The contribution of religion and of his superstitious mother's machinations to Alexander's successes will always be uncertain, but we can at least be sure that a crucial factor in his achievements was money. Under Philip, the disposable income of the Macedonian mon-archy had increased massively. He developed and kept under his fami-ly's control a new mining program, exploiting the natural resources of gold and silver around his domain. He received as much pure annual profit from the mines as a thousand talents. The visual impact of the dazzling golden grave furniture and ornamental wreaths, with their clusters of acorns, found in the two-roomed tomb believed to be his at Vergina, is nothing if not ostentatious. Philip also built economic power by circulating Macedonian money. He expanded Macedonian territory into densely forested regions on the edges of the Strymon river valley, supplying almost unlimited quantities of the fir, pine, and oak needed to maintain an increasing demand for ships. In Macedo-nia, substantial rivers supplied routes by which even the largest planks could be floated to the coastal shipyards all year round.

Monetary resources were thus available to support Macedonian military flair. Philip studied the famed strategies of the Theban army and invested in a professional infantry of Macedonian peasants, organized according to their several tribes, whom he supplied with the most up-to-date weapons. The Macedonian kings' famous infantry guard, or *hypaspists*, were, however, a crack troop of perhaps three thousand men specially selected from *all* tribes. They were encouraged to think of themselves as his personal bodyguards. Philip also created and commanded a companion cavalry of landed gentry that swiftly became the most powerful the Western world had ever seen, partly by inviting horsemen from elsewhere in Greece and granting them tracts of land. He abandoned the traditional pause in military activity over the winter months: Philip refused to be season-bound and expected his troops to campaign every day of the year. The importance of preeminence at sea was not lost on the Macedonians, either; Alexander could never have taken so much of Asia at such speed if his admiral Nearchos had not kept control of the ports of Anatolia, forcing the Persian fleet to take massive detours and denying them access from the sea to their king's domains.

Under Philip and Alexander, the relationship between warfare and heavy engineering was cemented and siege warfare transformed in favor of the attacking army. The arrow-firing catapult had been invented in Sicily in the early fourth century, but it was under Philip or Alexander, who could afford the salaries of the world's most distinguished engineers, including Polyeidus of Thessaly, that the torsion spring was introduced. This increased the size of the missiles that could be mechanically launched from a small stone to a rock weighing 176 pounds, which on impact could knock a man's head off or remove a whole battlement. Missiles could be launched accurately and repeatedly at defensive ramparts, making swift work of them. Along with massive movable siege towers and battering rams of unprecedented size, the Macedonians' terrifying catapults transformed the experience of both besieger and besieged. The invention of the torsion-sprung catapult was instrumental in the emergence of both the Macedonian and the Roman Empires.

Philip and Alexander also turned the Greek habit of acquiring expertise from outsiders into a systematic commercial operation.

Philip invited Greeks from far afield to entertain his court and to improve his weapons. Nearchos was actually the son of an islander from Crete who had been invited by Philip to settle in Macedonia, presumably to advise him on naval affairs, since the Macedonians had never been great sailors. The Macedonian kings had been purchasing cultural prestige since the later fifth century, when Euripides, along with other Athenian glitterati, was invited to the northern kingdom; Alexander followed suit by summoning outstanding artists to enhance his image—Apelles, who painted several portraits of his patron and a series of pictures of goddesses regarded as masterpieces; Lysippos the sculptor; Pyrgoteles, engraver of gems.

Yet of all the brilliant men who helped Macedonia conquer the world, the most important was Aristotle, tutor and inspiration to both Alexander and his confidant, Hephaestion. Aristotle raised the bar on intellectual inquiry in a way that still profoundly affects science, literature, philosophy, and political theory. It is difficult to imagine a more formidable and cosmopolitan source of support available to Alexander. Aristotle came from Stagira, in northern Greece, originally a colony established by Ionian Greeks from the island of Andros in the seventh century. Stagira had been strategically more important than its size might suggest, and had seen a variety of conquerors. Xerxes occupied it during his invasion of Greece. It was a member of the Delian League and thus allied with Athens, but it withdrew from the league in 424 and had then sided with Sparta. Aristotle's birth occurred during the reign of Philip's father, Amyntas III. Stagira was dominated by its increasingly mighty neighbor to its north and east and was indeed destroyed by Philip in 348, when he and Aristotle were both in their thirties. Aristotle was an almost exact contemporary of Philip, who was born just two years after him, in 382. Since Aristotle's father was physician to Philip's father, King Amyntas, it is inevitable that the two boys, Philip and Aristotle, knew each other well from an early age.

As a youth Aristotle traveled to Athens to study with Plato at the Academy. He stayed for twenty years. Much of his work can be read as a response to Plato's ideas, although the differences are significant. Aristotle left Athens in about 348, at the same time Philip destroyed Stagira. He traveled in Lesbos and Asia Minor but in 343 took up the appointment of tutor to the young Alexander. It was not until eight years later, in 335, when Alexander had succeeded Philip and already taken control of Athens, that Aristotle returned there to found his Lyceum and, it is thought, write most of his numerous treatises. For eight of Alexander's most important years, therefore, he was in constant and intimate dialogue with the famous thinker.

Aristotle's contribution to intellectual history, not only to Western philosophy, is incalculable. His *Metaphysics*, in particular, was instrumental in founding Arabic philosophy (*falsafa*) in the ninth century AD. It elicited a massive commentary by the Spanish Arab philosopher Ibn Rushd (Averroes), himself studied keenly in the West. There was no constituent of the universe in which Aristotle was not interested, whether it was empirically discernible to the senses or beyond the perceptible surface of things. All Aristotle's writings are unified by the methods of reasoning he developed, expressed in a group of works on logic that later ancient philosophers assembled and named his *Organon* (Instrument). The contents of these works monopolized the entire history of philosophical logic until the critiques of Aristotle by Gottlob Frege and Bertrand Russell appeared in the nineteenth and twentieth centuries. Contemporary philosophers are rehabilitating many of Aristotle's logical concepts again today. It is still astonishing that Aristotle could take the methods of philosophical reasoning that he found in Plato and his predecessors, and treat the inferential systems as the topic of analysis themselves. That is, he was interested not only in what made the world work in the way it did, but in the exact workings of the arguments on which thinkers based their conclusions about the world. Philosophy itself had become the object of philosophical analysis.

All the works on logic ask about how we make deductions (which Aristotle called syllogisms) or inductions from evidence and the positing of premises. His other works *use* these systems of inference in order to examine the nature of other phenomena. Aristotle also applied consistent categories of explanation in all the different branches of inquiry—for example the fourfold division of causal properties in things, or the "four causes": material, formal, efficient, and final. In the case of a kitchen table, its material cause is the matter out of which it is made (wood), its formal cause is the shape that makes it a table and not something else made of wood, its efficient cause is the agent who shaped the wood (the carpenter), and its final cause is the purpose, end, or goal (*telos*) for which it was made: providing something for people to put their plates on when they eat. The final cause held a crucial position in what is known as his teleology: The horns on an animal are produced from the interaction of form and matter that always had an inherent potential encoded within it to produce horns, the *telos* of which is the self-defense of the animal.

As we have seen, Aristotle's father practiced medicine, and it is no coincidence that the philosopher was brought up in that tradition, since it was the Hippocratics who had produced the only methodical study of living bodies by the fourth century. Aristotle undertook a systematic and comprehensive study of animals, which also functions to explain and defend his self-consciously applied analytical method. It was not until the European Renaissance that any comparable contribution to zoology was ever produced. The power of his intellect in inventing systematic zoology almost from scratch still takes scientists' breath away. The Victorian anatomist Richard Owen said that zoological science sprang from Aristotle's labors "we may almost say, like Minerva from the Head of Jove, in a state of noble and splendid maturity."

Aristotle was as interested in culture as he was in nature. His handbooks on rhetoric and tragic poetry analyze their constituents but have an ethical component and are prescriptive as well as descriptive. They can improve the output of the trainee public speaker or tragedian partly because they do not let him forget the goal at which his art is aiming: persuasion in the case of rhetoric, but in the case of tragic theater, guiding the audience to understand painful matters better. Alexander must have been helped by Aristotle to become an outstanding speaker, and he loved poetry, especially Homer and the tragedian Euripides. He knew whole speeches from Euripides' plays by heart and recited them at parties. He even provided theatrical performances for his soldiers on campaign. But it was probably Aristotle's works on ethics and political theory that Alexander found most helpful. In his two books on ethics, the *Nicomachean Ethics* and the *Eudemian Ethics*, Aristotle posits happiness (*eudaimonia*) or "living well" as the fundamental goal in human life. *Eudaimonia* is an activity rather than an abstract state, and the function of human life is to perform this activity. Living well is equivalent to living rationally, in an examined and carefully considered way, in accordance with virtue (*arete*). Aristotle's political theory was an extension of this ethical position to the whole community or city-state (polis), since happiness is the goal of the city-state and the reason for its existence. In his *Politics*, he notoriously argued for the superiority of Greeks and their natural right to rule other peoples and to enslave them through warfare, a political philosophy that matched Alexander's aspirations perfectly.

Aristotle's reaction to Alexander's premature death in 323—he fled Athens for Euboea—illuminates the dangerous chaos into which the whole Greek world was cast. The philosopher died the following year and thus avoided watching his student's henchmen, the other Macedonian strongmen of the era, embark on their competition for the highest stakes—the largest empire—the world had ever seen. The surviving warlords and their sons after them fought each other almost incessantly for control of the different regions of his empire. Both generations, fathers and sons, married each other's sisters and daughters and had children with them, thus creating an ever-more complicated set of dynastic alliances and rivalries. Within a few decades, these Macedonians had created a completely new political map of the eastern Mediterranean, northern Africa, and Asia. It forms the psychic and cartographic horizons of the early Hellenistic era.

When Alexander died, Perdiccas became regent for the whole empire, with Antipater in control of Greece. Antipater became guardian of Alexander's infant son by Roxana. After machinations, Antipater's son Cassander replaced him. Cassander disposed of Olympias and had the boy heir and Roxana murdered. Yet amazingly, Cassander's twenty years on the throne of Macedonia (316–297 BC) were relatively peaceful and prosperous. We must thank Cassander for one of the most famous ancient visual images, since he commissioned from the painter Philoxenos the picture of Alexander in battle against Darius III of Persia that almost certainly was imitated in the exquisite "Alexander mosaic" from Pompeii: Alexander, with determined jaw and staring eyes, charges on his chestnut warhorse toward the terrified Darius, gesturing helplessly in his chariot.

In the rest of Greece, however, the rise and division of the Macedonian Empire left an uncertain legacy. Significant areas of mainland Greece were subject to frequent changes of ruler. From the death of Alexander in 323 BC to the Roman defeat of the Achaean League of several city-states in the northern Peloponnese in 146, life was often unstable. The wars between the Successors took four decades to resolve; then, in the 270s, Pyrrhus of Epirus, a descendant of Olympias's family and thus related to Alexander, invaded the Peloponnese. Between the 260s and the 240s there were several attempts by Peloponnesian communities to rebel against Macedonian rule; in the 220s, Sparta failed to revive its obsolete empire.

Alexander's most trusted general, Ptolemy, concentrated on making himself king of Egypt and founded the long-standing Ptolemaic dynasty there (see chapter 8). Perdiccas was assassinated by his own officers within two years. One of the assassins was Seleucus, who became Seleucus I Nicator, or Seleucus the Victor. Although originally given the satrapy of Babylon, which was wealthy but unimportant in military terms, Seleucus took years to achieve dominance there. But by 302 he had taken control of the eastern conquests of Alexander as far as the Indus Valley. He founded ten cities in what are now Turkey and Syria. They included Seleucia Pieria on the coast as a basis for naval operations, and Antioch as the center of power. Although he failed to extend this empire westward or to recover Macedon and Greece themselves, he founded a dynasty and an empire boasting a high level of Greek sophistication and culture that was to last until 63 BC.

Yet the most personally formidable of these prodigious Macedonians, Antigonus, never relinquished his desire to conquer the whole world for himself. Born in 382 BC, he was an exact contemporary of Philip, although he outlived him for decades. Antigonus was called the One-Eyed because, like Philip, he had lost an eye. Having alienated most of the other Successors, he died fighting their alliance in the battle of Ipsus at the astonishing age of eighty-one. But he had come through the first of the Wars of the Successors in possession of Syria and Asia Minor, and by 307 his son Demetrius had taken Athens and Cyprus into their joint power. Antigonus was the first of the Successors to declare himself king, in 306. In 302 he and Demetrius announced the renewal of the Panhellenic League, which united most of southern mainland Greece under their rule.

Demetrius was as intimidating as his father. Because Rhodes had refused to help him in his bid (which failed) to oust Ptolemy from Egypt, he besieged it for a year with engines the likes of which the world had never seen. One, a siege tower on wheels said to have been 125 feet high, was given the nickname Helepolis (City Taker). The siege of Rhodes was an ambitious project even for Demetrius. Rhodes was a magnificent, strategically crucial city; founded in the late fifth century, according to the grid design of the renowned architect Hippodamus of Miletus, it had no fewer than five harbors. Its proximity to Asia attracted merchants in great numbers who made Rhodes rich. Despite his terrifying war machines, Demetrius eventually backed off, and the Rhodians celebrated by building a colossal statue of their favorite god, Helios, that was almost as tall as the siege tower had been. Erected in the main sanctuary of Helios on the east side of the resplendent acropolis, it loomed above the harbors lower down and the sea. It was quickly identified as one of the Seven Wonders of the World. But Demetrius had earned his title, *Poliorcetes* (Besieger), and continued to instill terror into his enemies. By murder and mayhem he grabbed Macedonia, ousting Antipater's dynasty. Demetrius was then engaged in incessant struggles with Pyrrhus of Epirus, who had been personally forced out of Macedonia in 288. But Demetrius's reign consolidated the Antigonids' hold on power there until the Romans conquered his descendant Perseus in 168 BC.

The satrapy of Thrace, including cities near the Hellespont, had initially been allotted to another of Alexander's intimates, Lysimachus, who had performed outstandingly in India. He consolidated his power by campaigning against the barbarian tribes on the fringes of his territory and extending his influence to Asia Minor and his favored city of Pergamum. After the battle of Ipsus in 301, as one of the Successors allied against Antigonus, Lysimachus received the whole kingdom of Anatolia. But unlike Ptolemy in Egypt and Seleucus in the east, Lysimachus failed to found a dynasty, despite having sons by two of his three wives and an additional one by a concubine. In an outstandingly nasty court intrigue, his eldest son, Agathocles, was framed by the mother of three of his other sons. This powerful woman was none other than Ptolemy I's daughter Arsinoe. Lysimachus, a mean and difficult man, had his promising heir arrested and murdered in prison. Agathocles' widow escaped with her children to Seleucus's court, and Lysimachus then faced uprisings in several of his cities in Asia Minor. Arsinoe fled with her sons. The crisis came to a head in 281 BC at the battle of Corupedium, where Lysimachus, now thoroughly discredited, was killed.

So there was to be no Lysimachid dynasty. Who was to succeed Lysimachus? The man in the right place at the right time was his former general Philetaerus, son of a Greek called Attalos and an Asiatic mother. Lysimachus had made him commander of Pergamum, but he had defected to Seleucus's side. The famous dynasty that ruled from Pergamum was therefore the Attalids. Philetaerus reigned from 281 BC to 263 BC. Since he could not have children (the result of damage to his genitals in a childhood accident), he adopted his nephew, who, on his death, succeeded him as Eumenes I, second Attalid king of Pergamum.

These were the key players in the intricate, bloody, and dangerous Wars of the Successors in Egypt, Asia, Macedonia, Thrace, and Greece. But the most interesting immediate legacy of Alexander's imperial project was manifested farther east. He had left more than thirteen thousand horsemen and infantrymen in Bactria, which formed part of modern Afghanistan. Following his normal policy, these soldiers married local women, and the result was an ethnically hybrid Greek state. The Greeks in Bactria felt confined, since Bactria was a landlocked stronghold protecting Iran against nomadic tribes to the east. More Greek settlers had arrived in the third century. By around 228 the Bactrian satrapy became independent of the empire of the Seleucids. A Greek named Euthydemus from Magnesia on the Maeander declared himself king. In 189 BC his son Demetrius succeeded him to the throne and made diplomatic gestures toward the rulers of the new Mauryan Empire, of which the capital was Patna, on the Ganges. After trekking across the mountains of the Hindu

Kush that separate northern Pakistan from Afghanistan, the Greeks advanced into India. In a remarkable fusion of Indian and Greek culture, they took over territories in the northwest.

Menander I, Demetrius's general, married Demetrius's daughter and became the most renowned of the Bactrian kings in India. He reigned for three decades in the mid-second century BC, probably from his base in Sagala (now Sialkot, in the northern Punjab area of Pakistan). After his death, he was succeeded by Queen Agathocleia and Strato I Soter, but within four decades new conquerors arrived in western India from central Asia. The Greek Bactrian dynasty came to an end. Menander was probably born and brought up as a Greek in Bactria, but coins issued during his reign, with beautiful Greek head portraits and inscriptions in both Greek and Kharosthi (an ancient Indian script), have been found as far north as Kashmir, as far west as Kabul, and as far east as Mathura (now in Uttar Pradesh).

Menander was eventually forced back into Bactria, but he had impressed Indian Buddhists, as they did his Greek subjects. There is an astonishing parallel between the traditional division of the Buddha's cremated remains into eight portions, one for each of the eight kingdoms of northern India, and the Greek writer Plutarch's account in his *Political Precepts* of what happened after King Menander's death: "But when one Menander, who had reigned graciously over the Bactrians, died afterwards in the camp, the cities indeed by common consent celebrated his funerals; but coming to a contest about his relics, they were with difficulty at last brought to this agreement, that his ashes being distributed, everyone should carry away an equal share, and they should all erect monuments to him." It is on Menander I of the Bactrians that the character of the speaker Milinda is based in the *Milinda Pañha* (Debate of King Milinda), one of the oldest Buddhist books, written in the Pāli language in northwest India in about 100 BC. It takes the form of a prose dialogue, not unlike those by Plato, in which Milinda is persuaded of the cogency of Buddhism by a Socrates-like spiritual figure named Nagasena. As specialists in the Indo-Greeks have pointed out, embracing Buddhism would have been strategically shrewd for a monarch in Menander I's position.

Yet the most colorful descendant of Macedonian imperialists was

Mithridates VI Eupator, King of Pontus (134–63 BC), who made a concerted stand against the might of Rome. With the exception of Hannibal, Mithridates was the most intimidating foe the Romans ever faced. He was also a star of the eighteenth-century stage, the protagonist in operas by both Scarlatti and Mozart. The trajectory of his life was inherently dramatic. He came to power only after his father was poisoned and his mother plotted against him in favor of her other son. Mithridates expanded the Pontic empire to an unprecedented size, to encompass coastal regions adjoining the northern, eastern, and southern Black Sea and some of Anatolia. He was as formidable at sea as on land, maintaining a potent navy. At one point, during the first of the three Mithridatic wars in which he challenged the expanding Roman Empire (88–84 BC), he occupied Cappadocia as well as Asia Minor and had even established his authority as far west as Athens, which he ruled through a vassal magistrate.

Mithridates stayed on the throne for more than fifty years, competing for territory with such eminent generals as Sulla, Lucullus, and Pompey. During the first war, he coolly authorized the massacre of 80,000 Romans and Italians in Asia. He won the second war (83–81 BC), inflicting a defeat on the Roman general Murena, who had invaded the Pontic kingdom in an attempt to bring Mithridates to heel. In the third and last war (73–63 BC), Mithridates led the Romans on a merry dance across the Black Sea and Armenia before Pompey finally brought Armenia under Roman control. It is not surprising that vivid stories circulated about Mithridates. He was said to have invented an antidote, containing over fifty ingredients, effective against any kind of poison. When his mother tried to kill him by making him ride a dangerous horse, he did not die. He is supposed to have spent his teenage years in the wild, toughening himself and living off the game he hunted. He survived being struck by lightning. It was said that he could control a chariot team of sixteen horses, and that he employed a horse, a bull, and a stag as his bodyguards.

Of mixed Persian and Macedonian descent, Mithridates exploited his hybridity to bolster his claim to be a new Greco-Persian unification hero. His name means "gift of Mithras," and on his father's side he claimed the Zoroastrian Darius I as ancestor; when it was strategically advisable, as in relation to some eastern tribes, he presented himself as Persian. On the other side, he claimed direct descent from Alexander the Great and took care to present himself as the heir to Alexander's imperial mission as well. Like Alexander, he encouraged artists and coin designers to identify him with Dionysus, Heracles, and Perseus, along with his winged horse Pegasus; although Perseus was Greek as could be (he was held to have founded Mycenae), his name had led Xerxes to identify him as ancestor of the Persians hundreds of years before.

At first, Mithridates emphasized his Greekness to unite Pontic Greek city-states against Scythian and other indigenous Black Sea tribes. In about 108 BC, it was as a fellow Greek that he represented himself coming to the defense of the Greeks of Tauric Chersonesos (now Sevastopol). As his success grew, he presented himself as the liberator of the Hellenes from oppressive, uncultured, venal Roman overlords. It was not difficult to maintain this propaganda when the Romans substantiated its truth. Sulla caused outrage during his war with Mithridates when he ordered the confiscation of sacred items of treasure from the sanctuary at Delphi. He even dismantled priceless artifacts to make them easier to transport.

At home in the Black Sea, Mithridates encouraged his court to revel in its fusion of Greek and Persian elements. In his own administration, the majority of the senior officials and bureaucrats were cultured Greeks, but the balance was the other way around among the peoples whom they governed. Mithridates ensured, however, that he could make his wishes clear to any and all of his subjects; "Mithridates, who was king of twenty-two nations, administered their laws in as many languages, and could harangue each of them, without employing an interpreter," said Pliny the Elder. But this polyglot prodigy also wanted to promote himself as a lover of Greek intellectual culture, inviting experts in poetry, philosophy, and history to adorn his northern salon. He was fascinated by pharmacology, especially poisons and their antidotes, and corresponded on this topic with famous medics near and far.

When finally put on the defensive by Pompey, Mithridates retreated to his capital at Panticapaion (now Kerch), where he faced rivalry from his own sons. Before the younger son finally betrayed his aging warrior father to the Romans, Mithridates had murdered the older one. But the king of Pontus was not the type of man to go in chains to Rome and be paraded in triumphal procession by the victorious Pompey. He tried to commit suicide, but failed since for many years he had deliberately inured his body to different poisons by taking small amounts—one of the reasons for his unofficial title, the Poison King. Determined not to be beaten, he then ordered his loyal bodyguard from Gaul to kill him with a sword. He was buried in Sinope, where he had been born more than seven decades previously.

Although such exotic kingdoms ruled by autocrats descended from the rivalrous Macedonian henchman of Alexander survived for several centuries, the ancient Greeks and Romans looked back on the brief ascendancy of Macedon with amazement. Dionysius of Halicarnassus, a Greek historian who worked in Augustan Rome, asked how the Macedonians had ever risen to power when "they had but lately shed their rags and were known as shepherds, men who used to fight the Thracians for possession of the millet-fields." How did they "vanquish the Greeks, cross over into Asia and gain an empire reaching to the Indians"? Yet only a few hundred years later, comments Dionysius, "if you should pass through Pella, you would see no sign of a city at all, apart from the presence of a mass of shattered pottery on the site." The rise and fall of Macedon had already entered the sphere of legend and hyperbole.

Nineteenth-century engraving of the townscape of Alexandria with a reconstruction of the Pharos lighthouse. Free adaptation of *The Pharos of Alexandria*, by Johann B. Fischer von Erlach, in *Entwurf einer historischen Architektur* (Leipzig, 1725), plate 9. *(Author's personal collection)*

8

God-Kings and Libraries

The outstanding generation of bellicose Macedonians who, with Alexander, conquered the world—Ptolemy, Antigonus the One-Eyed, Antipater, Seleucus—survived him and founded the Hellenistic kingdoms in which most Greeks lived until the Romans conquered them. The incessant competition for power characteristic of the Macedonian soldier-statesmen evolved into a centuries-long competition between them and their descendants for the status of rulers of the most impressive individual empire. The Successors poured untold wealth into the creation of fabulous capital cities, adorned materially with dazzling edifices and culturally with the best thinkers and artists the Greek world could offer. The pursuit of excellence that had always characterized the Greeks, at least since the early days of the Panhellenic cult centers and the institution of athletics competitions, became the abiding preoccupation of the new, fabulously wealthy Hellenistic kings. In Ptolemaic Egypt the desire to excel produced an obsession with being superlative at everything—to house the greatest community of intellectuals in the world, centered on the greatest wonder of ancient scholarship, the fabled library of Alexandria. The library was a new kind of institution altogether, one where the task of assembling all the world's knowledge was seen as the precondition of maximizing new advances in every realm of intellectual endeavor—literature, history, philosophy, mathematics, and what we now call pure and applied sciences. This chapter inquires into the library's role in fostering the world-beating ambitions of the Ptolemy family, the thinkers it attracted, the quality of the ideas and writings they were able to produce in it, and the stimulus provided by competition with rival centers of cultural excellence in Athens and Pergamum.

The word "Hellenistic" was originally used in English as an equivalent of "Hellenic" or "Greek." But by 1678 it described the Greek-speaking Jews of Alexandria. Thence, mysteriously, it came to designate the entire period of Greek culture from Alexander's death in 323 BC through Cleopatra's in 31 BC. The four main Hellenistic kingdoms that emerged from the Wars of the Successors were Ptolemaic Egypt, Macedonian-ruled Greece, Attalid-run Pergamum, and the vast empire based in Syria ruled by the Seleucids. The families who ran these monarchies were ruthless, autocratic, and self-promoting. Any lingering manifestations of the old Greek ideals of self-governance and individual self-sufficiency disappeared among their subjects. Of the ten ingredients in the recipe of Greekness, dislike of authority becomes far less visible in the age of the Hellenistic kings, although the Greeks continued to exhibit the other ingredients—not only the quest for excellence but curiosity, laughter, verbal artistry, and love of pleasure—in abundance. It was the great age also of Greek sea power, with superb navies and merchant vessels incessantly gliding in and out of the new, elaborately constructed harbors of the Mediterranean.

The most stable Hellenistic kingdom was Egypt. It was also the realm where the quest for cultural supremacy—for the creation of a city that excelled any the world had ever seen before—was most evident. Ptolemy I of Egypt was a pragmatist. Already about forty-four when Alexander died, he had always been in the younger man's shadow. He was the first Successor to realize that Alexander's empire could not be held together. But he refused to lose out on his one chance of some supreme power. Having picked Egypt as his satrapy almost the moment Alexander died, he stuck to his guns and was sensibly conservative, always preferring to consolidate his dominion there rather than attempt to spread it much farther afield. His rewards were to become the first in a long dynasty of Greek pharaoh-kings of Egypt, to ensure that he and his heirs were worshipped as gods, and to lay the foundations of the finest scholarly and cultural achievement in Mediterranean history.

Ptolemy shared with Philip II and Alexander a genius for public relations. Indeed, by encouraging the rumor that he was Philip's illegitimate son, Ptolemy suggested that he was half-brother to Alexander. He also wrote an account of Alexander's campaigns, to justify his own claim to the kingdom of Egypt and to enhance his own reputation as an intellectual as well as a soldier-statesman. It was Ptolemy who stole the body of Alexander when it was en route to Macedon and brought it instead to Memphis in Egypt in 322. He later removed it to a magnificent tomb at Alexandria, where it became a tourist attraction. At Memphis, Ptolemy learned about Apis the bull-god, worshipped there by the Egyptians alongside Osarapis, whom the Greeks called Sarapis. Within a few years he built a massive temple for Sarapis in the new city of Alexandria and created a synthetic cult that would please both incoming Greeks and resident Egyptians. He commissioned a statue that fused Sarapis with the Greek deities Zeus and Hades.

Ptolemy fought off other Successors' attempts to unseat him or destabilize his borders. He made an alliance with Cyprus and acquired control of Cyrene in Libya. He supported the island of Rhodes throughout the siege it suffered at the hands of Antigonus's son Demetrius Poliorcetes. By 305 Ptolemy had taken the title of king. He accepted when the Rhodians, on the advice of the oracle of Zeus-Ammon in Libya, bestowed on him divine honors and the title *Soter* (Savior). He did not demur when they built a shrine, the Ptolemaion, in which to honor him. Whether he personally believed in his own divinity is not the point: He realized that divine kingship would help him retain power and make Alexandria the most impressive cultural center in the world.

The wily Macedonian married two women from his homeland and had children by both of them. When he chose which son to favor as his heir, it was Berenice's child Ptolemy, although he was junior to Eurydice's child Ptolemy Keraunos by a decade. The victor became Ptolemy II (Philadelphus). In a series of appointments typical of the Ptolemies' obsession with importing to Alexandria the most acclaimed experts whom money could buy, Ptolemy II had received the finest education. His tutors were none other than the nonpareil poet Philetas of Cos and Zenodotus of Ephesus, a world expert on the text of Homer and the first head of the Alexandrian library.

The Ptolemies saw kingship as a family business. Ptolemy I chose to rule jointly with his well-educated son from 285 until his death in 283, when he was formally deified. The League of Islanders in the Ptolemaic realm set up an inscription on Delos vowing to send delegates to sacrifice to Ptolemy in Alexandria, crown him with gold, and provide athletes to compete in the new games in his honor, the Ptolemeiaia. The Greeks, who had once told the king of Persia that they did not prostrate themselves before mere mortals, had learned to worship a Greek as a god. On the instructions of Ptolemy II, they also worshipped Berenice as a goddess.

The divinity of the subsequent Egyptian monarchs was made easier for their subjects to accept by the reuse in every generation of the male name Ptolemy, and just a small range of names for girls who might become queens, including Cleopatra. To keep things even more in the family, in the mid-270s Ptolemy II divorced his first, Macedonian wife (Arsinoe I) and took the extraordinary step of incestuously marrying his resourceful full sister (Arsinoe II). She was known, as he was subsequently, as *Philadelphus* (Sibling-Loving). He issued coins that show them as joint rulers, the similarity between their facial features emphasized. A new aesthetic combined Egyptian and Greek elements in the portraits of the ruling family. The Metropolitan Museum in New York houses an exquisite limestone statuette depicting Arsinoe II in a style that fuses strikingly Egyptian posture, hairstyle, and costume with a cornucopia, which Hellenistic Greek sculptors used to signify godhead. In 270, when she died, Ptolemy II of course declared Arsinoe II, like the parents he shared with her, divine.

Ptolemy II was succeeded by his son Ptolemy III Euergetes (Benefactor), who reigned from 246 to 222 BC. The third Ptolemy took a wife from outside the immediate family, Berenice of Cyrene in Libya, to consolidate Egyptian influence there, creating a North African superpower. Berenice's claim to superhuman status was bolstered even in her lifetime by the circulation of the (preposterous) claim that some hair she had shorn from her head and dedicated in the temple of Aphrodite had been turned into a visible constellation, to this day known as the Coma Berenices (Lock of Berenice). The man who identified this group of stars as the queen's tresses was the court astronomer,

Conon; the one who wrote the artful but embarrassingly sycophantic poem that commemorated the transformation was Ptolemy II's right-hand literary advisor, the dazzlingly clever Callimachus, who, like Queen Berenice, was a North African Greek from Cyrene.

Ten more male Ptolemies sat on the opulent Egyptian throne between 222 BC and the fall of Ptolemaic Egypt to the Roman Empire nearly two centuries later. Some married their sisters and ruled with them; others came to the throne as small boys and were caught in the crossfire between ambitious regents, aunts, uncles, and court officials. The hybrid Greco-Egyptian political culture of Hellenistic Alexandria that they fostered was magnificent but remains perplexing. To scholars used to the argumentative and meritocratic strain in archaic and classical Greek literature, the Ptolemies' presentation of themselves as god-kings and the marriages between full brothers and sisters, pharaoh-style, are repellent. But the festivals and public amenities they created were astounding. The character of their public presence was consummated in the grand procession—or rather, sequence of processions—that took place during the reign of Ptolemy II, probably in 275 or 274 BC. The procession celebrated the divinity of Ptolemy's parents, but in a particular way which identified the whole family as the descendants, through Alexander the conqueror of the East, of no lesser a god than Dionysus.

It is hardly surprising that the Greeks had believed Alexander when he claimed Dionysus as ancestor. In the tragedy *Bacchae*, written by Euripides, perhaps in Macedon, the god Dionysus had long before told them he had "left the rich lands of Lydia and Phrygia, the sun-struck plains of Persia, the walls of Bactria, the wintry country of the Medes, blessed Arabia and all that part of Asia which lies by the briny sea, where Greeks and barbarians live together in cities of beautiful towers." This must have sounded like an unmistakable precursor of Alexander's conquests. In response, Dionysus's journeys were systematically reconceived by the Ptolemies as a sequence of colonial annexations extending to India. At the center of the event was a gargantuan public Dionysiac feast in a specially constructed pavilion. It contained a hundred and thirty couches for the feast and pillars that looked like palm trees. A glittering array of dining equipment, gold and silver and bejeweled, awaited the lucky diners. Marble statues of animals and lovely paintings were arranged around the pavilion. The entire city was decked with flowers; blossoms were strewn beneath everyone's feet and made into chaplets to crown them.

The procession included a statue of Dionysus, three times an average man's height, with retinues of young women and satyrs clad in scarlet and purple. Some of them rode asses. They were followed by chariots drawn by outlandish animals. Dionysus, drawn on a wagon by 180 men, was led in by his priest along with victory tripods for the athletics competitions. He was followed by a cavalcade of floats, one holding an enormous wine sack made of leopard skins, which squirted continuous streams of wine over the road. More floats followed, drawn by more exotic animals—antelopes, elephants, buffalo, ostriches, zebras, camels, and lions. The king's military power was then demonstrated by a march of nearly 60,000 infantry and 23,000 horsemen, all in full armor. "Nothing in excess" was one of the mottoes inscribed on the temple of Apollo at Delphi. This was not a mantra of the Ptolemies. Like no Greeks ever before them, they understood the politics of scale. Ptolemy IV commissioned a massive galley with forty banks of oars. The ship's personnel included four thousand rowers and four hundred other sailors; on her upper decks she could accommodate three thousand armed militiamen. This monster ship never actually sailed; she was designed as a civic exhibition. But her very conception shows that each generation of Ptolemies wanted to outdo their forefathers in visible accomplishments of tremendous scale.

But Ptolemy IV's galley, however ersatz, reflected a truth about the Hellenistic maritime economy. Much bigger ships, with four and five rows of oars, had been adopted in the late fourth century. At a battle in Cyprus in 306 between Ptolemy I and Demetrius Poliorcetes, enormous navies comprised of ships with four, five, seven, and even ten banks of oarsmen had confronted one another. There was an exponential growth in the movement of goods by sea internationally. Incomparably more shipwrecks have been documented from this period of ancient Greek history than any other. The Ptolemies exported tons of grain and imported in equivalent amounts the wine and olive oil that Greeks always needed. Eastern Mediterranean trade was facilitated by the widespread use of coins minted to a common standard.

The idiom of enormity had been established by Ptolemy I, whose deification had prompted the procession in the first place. He dreamed of building the greatest city the world had ever seen, to house its largest library. Alexandria was constructed on a grid pattern, with walls, shrines, and Alexander's tomb near the center. The lavish palace area, called the Brucheion, took up a quarter of the city and included the famous museum, library, and perhaps the Sarapeum (temple). Ptolemy also ordered the construction of the jetty connecting the city to the island of Pharos, which was nearly a mile in length, creating two harbors, one on either side. At the eastern end of Pharos, where the waters were shallow and rocky, he planned the famous lighthouse. It was erected by 297. In accordance with the Macedonians' policy of always thinking big, it was nearly four hundred feet high, its three main stories made of gleaming white stone. Reflective plates beamed its light across many nautical miles, announcing to all comers that they were entering the world's supreme center of civilization. This Wonder of the World was dedicated to the Savior Gods—the completely human Ptolemy and his preferred wife Berenice, although the soubriquet also applied to Zeus and several other Olympians. Poseidippos, the Ptolemies' guest poet, from Pella in their ancestral kingdom of Macedonia, celebrated the lighthouse in an epigram: "all night long the man who sails swiftly on the wave can watch the great fire burning on its summit."

Since the early 1990s, two rival French teams of underwater archaeologists have photographed hundreds of objects from Ptolemaic Alexandria resting on the seafloor in and near the harbor. One is part of a statue of Poseidon that may have stood beside the lighthouse. There are Corinthian columns, chunks of masonry, obelisks, and sphinxes. Some of them date from as early as the reign of Rameses II in the thirteenth century BC, which proves that the modish Greek kings of Alexandria liked to ornament their city with indigenous antiques. Outlines of the wharves can be discerned, but the appearance of the stunning public buildings of Ptolemaic Alexandria, including the lighthouse, must still be imagined. To sense their gargantuan aesthetic, we need to look at other buildings erected by Hellenistic monarchs, especially the great altar of Pergamum in what is now northwestern Turkey, constructed in the second century by Eumenes II and his successor, Attalos II. It stood in a prominent position on a terrace below the citadel and was the largest and most important marble building in the city. But it was far from the only one: The entire acropolis was designed to impress visitors. Other Pergamene buildings included a temple and theater of Dionysus, a Doric shrine where the now divine Attalids could conveniently be worshipped, a temple of Athena housing a library, and a large marketplace.

The altar functioned as the site for the sacrifices and burnt offerings that defined pagan Greek religion. The gods to whom it was dedicated were probably Zeus and Athena. The oldest reference to it occurs in the Bible, in Revelation 2:12–13, where Pergamum is the place where "Satan has his throne"—a description probably inspired by the altar's grotesque serpent-footed mythical bestiary. It was destroyed by the early Byzantines in the seventh or early eighth century when they needed stones to erect fortifications against Arab invaders. In the late nineteenth century, excavations organized by the Berlin Museum brought the altar's fragments to light, and soon to Berlin itself. The altar is still in the Berlin Pergamum Museum, where it makes an awe-inspiring impression. More than 115 feet wide and almost as deep, it was approached by the worshipper via an imposing frontal row of steps. The sense of monumental scale is psychologically heightened by the epic themes of the deeply carved relief friezes—the battle between the gods and the giants (gigantomachy), and the adventures of Telephus, son of Heracles and mythical founder of Pergamum. The gigantomachy frieze, at 370 feet long, is the longest ancient Greek frieze in existence except for that of the Parthenon.

Hellenistic Alexandria possessed similar architectural glories, which, alas, have not survived. The Ptolemies' unbounded *intellectual* ambitions, however, still reverberate. They began to be realized in the early third century BC, at the moment when Demetrius of Phalerum, the exiled Athenian statesman, docked in the Alexandrian harbor to advise Ptolemy on his library. Demetrius was a renowned student of Aristotle's school and therefore brought the prestige the Ptolemies craved to their project, the wholesale relocation of world intellectual prowess to Alexandria. Demetrius supervised the book-buying program that his patrons now bankrolled. Scouts with limitless cash scoured the book shops of cultural centers including Rhodes and Athens. The busy harbors of Alexandria saw the confiscation of books found in any ships that docked there. The originals were kept by the Alexandrians, who only handed copies back, swiftly made, by dictation to armies of scribes. Demetrius imitated on a larger scale the organization of Aristotle's Lyceum, with its community of scholars and its dedication to the Muses. He structured the new library's collections according to the system Aristotle had used for his own. No wonder that the ancients sometimes said that it was Aristotle himself who had taught the Egyptian Greek kings how to run a library.

The library was located within the precinct of the Muses, the Museum. The buildings adjoined both the harbor and the palace complex. They included a walkway and a dining hall for the Museum's scholars. The tomb of Alexander was part of the complex and remained there until the Romans arrived. It was therefore not far from the book collections and the work of scholarly editing. The preservation of the cadaver of the man who had conveyed Hellenism to parts of the world it had never before reached thus physically symbolized the preservation and adulation of the literary records of Hellenism.

One of the earliest intellectuals Ptolemy sponsored was Euclid, the author of the seminal treatise on mathematics and geometry, the *Elements*, which still influences these fields today. To supervise the administration of the library and its scholarly activities he summoned from Ephesus, in what is now southwest Turkey, the learned grammarian Zenodotus, who edited the texts of Homer. Under Ptolemy II an invitation was sent to the most distinguished literary figure associated with the library, the scholar and poet from Libya, Callimachus of Cyrene. Callimachus claimed royal blood, as a descendant of Battus I, the founder of Cyrene. Callimachus was a man of letters in the fullest sense of the term. He knew more about ancient Greek literature than anybody before or since. Although he was not himself ever made chief librarian, he is also the founding father of all library cataloguing systems; the genre-based classifications he devised were as influential in antiquity as

Melville Dewey's decimal system, created in 1876, is in libraries today. The one hundred and twenty books of Callimachus's *Pinakes* (writing boards) consisted of a prose list, with commentary, of all the library's holdings (said to number half a million rolls). It classified each by genre, describing the author, quoting its opening, and stating the number of lines it contained. This alone would constitute an impressive life's work. Callimachus wrote other reference works in prose, including a study of Democritus's vocabulary or sayings, one on nymphs and one on the Wonders of the World. But Callimachus did not just categorize and organize all the literature in Greek that the Ptolemies' book-acquisition scouts, with their limitless cash, could get their hands on: By composing many poems, he added to that literature substantially.

Callimachus, along with his students and colleagues, altered the course of Western poetry. Their project was immense: It was to create a new wave of Greek literature, steeped in the earlier literary culture they had collected at the library but fundamentally breaking away from it. It was to be centered on life in Ptolemaic North Africa. They were writing for monarchs who fostered Egyptian deities, Sarapis/Osiris and Isis, as well as the gods of Greece. Egypt itself fascinated the court; with the encouragement of the first two and possibly three Ptolemies, the bilingual Egyptian priest Manetho wrote a comprehensive history of Egypt, using sources in both languages, the preserved parts of which remain an incomparable source for Egyptian chronology. But the poets of the immense new Greco-Egyptian kingdom developed a poetic style that, paradoxically, abhorred immensity. Everything about Ptolemaic culture was big, except for its literary aesthetic. In this one cultural arena, Callimachus led (and came to symbolize) the movement away from literature with hefty ethical, philosophical, and civic questions at its core. Instead, Alexandrian poetry celebrated the Ptolemaic regime, or reworked canonical works of literature in intricate and innovative ways, or talked self-consciously about other poets and the nature of poetry itself. Along with content, Hellenistic poetry changed in form. It is not that it abandoned old generic and metrical structures—indeed, it played with them incessantly, creating new effects by juxtaposing old elements. The important change was in scale and tenor. It is perhaps surprising that the

Ptolemies did not, apparently, require the poets they patronized to produce enormous epic poems to glorify their deeds and ancestry, although Callimachus was commissioned to write something, perhaps an epyllion (miniature epic), to celebrate the marriage of Ptolemy II to his biological sister.

The concerns of Callimachus and his circle, loyal servants of their wealthy patrons to a man, were the creation, within elegant and lapidary verses, of sophisticated tonalities, erudite allusion, and the placement of the exemplary mot juste. They cultivated a sophisticated knowingness, a style, a grace, the appeal of chiaroscuro, of studied asymmetry, and a refined sensibility. Their poetry was a complex fusion of traditional elements and experiment. It is as if they took apart all the Greek literary classics, creating a toy box of building blocks—meters, dialects, tropes, phrases—and reassembled them in novel ways. The poems of Callimachus were so dense, erudite, and cryptic that even within a generation of his death readers needed help in understanding him. These poets of Alexandria aimed at producing an effect that was "subtle" (*leptos*) and playful. They liked to use old poetic words in unexpected new contexts. They did not prize continuity, instead welcoming sudden, disruptive voices and unexpected shifts in perspective, topic, and timber. Callimachus opened his *Aitia* (Origins) with his literary manifesto, aimed at critics who had complained that he did not write "a boring uninterrupted poem, featuring kings and heroes in thousands of lines."

Callimachus was also a pioneer in the concept of the poet and his relationship with his art. His *Hymns* and *Epigrams* survive. His six *Hymns* are elaborate poems that praise Zeus, Apollo, Artemis, Delos, Athena, and Demeter. Their style combines the formal apparatus of the archaic Homeric *Hymns* with allusions that only make sense in the context of the Ptolemaic empire. But they were arranged to interact with one another artfully as a reading experience and must therefore be regarded as our first surviving poetic book. The *Epigrams* include a series of sparkling, concise explorations of erotic themes, original in their comparison of love and sex with the experience of poetry: "I hate recycled poetry," Callimachus says, as much as he dislikes "a boy who sleeps around." No wonder the great Latin love poets—Catullus, Propertius, and Ovid—admired him.

The fragments of Callimachus's other poems, especially his *Hecale*, suggest that we have lost innovative works. I find this poetry, at least in the fragmentary form we can read it, exasperating. I would like to know much *more* about Callimachus's subjective experiences, especially as he hints that it was as a boy in Cyrene that he was visited by Apollo and became a poet. In his fascinating *Aitia*, he says his beard was just beginning to grow when he dreamed he moved from Libya to Mount Helicon, an African Hesiod. He looked at the world through a kaleidoscope in which myth, realism, and literary stereotype were jumbled up, all equally valid as modes of seeing. In his *Hecale*, for example, he reveled in the rather kitsch description of the encounter between a poor old peasant woman living in the hills near Athens and the feisty young hero, Theseus.

Callimachus was a favorite of the royal family, and his refined poetry was designed to be performed in live recitals at the palace rather than studied in the library. The leisure enjoyed by the Macedonian Greeks who ruled Egypt from Alexandria, along with the resources of the library, prompted experiments in literary recreation. They enjoyed live entertainment ranging from large-scale festival performances of tragedy to bawdy comic sketches. Our picture of the live theatricals they enjoyed was transformed in 1891 by the discovery of a papyrus at Fayum containing nine comic playlets known as *Mimiambs* by a writer named Herodas. They would have been performed, possibly without masks, by actors specializing in the impersonation of the low-life urban characters in which Herodas reveled—randy housewives, dildo retailers, and prostitutes. One category of specialist actor was a youth who impersonated effeminates and transvestites. Herodas's second *Mimiamb* is a parody of a law court speech delivered by a transvestite pimp who claims that the man he is prosecuting assaulted one of his prostitutes and trashed his brothel. But the speech itself is a careful parody of some of the most famous speeches of the classical orator Demosthenes and would therefore have been found particularly amusing by members of an educated male audience, all of whom would have received training in the masterpieces of rhetoric. It required ten minutes to recite. In the hands of a skilled transvestite-impersonator it could transcend its intellectual complexity to produce, at least in an audience that shared its cultural touchstones, sidesplitting entertainment.

The Hellenistic poet with the deepest impact on Western culture since the Renaissance is Apollonius the Rhodian, whose epic *Argonautica* immortalized the story of Jason and the golden fleece. Two famous films have ensured that Apollonius's epic has penetrated deep strata of global popular culture through the twentieth century's new medium, cinema. Revolutionary special effects were created by animator Ray Harryhausen for *Jason and the Argonauts* (1963, directed by Don Chaffey). Pier Paolo Pasolini's *Medea* (1969) uses the barbarian culture portrayed in the ancient epic to criticize Western cultural imperialism.

Apollonius responded to the Egyptian context of Ptolemy's brave new kingdom by incorporating Egyptian allusions into his Argonauts' adventures. Alexander the Great had been declared the son of the supreme Egyptian god Amun-Re, syncretized with the Greek Zeus. The cult of Amun-Re was fostered by the early Ptolemies, whose coins implied that each one of them was his offspring. Apollonius says that the golden fleece, guarded by the serpent in the faraway Black Sea, emitted a golden light. An Egyptian Greek audience would have been reminded of popular representations of Amun-Re as a ram, with golden horns and a snake on his forehead. Amun-Re traveled in a magical solar boat, which had oracular powers and invited a parallel with the *Argo* and its prophetic keel.

The wit of Apollonius is shown in his choice to make his Argonauts arrive, after being blown off-course, at a place in North Africa near Cyrene, the homeland of his rival poet Callimachus. Apollonius implies that the sea there is too dangerous to reenter, and that the land is desolate, as dry and unwelcoming as Callimachus's poems. The Argonauts succumb to a catatonic depression until some nymphs and Poseidon help them out. They are directed to carry the *Argo* until they find water on which she can sail. It takes them twelve days of agonizing labor, including carrying the boat on their shoulders as they trudge across the northern Sahara.

The ancestral kingdom of Macedonia had never been known for its homegrown poets, but when one was found, he was inevitably summoned to Alexandria to endorse Ptolemaic values. Poseidippos of

Pella praises the bronze statue of the poet who tutored Ptolemy II, Philetas of Cos, and thanks the benefactor who has dedicated it in the Museum, "Ptolemy, God and King alike." In 2001, the classical world was astounded by the publication of over a hundred of Poseidippos's epigrams, newly discovered on a papyrus in Milan. Some are devoted to omens, statues, tombs, victory monuments, and people who have died at sea or been cured of illnesses. A group of poems about stones, the *Lithika*, reveal the Ptolemaic maritime empire to be under the protection of the gods. But the Macedonian poet's thoughts do sometimes return to his rugged homeland. One epigram voices his desire that, after his death, at an advanced age, he will be commemorated in the Pella marketplace by a statue reading from a roll of papyrus, and his deceased self will follow the sacred path taken by all Macedonian mystery cult initiates to the judge of the dead, Rhadamanthys.

If the poets were to avoid praising the Ptolemies, they had to fly from history and reality altogether. Among the *Idylls* of another of Callimachus's contemporaries, Theocritus, the pastoral examples have been admired for this reason. They are the first bucolic poems to use their setting as a formal frame for the discussion of the poet's vocation on an almost abstract level. They have exerted their influence on the pastoral in the visual arts and opera, as well as pastoral poetry, through or alongside the Latin *Eclogues* of Virgil and the pastoral ancient Greek novel by Longus, *Daphnis and Chloe*. But of equal significance in the history of poetry have been the aesthetic form and tone of the *Idylls*, medium-length poems giving the impression of a dialogue. They combine superficial simplicity, faux innocence, and nostalgia. This aspect of Theocritus's presence was prized by late eighteenth- and nineteenth-century poets including Leopardi and Tennyson.

Theocritus's 15th *Idyll*, set in Alexandria, features the visit of two Greek women to the palace exhibition put on for the festival of Adonis by Arsinoe II. This poem includes a performance of an aria by a woman singer and a visual display. But its first vivid scene invites us into the home of private citizens of Alexandria and introduces us to a pair of talkative young wives. The hostess, Praxinoa, has a baby, a typical feature of the literature of this era. Hellenistic consumers had a penchant for terra-cotta figurines of child-minding satyrs, nurses, and slaves holding babies. The comedy that appealed to these Hellenistic Greeks was not the raucous political satire of Aristophanes but a new kind of apolitical domestic drama, and its plots often revolved around newborn foundlings, identified by the trinkets in their cradles. Even the epic world of Apollonius introduces us to Achilles as a cute baby, held in the arms of the centaur Cheiron's wife, waving the *Argo* off on its legendary voyage, and Eros, driving his mother to distraction with his infantile games.

The sentimentalization of early childhood is a peculiar feature of Hellenistic culture and encapsulates its fascination with the miniature and the playful, as well as its abject flight from the grown-up business of politics. On the other hand, it can be read as a reflection of real shifts in the aspirations of the Greek family. In their vastly extended world, in cities where Greeks were often in the minority and yet of the ruling class, did children come to play a different role in public life and its self-representations? The royal families, concerned to legitimize the supremacy of their own dynasties, discussed their children more publicly and promoted what we would call "family values." When Ptolemy III and his wife inscribed a dedication for a temple to Isis, they drew ostentatious attention to their own "little ones."

The Alexandrian dominance of literary production in the Hellenistic age was by no means complete. Alexandria was at the center of a network of cultured Greek cities allied with her, including not only Rhodes and Pella but Cos and Syracuse, associated with Apollonius, Poseidippos, Philetas, and Theocritus, respectively. But one poet whom we have no reason to think ever visited Egypt was Nossis of Locri Epizephyri, a south Italian city allied with Theocritus's Syracuse. Nossis's third-century epigrams reveal the psychological world shared by the women in her community. Some describe the dedications made by women in the local temples of goddesses and celebrate the erotic charms that Aphrodite (in Locri atypically conflated with Persephone) has bestowed on the celebrants. Another poem begs Artemis, the goddess who oversaw women's biological lives, to aid a woman in the agony of childbirth. The femininity of the world of Nossis, who equates herself with Sappho, is intriguing because one ancient source suggests that the nobility of Locri, most unusually for a Greek city, traced their ancestors via the mother's line. In

Nossis's poems the mother-daughter relationship is paramount. One poem describes the linen mantle woven for Hera by three generations of women from the same family—Nossis, her mother, and her grandmother. Another describes a portrait of a girl called Thamareta and says that her *female* puppy wags her tail at the sight of her mistress's painted face.

Nossis had read some earlier poets, including Syracusan dramatists and Sappho. But did the ancients ever ask whether the existence of libraries on the scale of Alexandria might actually be detrimental to the writing produced by the culture that had created these collections, let alone detrimental to its emotional and spiritual health? The answer is "yes, a few." When it comes to historiography, there is one early voice raised loudly against the use of libraries by the writer. It is the voice of Polybius, a Greek who (as we shall see in the next chapter) rose to prominence at Rome in the second century BC and traveled incessantly. In his *Histories* he criticized an earlier Greek historian, Timaeus of Sicily. Timaeus spent four decades in Athenian libraries writing his mammoth forty-book *Histories* of Greece. Polybius has at least two axes to grind against Timaeus, one political and one more private and Oedipal, but even so, what he says about libraries reveals one strand in the discussion to which we rarely have access. Timaeus, complains Polybius, substituted reading books for interrogation of witnesses, because it required traveling to the places where history had happened.

> Inquiries from books may be made without any danger or hardship, provided only that one takes care to have access to a town rich in documents or to have a library near at hand. After that one has only to pursue one's researches in perfect repose and compare the accounts of different writers without exposing oneself to any hardship. Personal inquiry, on the contrary, requires severe labour and great expense, but is exceedingly valuable and is the most important part of history.

Polybius had a point: How many of us have had our perspectives on a poem or historical event altered by visiting a physical place related to it or talking to an eyewitness? The experimental ways in which the traveler

Herodotus and the soldier Thucydides wrote history, in an era before libraries and with few predecessors in historiography, would have been compromised if they had stayed in Athens all their adult lives.

When it comes to poetry rather than prose, there were also a few who believed that libraries were not always beneficial to the artistic quality of new works produced. The most famous is the satirical poet Timon of Phlius (near Corinth), who spent time in Asia Minor and then Athens. He was a contemporary of the great Hellenistic poets and scholars Theocritus, Callimachus, and Apollonius. But the independent-minded Timon despised the Alexandrian literati's project of editing Homer. When asked how best to obtain the "pure" Homeric text, he replied that the only way would be "if we could find the old copies, and not those with modern emendations."

Timon, who was *not* financially supported at Alexandria, sarcastically expressed his views on its library in another famous quip. This is traditionally translated, "Many are feeding in populous Egypt, scribblers on papyrus, ceaselessly wrangling in the *talaros* [bird cage] of the Muses." Timon's brilliant image was often understood as caricaturing the Alexandrian versifiers as unimpressive poetasters who were salaried but caged, suggesting that they were censored by the blue pencil of the autocratic Ptolemies. It is true that these poets, self-conscious about their craft, discussed their disagreements within their poems. But the famous image of the cage is a misleading translation of *talaros*, which means something dish-shaped and plaited out of twigs—more likely nest than cage. The image is, rather, of rivalrous chicks in a nest, trying to outsquawk each other to get the most feed from their Ptolemaic parents. The term *talaros* is often used of women's work baskets containing wool ready for weaving, thus implying that these dependent poets have become effeminized. The unmanly poets, who are financially supported in Ptolemy's library and guzzle his food, are all scribbling on the papyri but are also, of their own free will, *vying* for attention and stipends. Perhaps Timon contrasted this tame way of life and poetic output with his own far more independent and freely spoken satires. These, interestingly, did *not* survive for us to read in more than pitiful quotations. Perhaps not enough ancient librarians believed that they were worth copying out for posterity. I wish they had.

Might we have enjoyed better poetry from these men if they had *not* been so immersed in the contents of the library, let alone so focused on praising the monarchy that bankrolled it? The aesthetic and the political became entwined in early Alexandria in a wholly new way, precisely because of the presence of all those old books. The weight of the past Hellenic literary tradition lay heavy on the poetry of the new political order. That generation of Hellenistic poets were pioneers of a sort, bringing self-conscious poetics and the pursuit of tonal effect to an unprecedented level. But almost as quickly as Ptolemy had brought the finest poets of his empire to its headquarters in Alexandria, innovation in Greek poetry ceased almost altogether; the only genres in which experimental advances are subsequently perceptible are epic and epigram. But these forms were themselves antique, first brought to perfection centuries earlier by Homer and Simonides of Ceos.

Hellenistic Greek poetry is controversial. It has enjoyed a revival among recent researchers. One reason has been the current postcolonial fascination with hybridity, migration, and diasporas, which has renewed interest in the whole Ptolemaic project of creating a new Greek metropolis in Egypt, with all the cultural syncretism in relation to indigenous Egyptian religion and ceremonial practices which that entailed. But another reason is aesthetic. Our own postmodern aesthetics are arguably far too welded to past forms of literature: At the cinema, we have entered an age of nostalgia, of remakes and pastiches of old movies and television programs, as if seams of creativity have run dry. Our current obsession with recycling inherited artifacts inevitably makes us relate to the allusive, pseudo-archaic *Hymns* of Callimachus or the whimsical, gothic response to Homer in Apollonius's *Argonautica*.

I have come perilously close to claiming that the emergence of great libraries of literature killed off fresh innovation in Greek poetry, and must stress that they were essential in the development of many prose genres—geography, scientific treatises, biography, moral essay. The third director of the Alexandrian library was Eratosthenes (who, like Callimachus, came from Cyrene), an incomparable geographer who calculated the circumference of our planet to within fifty miles. The Alexandrian library, which may eventually have stifled experimentation in Greek poetry, was a crucial stimulus for poetry in *Latin*.

By 30 BC, the time of the deaths of the last Ptolemies on the Egyptian throne, Cleopatra VII and her son by Julius Caesar, Ptolemy Caesar (Caesarion), the Romans were systematically appropriating Greek culture, adapting it to their own language and civilization. None of the famous poets of late Republican and Augustan Rome—Catullus, Propertius, Virgil, Horace, Ovid, and Tibullus—could have achieved what they did without the Alexandrian Greek luminaries.

Alexandria also set the fashion for Hellenistic libraries elsewhere. In Pergamum, the Attalids competed for cultural prestige with the Ptolemies and founded their own magnificent library. It was routinely mentioned as one of the greatest collections of books that had ever been amassed. Like the Ptolemies, the Attalids knew that money made it possible to acquire the accessories of artistic excellence. Attalos I wanted Aegina, which contained prestigious artworks, and so paid the Aetolians (to whom the island then belonged) the sum of thirty talents. The Attalids courted the philosophical schools in Athens and invited several of their celebrities to Pergamum. Most refused, perhaps despising the Attalid family as parvenu. Perhaps the Attalids didn't offer salaries equivalent to those paid by the rival dynasty in Alexandria. But Crates the Stoic, from nearby Mallos, a distinguished Homeric scholar, did accept the post of head of the Pergamene library, and under him its reputation escalated. Although no Greek intellectual since Aristotle had seriously doubted that the earth was a sphere, it was Crates who first made a spherical model of the world—a globe—to show the location of known land masses.

Yet Alexandria held on to its reputation as the hotbed of scientific research and discoveries. The roll call of superb minds who worked there is never-ending. In the third century, Bolos of Mendes (in the eastern Nile Delta) came with advanced alchemical lore and conducted experiments in metallurgy. Philo came from Byzantium to write a comprehensive survey of mechanics. It covered levers, harbor construction, war machines, pneumatics, siege works, and automata. Archimedes from Syracuse was a resident in Alexandria; besides shouting "Eureka" when he discovered the law of hydrostatics in the bath, he brought his screw pump, which enabled water to be lifted, thus making a huge leap forward in farm irrigation technology. In optics he enriched the understanding of parabolas (sections of cones) and the practical applications of their focal and reflective properties. From Samos there came Aristarchus, the "Copernicus of antiquity," who was able to infer, from his study of solstices, the hypothesis that the sun was fixed in one place and the earth revolved around it. He also proposed a sequence for the position of planets that contains some truth: He put the moon first, followed by Mercury, Venus, the Sun, Mars, Jupiter, and Saturn. Aristarchus used calculations, rather than guesswork, to assess the size of the planets and distances between them. In the next century, Hypsicles made further astronomical strides in Alexandria, adopting the Babylonian system of dividing the circle into the 360 degrees still marked on our protractors today. From Knidos came Agatharchides, who wrote a seminal account of the ecosystem of the Red Sea.

During the Hellenistic period, the Greeks called both astronomy and astrology *astrologia*, since they believed that the unchanging physical phenomena that constituted the heavenly bodies must affect the ever-shifting world of humans as experienced on earth. Aratus of Soloi wrote a meteorological poem, the *Phainomena*, that describes the heavenly constellations in allusive, mythical terms. Eratosthenes of Cyrene, head of the Alexandrian library from about 245 BC, produced an elaborate work, *Catasterisms* (Transformations into Stars), explaining the supposed mythical origins and observable characteristics of the major constellations. But he also wrote treatises on methods for measuring the earth and for explaining the existence of former signs of marine life many miles from the sea. Eratosthenes was brave enough, in the face of Ptolemaic royal propaganda, to complain that the Indian adventures of Dionysus had been invented merely in order to burnish the reputation of Alexander the Great.

The greatest astronomer of antiquity was (for us, confusingly) named Claudius Ptolemy, direct heir to the tradition of Eratosthenes. Drawing on the work of earlier astronomers but adding his own measurements of the heavenly bodies, he changed the way people thought about the physical universe. His book on astronomy, the *Almagest* (more correctly known as *Mathematike Syntaxis*), was based on such systematic observations that, even in the sixteenth century, Copernicus still adopted Ptolemy's figures relating to the orbit of Venus. But Ptolemy's observations added up to more than data: He used them to argue that the intricate movements of the stars and planets were mechanical and repetitive. He realized that if all celestial movements were scrupulously recorded, it would be possible to predict when, for example, eclipses would take place. This marks him out from his contemporaries and underlines his originality. Scholars have recently studied papyrus texts dealing with astronomy from the ancient garbage dumps of the Greek town of Oxyrhynchus, in the Egyptian interior. These show that other astrologers of Ptolemy's time were not yet able to calculate the positions of the planets by using geometric theorems. They were still producing very inaccurate predictions by adding up and subtracting periods of time, a method they had adopted from Babylonian precursors in the field.

The old intellectual powerhouse of Athens did not disappear from view in the Hellenistic era altogether. Alexandria outstripped her in literature and science, but in philosophy Athens's leading role was never seriously challenged. Aristotle's associate Theophrastus, an outstanding botanist and polymath, succeeded him as head of the Lyceum in 322 BC. Teaching and research continued at the Lyceum until the first century BC. Plato's Academy evolved into the center of Skepticism, and Epicurus, who was of Athenian descent, founded his Epicurean Garden nearby in 306 BC. From the Cynicism of Diogenes, there evolved Stoicism, the most popular of the philosophical approaches to life in antiquity. Although Zeno, the founder of Stoicism, was from Cyprus, and rumored to be not a Greek but a Phoenician, it was at Athens at the end of the fourth century that he began teaching in a public art gallery in the shape of a long colonnade, or stoa, known as the Painted Stoa, after which his ideas were named. His most famous work, his *Republic*, propounded egalitarian and communistic ideals.

Yet the grand Athenian genre of tragedy, perfected under the democracy, became detached from its city of birth altogether. Hellenistic tragedies were no longer by Athenians but by dramatists from all over the Greek world, and composed for performance at the new Hellenistic festivals such as the Ptolemeiaia in honor of the god-kings of Alexandria. In comic drama, however, Athens retained her preeminence, if not in performances then at least in composition. Although he had rivals, the most significant Hellenistic dramatist was the Athenian comic playwright Menander, who won many prizes at local festivals in the late fourth and early third centuries BC. It is possible that Menander was invited to Alexandria by Ptolemy I, but he refused to go. He loved his home in the Athenian port at Piraeus, where he died while taking a swim.

Menander's impact on antiquity was huge. His plays became fashionable reading in Augustan Rome. Papyri of Menander have been found in abundance in Egypt, showing how widely he was read and, I believe, performed there. A treatise comparing Aristophanes and Menander attributed to Plutarch states, "Out of all the works of beauty Greece has produced, Menander made his poetry the most widely accepted subject in theatres, conversations and dinner parties, for reading, education and theatrical competitions." Speeches excerpted from Menander were performed at symposia; in a dinner-party context Plutarch suggested that Menander was beneficial because he was not too erotic, thus encouraging men to be content with their marriages! The Roman teacher of rhetoric, Quintilian, recommended the study of Menander to trainee orators.

The influence of Menander on comedy since the Renaissance, though profound, has been subterranean: The plays read, performed, and imitated by humanists and their students all over Europe were the Latin comedies of Plautus and Terence. Shakespeare's *Comedy of Errors* absorbed elements from both Plautus's *Menaechmi* and Terence's *Andria*. But these republican Roman comedians adapted scenes and sometimes whole plots from the Greek originals of Menander and his peers, written at Athens a century earlier. The surviving texts of Menander's comedies were not discovered until the twentieth century, too late to exert a direct influence on Western culture equivalent to the other great names in ancient Greek literature. But the papyrus finds, especially the *Dyskolos* (Ill-tempered Man), have furnished substantiation of Menander's claim to have founded the European "comedy of manners."

To Hellenistic Athens, therefore, we must give the continuing credit for supremacy in philosophy and comedy. There can be no denying, however, that Hellenistic Alexandria left a deeper impression on history. The men who worked there, whether they were born in Sicily, Macedon, Cyrene, or Egypt, shared many of the qualities that defined the pagan Greek mind-set across the centuries. Their relationship with the sea took a new turn with transformations in the economy; they remained articulate, witty, and competitive; they sought pleasure and happiness. But the Hellenistic Greeks needed to conform to an autocratic monarchy, and in the process their rebellious streak was suppressed, along with at least some of their psychological candor. Fortunately, the Ptolemies fostered inquisitive and analytically minded individuals, provided their questions were not overtly political, and furnished them at the library with an ideal place to push at the limits of knowledge.

Alexandria continued to attract brilliant thinkers for centuries. The Greek intellectuals discussed in the next chapter, "Greek Minds and Roman Power," include several who lived in or visited Alexandria. All fed off the intellectual culture that the incomparable library represented. Through them, Alexandria contributed an inestimable amount to our internal mental landscapes. But Alexandria's material self has not survived so well. Parts of the library suffered damage several times, at the hands of Julius Caesar and of Christian bishops long before the Arabs arrived in the seventh century AD. An earthquake and tsunami on July 21, AD 365, obliterated almost all Alexandria's architecture. The earthquake began underwater near Crete. But soon afterward, as the historian Ammianus Marcellinus wrote, "fearful dangers suddenly overspread the whole world, such as are related in no ancient fables or histories." In Alexandria, the tremors and ensuing winds were so violent that large ships were spewed out by the sea and landed on rooftops. Most of the last visual remains of the Ptolemaic Greco-Egyptian dream city, home to the best minds and the greatest collection of books the world had ever seen, sank out of sight forever.

Galen conducting an operation, engraving
by C. Warren, originally created to illustrate
Cooke's Pocket Edition of Sacred Classics (London,
1796). (*Author's personal collection*)

9

Greek Minds and Roman Power

The inhabitants of the mainland Greek peninsula were forced to accept Roman dominion in the mid-second century BC. Under its last monarch, Perseus, the once glorious kingdom of Macedonia fell to Rome at the battle of Pydna in 168. The events were narrated by the Greek historian Diodorus of Sicily, in his *Library of World History*. Diodorus accepted the inevitable rise of the Roman regime but had reservations about Roman culture and behavior. The ambivalence of his Greek contemporaries was crystallized in his work. His *Library* is peppered with formulaic praise of Roman virtues, yet between the lines it reveals another story. Consider his account of the punishment of Perseus, the last king of Macedonia, in Italy after his defeat. While the victorious Roman general Aemilius Paullus celebrates a triumph,

> The adversities faced by Perseus were so grave that his tribulations seem like the inventions in a novel. But despite them all, he still did not want to die. Before the Senate had made a decision as to how to punish him, one of the city magistrates had imprisoned him and his children at Alba. This prison is deep underground, smaller than a dining room, dark and foul-smelling from the large numbers of men it accommodated. They were men condemned for capital offenses, for at this time Alba was the jail where most who

fell into this category were imprisoned. Since so many of them were confined in such a small space, the miserable wretches began to look like animals, and since their food and everything else related to their bodily functions was disgustingly combined, the stench that met anyone who approached them was unendurable.

Perseus is eventually removed to a slightly less barbarous Roman prison, where his state of mind improved, says Diodorus cryptically, "on account of the Senate's kindness."

Two decades later, the Romans completed their conquest of Greece by annexing the Peloponnese. In 146 BC the rebellious Achaean League, which had earlier striven for Greek autonomy under the magnificent "last of the Greeks," the Arcadian military tactician Philopoemen, was overwhelmed by the Roman republican army at the battle of Corinth. The Romans obliterated the beautiful ancient port city, a long-standing symbol of Greek commerce, sea power, and alluring temple cults. Polybius, a historian from Arcadia who witnessed the aftermath of the destruction of Corinth, describes boorish Roman soldiers with such contempt for high culture that they threw masterpieces of Greek painting on the ground, including two world-famous pictures of Dionysus and Heracles, and used them as checkerboards.

The career of Polybius, born in the late third century BC but surviving until he was over eighty, typifies the Greek attitude to Rome. He had nostalgia for the glory days of Greek freedom and a conviction that Greek culture was superior to all else. But any sentimental patriotism was leavened by an admiration for the Romans' efficiency, a fascination with Roman history reflected in his brilliant account of the Punic Wars, by ties of affection with individual Roman friends, and by a desire for peace at almost any cost. Although his father was loyal to the Achaean League, Polybius was a soldier and a realist who appreciated the quality of the Roman army. During the conquest of Greece he had supported a policy of cooperation with (although not acquiescence to) Rome against Macedon. But in 167 BC, soon after the death of Philopoemen, Polybius was sent as a hostage to Italy. He was fortunate enough to be appointed tutor to the sons of L. Aemilius Paullus. One of the boys was called Scipio Aemilianus, and when he grew up he secured Rome's famous victory over Carthage. Scipio took his old tutor Polybius with him to Carthage, and so it is from this Greek historian that we have received a precious eyewitness account of the siege and destruction. Polybius's friendship with Scipio changed his life. It enabled him to plead that the Greeks be treated with some leniency after Corinth was taken. He was then made responsible by the Romans for overseeing the transition of the Peloponnese to the new regime, a task he performed with tact and competence, though probably not enthusiasm.

Yet in an important sense, Polybius never stopped defending Greece. His moving account of the last stand of the Achaean League prevails in the historical record. This soldier and administrator was also a wordsmith. His discussion of political constitutions helped shape the modern world by influencing the ideas of a series of seminal thinkers from Charles de Montesquieu to the Founding Fathers of the United States, especially John Adams. For of all the defining characteristics of the Greeks, in the Roman imperial centuries it was their prowess in both the spoken and the written word that came to full fruition.

Diodorus and Polybius were just two of an extraordinary group of intellectuals writing in Greek under Roman rule, including the biographer Plutarch and the Stoic Epictetus. Their achievements form the subject matter of this chapter. First printed in Italy and what is now Switzerland in the early sixteenth century, and translated into modern languages soon thereafter, the works of these writers bequeathed to us vivid and definitive images of the ancient world: the Carthaginian Hannibal crossing the Alps with his elephants, the defiant suicide of the Jews of Masada, the colossal statue of Zeus at Olympia, and the slave revolt led by Spartacus. Under Roman power, millions of glittering ancient Greek words were poured out in hundreds of thrilling books we can read today, encompassing every aspect of life. These authors captured the world not by arms but in the words that they inscribed with such fluency on papyrus. They specialized not just in history but in medicine, temple cult, archaeology, geography, philosophy, self-help, and different genres of fiction. They told us about themselves and their intense personal experiences. Through their words we can experience this period of history with a directness and vividness possible for no earlier era.

Some accounts of ancient Greece end with the fall of Corinth. But under the mighty Roman Empire, the Greeks remained as Greek as ever—indeed, being under the administrative control of non-Greeks made them prouder of their heritage. They did not just write for Greeks, either: They colonized the minds of their Roman masters. There was scarcely an aspect of literary, artistic, philosophical, or scientific culture that the Romans did not adopt or adapt from their clever neighbors. Some Roman aristocrats developed a laughable mania for things Greek: Polybius records in a supercilious tone that Aulus Postumius Albinus, consul in 151 BC, "had from childhood set his heart on acquiring Greek culture and the Greek tongue. . . . He even went so far as to attempt to write in Greek a poem and a serious history, in the preface to which he begs his readers to excuse him, if, as a Roman, he has not a complete mastery of the Greek language and their method of treating the subject." The Roman poet Horace put it better than anyone: "captive Greece took her fierce conqueror captive" (*"Graecia capta ferum victorem cepit"*). This period saw the definitive conquest of the Western mind by the ancient Greeks, and their final elaboration of the mental landscapes we still inhabit today. There is more than one kind of colonization, and cultural hegemony has more lasting effects than political dominance. As Diodorus put it, "it is by means of discourse alone that a man can gain ascendancy over many."

These articulate writers shared several characteristics, besides being destined to inspire specialists in their respective fields when manuscript copies of their works were rediscovered during the European Renaissance. They were all prolific—this is the age of the multivolume history and the encyclopaedic handbook. They used the same Greek prose; by 300 BC, even the Macedonians in their original kingdom were using the *koine* (common [language]) to inscribe their monuments, a version of Athenian Greek that had become the standard dialect spoken by Greeks internationally. In the Successors' cities, almost all of which eventually came under Roman power, *koine* Greek was thus the official language. Anyone who wanted to build a business or a career in civic administration needed to speak it competently. This motivated native speakers of Aramaic, Syrian, Phoenician, and Nubian to learn Greek fast and well. Even before Alexander had crossed the Hellespont, an Athenian educator named Isocrates had written an oration, the *Panegyricus*, advocating a Panhellenic campaign against the Persians, in which he had defined what it meant to be Greek. Greeks, he said, were not united by blood but by a frame of mind (*dianoia*), which could only be acquired through education in Greek culture (*paideusis*), not by some process in nature. The men who possessed this Greek mind-set, polished by education in the established curriculum, especially the Homeric epics and rhetoric, were called the *pepaideumenoi*, or "educated ones." There was no requirement that their mother tongue was Greek, although mastering the curriculum, if Greek was a second language, was arduous. Several of the writers discussed here, including the Jewish historian Josephus and the Syrian satirist Lucian, did not speak Greek at home.

The other characteristic these authors shared was that they were well traveled. They came from different parts of the Greek-speaking world, and this chapter, which began with Diodorus of Sicily and Polybius of Arcadia, shifts next to northern Turkey and the Black Sea before traveling, via destinations including Jerusalem, to the cities of ancient Syria. But the famous writers of Greek under the Roman Empire toured its cities to display the results of their researches in public lectures. They are often called collectively Second Sophistic authors because they revived the classical Greek figure of the traveling sophist. They were as accomplished in showcase oral delivery of their studies as in formulating them for circulation in persuasive prose. Several of them worked for a time in Rome and had experience of the circles around the Roman emperors: They were celebrity intellectuals.

The most stellar was Galen (AD 129 to around AD 200), the ancient physician whose reputation is second only to that of Hippocrates. Galen's career offers a vivid route into Roman imperial culture. He was born into a well-to-do Greek family in Pergamum, always one of the Greek cities of Asia most accommodating to Rome. The son of an architect, he was given a superb education, and his career was chosen after his father had a dream in which the healing god Asclepius ordered him to make his son study medicine. Galen did not get along with his mother, whose hot temper the dispassionate young intellectual did not share. His father died when Galen was nineteen, and he took to traveling and studying abroad. He spent four years in Alexandria (AD 153–57) and read every previous medical writer he could access.

His first big career advance came in 157, when he was appointed physician to the gladiators owned by the High Priest of Asia back at home in Pergamum. The gladiators were required to perform in the imperial cult, and Galen was to refine his understanding of injuries while treating them. He won the job against competition by performing operations, publicly, on a monkey. He made an incision in its stomach to reveal the intestines and challenged the other physicians present to replace them and insert the necessary sutures. None took up the gauntlet. Galen recalls, in a ceremonial first-person plural:

> We ourselves then treated the ape displaying our skill, manual training, and dexterity. Furthermore, we deliberately severed many large veins, thus allowing the blood to run freely, and called upon the Elders of the physicians to provide treatment, but they had nothing to offer. We then provided treatment, making it clear to the intellectuals who were present that [physicians] who possess skills like mine should be in charge of the wounded.

From Pergamum, Galen went to Rome, where he eventually settled, working for the emperors Marcus Aurelius, his son Commodus, and Septimius Severus.

This enterprising Greek doctor turned curing patients into a competitive performance. On one occasion he was summoned to treat a slave with wounds to the chest that no other doctor had been able to heal. Galen excised the breastbone, and in a spectacular procedure exposed the heart, after which the patient recovered. When another physician denied that the kidneys were involved in the excretion of urine, Galen publicly enacted a vivisection on a male animal, which involved tying up its kidneys and penis, blowing into its bladder, and puncturing the tube that connected it to the bladder, thus releasing a spurt of urine.

So successful a doctor and self-promoter was Galen that he excited envy in his rivals, who spread rumors that he was a charlatan. Eventually he felt compelled to undergo a public scrutiny of his anatomical theories, an ordeal lasting several days. At the public venue of the Temple of Peace, other doctors repeatedly challenged him to defend his findings. He refuted them with his scalpel and practical demonstrations on patients and the cadavers of animals. These were inevitably bloody and theatrical, and he spectacularly pulled off the defense of his reputation, but the experience made him more critical than ever of other doctors. He regarded them as either incompetent or avaricious, and always as unscientific. His major contributions were to a systematic method of diagnosis, identification of cause of illness, symptoms and prognosis, described and reasoned in his massive fourteen-book treatise *On Therapeutic Method*. But he also advanced understanding of anatomy and of diagnosis by means of the pulse. Indeed, his readings were so sophisticated that he could pride himself on the case of Justus's wife, from whose pulse he had been able to diagnose not physical illness but infatuation with a dancer named Pylades.

Galen never married or fathered a child, and he was a workaholic. Despite having inherited a personal fortune, he was almost unbelievably prolific, producing at least five hundred treatises, of which more than eighty survive; these make up more than half of the entire corpus of ancient medical writing and a substantial proportion of *all* the ancient Greek we can read. Galen brought the long-standing tradition of Greek rational medicine to an unprecedented level. He also personally modeled many ideas about medicine in both the Arab and the Western worlds. His works were translated into Arabic in the ninth century, and thence into Latin. In Latin translation, several of them constituted core texts on the basic European medical curriculum by the late thirteenth century. As the Greek manuscripts began to appear in the West in the fifteenth and sixteenth centuries, a more detailed picture of the incomparable doctor's methods could be inferred from a comparative study of the textual traditions.

Galen's insistence on a scientific method based on empirical observation and dissection is especially impressive when compared with the religious view of medicine that many of his contemporaries still shared. A more typical attitude was held by Aelius Aristides, who was also an educated Greek from western Asia. Aristides was a Sophist, or practitioner of the art of declamation. During the Roman Empire, the live performance, or declamation, of elaborate set-piece speeches, on a prescribed theme such as praise of an individual or city, was a popular art form. Born near the Propontis in Asia Minor, Aristides was one of the best-traveled declaimers of antiquity. He toured Asia, North Africa, Greece, and Italy. A rhetorical superstar, his appearances often resulted in elaborate memorials erected by citizens proud to record his visit to their town. But today he is chiefly known as the ancient patient who left us details about his medical afflictions and as the founding father of the genre of personal memoir. He was obsessed with his health and suffered from extreme hypochondria. In his mesmerizing *Sacred Tales* he describes his psychological as well as physical sensations, especially while seeking a cure at the elegant town of Smyrna, his adoptive home. Smyrna boasted several beautiful baths fed by the local river, one of which, between the harbor and the ancient marketplace, was excavated by archaeologists in 2002.

Aristides was devoted to Smyrna. When it suffered an earthquake in AD 178, he interceded on its citizens' behalf with the reigning emperor, Marcus Aurelius. He pleaded so persuasively that the emperor was moved to tears and bankrolled the rebuilding of the city. The Smyrnaeans showed their gratitude to Aristides by lavishing offers of honorary offices upon him, but he accepted only the priesthood of the healing divinity Asclepius. He retained it until his death, which occurred at a greater age than he had anticipated.

About fifty fascinating orations of Aristides have survived, praising gods, men, and cities he visited, as well as two treatises on rhetoric. But his *Sacred Tales* allow us to listen with unparalleled intimacy to an individual Greek. He wrote them in middle age, after he had recovered from a baffling illness that lasted through his thirties and had devoted his life to the cult of Asclepius. The collection was designed to be an offering to the god who, Aristides believed, had made him well again. But it is the work of a skilled orator who keeps the reader fascinated, moving between pity for his agonies and wonder at the manifestations of divinity that he describes with both delicacy and awe. Aristides is our best witness to the personal experience of pagan religious devotion to survive from the ancient Greek world.

The *Sacred Tales* are interesting medically because we hear detailed descriptions of symptoms as they were experienced:

> I was beset by day and night by ferocious catarrh. I suffered palpitations and was short of breath. Sometimes I thought I was about to die, but I was unable to find the energy to summon any of my attendants. It was only with great effort that I could swallow some types of food. I could not lie down flat and was compelled to spend the night sitting up, my head resting on my knees, covered with garments made of wool and other warm fabrics.

Aristides also describes in minute detail the range of treatments recommended by doctors. These included dietary intervention, multifarious purgatives, and bloodletting. The texts' greatest interest lies, however, in Aristides' psychological isolation while he endured bouts of fever and pain, and his many visions of Asclepius and signs from gods.

On one occasion, when Aristides had just come home to Smyrna, Asclepius appeared to him along with Apollo. Asclepius stood beside his bed and assured him that this was not a dream but a real visitation. He ordered Aristides to bathe in a local stream. It was midwinter, and the temperature was sub-zero. An enormous crowd of doctors and spectators, not all of them supportive, gathered on an adjacent bridge to watch the famous patient take the plunge. Aristides continues:

> Once I had reached the river, however, I did not need encouragement because the sight of the god filled me with warmth. I removed my clothes, and without being rubbed down, I immersed myself in the deepest place in the river and remained there as if I was in a warm fish pond, swimming around and splashing myself with water. When I came out, my skin shone and my body looked healthy, and the crowd watching me shouted loudly the celebrated cry, "Asclepius is great!"

Aristides felt physically better and was filled with "an ineffable tranquillity of mind." He decided to devote himself fully to the cultivation of the god.

His religious conviction shines through his account of recovering from the plague, which afflicted Smyrna *after* he finally found a cure for his long-standing personal malady. All his slaves expired, and he became so ill himself that the doctors were convinced he would die. But the god did not give up on his priest-protégé. He came once again to Aristides in a dream, along with Athena, holding her aegis exactly as she is represented in Pheidias's famous statue. She told him not to give up, reminding him that Odysseus and Telemachus had undergone many ordeals before prevailing. Aristides must, she said, purge himself with Attic honey and eat goose livers and fish. But Aristides did not recover completely from the plague until the death of a foster-brother whom he loved. Aristides was convinced that the gods had bartered his foster brother's life for his own.

The overall effect of the *Sacred Tales* is chaotic. They often lend the impression that Aristides was a mentally unstable fantasist as well as a neurasthenic. They present the modern reader with the tension between a rational, scientific approach to medicine and one based in a mystical apprehension of gods' direct involvement in the physical world.

Galen and Aristides were both celebrities whose medical procedures, whether as star doctor or star patient, attracted crowds of spectators. They were both Greeks from the northwest of Asia Minor who cooperated with Rome while continuing to practice their Greek way of life. Their voluminous and eloquent prose writings show how they used their immersion in the classical Greek curriculum to offer us unparalleled routes into the ways that ancient Greeks under the Roman Empire thought about their bodily existence. Their corner of the Greek world in Asia Minor, where Greeks were enthralled by their classical past, also produced Pausanias, who gave us our seminal account of the appearance of the archaeological sites of Greece in the second century AD.

Pausanias was born in Lydia not far from Aristides' city of Smyrna. In his day, the Roman emperor Hadrian was promoting interest in Greece, and indeed reorganized a group of old Greek cities under the nostalgic heading of the Panhellenion in AD 131–32. But it is possible to overemphasize the presence of the Roman imperial project in Pausanias. Pausanias traveled, inquired, took notes, interviewed local people, and acquired memories for twenty years, and his efforts resulted in his ten-book *Periegesis* or *Guide*. His writings still form the basis of guides to Greek antiquities and have provided our understanding of the appearance of ancient Greek buildings and artworks. It is to Pausanias, for example, that we owe our detailed description of the only one of the Seven Wonders of the World that lay in mainland Greece—Pheidias's statue of Zeus at Olympia. It begins like this:

> The god sits on a throne, and he is made of gold and ivory. On his head lies a garland which is a copy of olive shoots. In his right hand he carries a Victory, which, like the statue, is of ivory and gold; she wears a ribbon and on her head a garland. In the left hand of the god is a sceptre, ornamented with every kind of metal, and the bird sitting on the sceptre is the eagle. The sandals also of the god are of gold, as is likewise his robe. On the robe are embroidered figures of animals and the flowers of the lily.

Pausanias invented travel writing. He thought that travel was worth it for its own sake. He assumed that art and architecture could only be appreciated by actually seeing them, in contrast to most of his contemporaries, who saw the evocation of works of visual art in words as admirable in itself. He placed all the artifacts and buildings he surveyed as far as possible in historical context. He researched the old epithets of the gods. He struggled to locate obscure sites, on one occasion undertaking an arduous journey on mountain roads mainly because he had heard about a particular statue of Demeter, only to discover that it had not been seen for years. He waited for hours in the hope of hearing the legendary singing fish near Kleitor but was disappointed on this occasion, too. He was an excellent epigrapher, deciphering and recording inscriptions in obscure local dialects on worn-out old stones. His accuracy in describing the location of antiquities was impressive: The archaeologist who excavated Troy, Heinrich Schliemann, used Pausanias to help him discover the historical Mycenae. Where Pausanias departed from modern travel writing, however, is that he did not expect his readers to be interested in his day-to-day experiences on the road. Sadly, he never tells us whom he traveled with, where he slept, and what he ate. Our regret is heightened by the occasional exception, especially his suggestive statement that there were far more women than men in Patras, and that he found them charming!

What Pausanias did for Greece was done for the geography of the entire Roman Empire by Strabo, born farther east in the city of Amasia (in modern central north Turkey). The year Strabo was born, 63 BC, Amasia became part of the Roman Empire on the death of the defiant Pontic monarch Mithridates. Strabo supported the burgeoning project of Roman imperialism. But he never doubted that the giants on whose intellectual shoulders he stood were products of Greek, rather than Roman, culture. Strabo thought hard about the intellectual discipline of geography. He maintained that measuring the earth and ignoring the human population upon it was to overlook the wood for the trees. He insisted that geographers, while taking their departure from measurements of the world in its entirety, have a distinctive role. This is to explain our "inhabited world," the *oikoumene* (from which we derive our word "ecumenical"). Strabo's seventeen-book *Geography* thus conceived the discipline ahead of its time, moving through the whole world the Greeks and Romans knew, beginning at the Pillars of Heracles in the Straits of Gibraltar and advancing clockwise around the Mediterranean and the Black Sea. It explains the nature of peoples in the context of places they inhabited, from Ireland to India, Libya to the Caucasus.

To call Strabo a geographer is a little misleading. His understanding of the physical world and his literary style were both inflected by his classical philosophical training. He also traveled extensively—to Egypt, Ethiopia, up the Nile to Kush in what is now Sudan, to Italy and Greece. His long life spanned the fall of the Roman republic, the Roman civil wars, the relatively peaceful years of Augustus's rule, and the first part of Tiberius's reign. It was probably under Tiberius, who became emperor in AD 14, that Strabo completed his life's work. The *Geography* is a reference book with a practical application, intended to help statesmen understand the peoples they governed. As such it was found valuable by the Byzantines and by the explorers of the Renaissance. Christopher Columbus read Strabo avidly. Napoleon Bonaparte was sufficiently inspired by Strabo's account of Egypt to invade it in 1798. The vision of the world that Strabo laid out during the early Roman Empire has shaped not only our own mental pictures but the course of political geography.

The last of this group of brilliant men from near the Black Sea coast of Asia Minor was the prodigious Greek philosopher Epictetus, originally a slave from Hierapolis in Phrygia. Epictetus brought to culmination the ethical program of Stoicism, perhaps the most beneficial contribution to human ethics made by classical antiquity. We have lost the writings of the founder of the Stoic school of philosophy at Athens in the late fourth century, Zeno of Citium, in Cyprus. But Epictetus can put us into direct contact with the doctrines of the early stoa. In the early 90s AD, the intolerant emperor Domitian banished philosophers from Rome, and Epictetus fled to the town of Nicopolis, in Epirus, northern Greece. There he taught philosophy for the remainder of his days; it is not certain whether he was ever formally made a free man. One of his pupils was Arrian, who was devoted to his teacher and has left us a fairly literal transcription in four books of his teacher's discourses as he heard them in about AD 108, along with an abridgment known as the *Encheiridion* (Little Handbook). These texts made a huge impression on cultured Romans and were acknowledged by the writer of the other great Stoic book to have survived from antiquity, the *Meditations*, written (in Greek) by the later emperor, Marcus Aurelius.

Epictetus's experiences on the fringes of the imperial court led him to make frequent—and negative—references to Roman values when discussing the prominent men whose greed and ambition were antithetical to Stoic principles. The figure of the tyrant, the antitype of the Stoic wise man, dominates Epictetus's writing, and the tyrant of whom he was thinking was Domitian. Domitian had been assassinated in AD 96, after ordering persecutions of prominent individuals. There is something intensely moving about the attitude to true liberty in Epictetus's thought. The first book of his *Discourses* opens with a discussion of freedom, and toward the end it addresses the man who has fully understood that the external trappings of wealth and power are worthless, and who can therefore stand up fearlessly even to the tyrant in his palace. The concept of freedom is mentioned over a hundred times in the four small books of Epictetus's works.

He argued that because God (whom he calls "Zeus" or occasionally "the gods") is benevolent and rational, he created human beings to be rational, too, and capable of rational actions if they use their impressions of the world reflectively. In fact, our minds are small parts of Zeus's mind, and so our mental power is part of the power that runs the universe. We are accountable for our choices because we are free to make them and are capable of so doing. We seek through our choices to act to our own advantage, but since our own interests are part of a much larger system, we are able to see that, for example, choosing our own death can sometimes be the best decision. Stoics were famously prone to dignified suicide. For Epictetus, objects external to ourselves are neither unconditionally good nor unconditionally bad. The inner self is paramount, and externals are to be evaluated only in relation to the self. Epictetus understands that happiness is achievable only if humans are not dependent for their happiness on wealth or possessions or any other external phenomena. The emotions that make us miserable (fear, envy) are responses to the false idea that externals can make you happy. Equally false is the idea that the actions of another need affect us detrimentally. However, this does not mean we should not make efforts on behalf of other people, especially family and close associates.

Epictetus's thought was so attractive in antiquity because he gave practical advice on how to cultivate the peace of mind that Stoic theory described in the abstract. His thought is compatible with taking part in public life and taking an active role in any community. It can help people without control over the external circumstances of their lives (slaves, the poor, persecuted critics of the emperor) to find maximum contentment within those circumstances. But it takes a long-term commitment to self-improvement, and reflection about perceptions and choices. The most important thing is to slow down, absorb information carefully, and take time to reflect before action.

The clarity and good sense of this advice, which we might regard as nearer to psychological than philosophical, explain why Epictetus's *Encheiridion* is so often the starting point for people interested in non-religious self-improvement today. Epictetus has always been in tune with the American character and was recommended by both William Penn and Benjamin Franklin. He has been published in dozens of translations and played an important part in the development of the self-help movement through his influence on Dale Carnegie. Former US president Bill Clinton claims he rereads Epictetus every year.

A more esoteric alternative to Stoicism was Epicureanism, a philosophy grounded in a materialist conception of the universe. Epicureans believed that we are all made of atoms, and come into creation and pass away as part of a universal cycle of agglomeration and dispersal. Epicureanism aimed to free people from fear, especially fear of death, by showing that all religion was superstition. Knowledge of the world and the self could facilitate a freedom from desire, anxiety, and pain and thus true tranquillity (*hedone*, from which we derive our word *hedonism*, although with a debased signification). Epicureanism was voguish among Roman literati, who sought out experts from the eastern provinces of the Roman Empire (Asia Minor, Syria, and parts of North Africa) to school them in this arcane Greek philosophical system. One of the private centers of Epicureanism outside Athens was the Villa of the Papyri, found in 1752 at Herculaneum near Pompeii. This was the vacation home of Julius Caesar's father-in-law, L. Calpurnius Piso, where the famous philosopher Philodemos of Gadara, a Syrian from what is now Jordan (Syrians were always skilled expositors of Greek philosophy), was custodian of his patron's magnificent collection of Epicurean texts. The modern technology of multispectral imaging has allowed their remains, burnt by the same volcanic eruption that destroyed Pompeii in AD 79, to be deciphered and published. Some of them are by Philodemus himself, and some are his summaries of the ideas of his teacher, Zeno of Sidon. Zeno was yet another "Greek" philosopher from Phoenicia, the leading Epicurean of his day; he died in about 75 BC. This Zeno impressed Cicero when he heard him lecturing at Athens. The Herculaneum papyri include fragments of Zeno's essays on the topics of anger and on frank criticism. In addition, they include priceless fragments of Epicurus's own seminal treatise *On Nature.*

Although all men versed in Greek culture—the *pepaideumenoi*—knew something about the major philosophical schools, few combined the roles of literary author and philosopher with as much aplomb as Plutarch (AD 46–120). It is a measure of the diffusion of Greek culture at this time that Plutarch is the only figure discussed in this chapter, besides the historian Polybius, who was both born and resident in mainland Greece. His has always been one of the most influential of ancient voices. The quality of his prose glimmers through even workmanlike modern-language translations. Plutarch had read every word of the Greek literary canon, and derived from it a rich vocabulary, a wonderfully rich and clear style, and a delight in allusions to his brilliant forebears.

It was in Chaeronea, Boeotia, that Plutarch was born, a day's walk east of Delphi, at the site of that historic battle at which Philip of Macedon had heralded the brave new world of Hellenistic empires by bringing Athens and most of southern Greece under his control. It seems appropriate that a man born in such a historic location has played such an incomparable role in creating our modern vision of ancient history, sometimes because his biographies have been adapted in the plays of William Shakespeare or famous movies. Plutarch's *Lives* depicts significant individuals, from as early as the legendary Theseus of Athens and Romulus of Rome to as late as Galba and Otho, emperors in AD 69. These biographies have been popular as sources for antiquity since they began to circulate widely in the Renaissance. Our ideas of Pericles, Alexander the Great, Antony, Cleopatra, and Caesar, of the Gracchi and Spartacus, of Coriolanus and Cato, owe more to Plutarch than to any other author.

Plutarch wrote about prominent Romans from history in the same way as he wrote about prominent Greeks. He used the method of writing "parallel lives," comparing the lives of two figures, one of each ethnicity, who had experienced what struck him as similar careers. He compared, for example, the Greek orator Demosthenes and Cicero, the Roman lawyer and philosopher. Plutarch did visit Rome, and he lectured in Alexandria, but he preferred his native land. He shows how Greek intellectuals could accommodate themselves to the reality of the Roman Empire and flourish under the relative stability it provided. Plutarch reveled in his Greek heritage: He studied philosophy and mathematics at Athens, served as a priest of Apollo at Delphi, and was an active member of his civic administration at Chaeronea, even serving as its mayor. He was also devoted to his large family and traveled as little as possible. He struggled to learn Latin, but he carefully maintained friendly relationships with Rome. He embraced the privileges of full Roman citizenship when a friendly Roman consul arranged it for him. Through his readable works, he became famous throughout the Roman world. Some scholars have argued that Plutarch's professed respect for Rome and its emperors was a prudent response to the reign of Domitian, and that his accounts of Greek history can be read as nostalgic evocations of the once-free Hellenes that, at least implicitly, subvert the regime under which he lived. But such "resistant" readings of Plutarch miss his overriding concern in life, which was not political. He wanted to be a moral educator.

A substantial proportion of Plutarch's works are not biographies but essays on moral, literary, and even personal themes: The most moving is his letter of consolation to his wife when their daughter Timoxena, the first girl after four boys, died in his temporary absence when she was only two. Plutarch, who knew as much about Epicureanism and Stoicism as about the Platonic and Aristotelian traditions in which he had been trained, believed in the practical application to human problems of classical ethics. His works have a philosophical purpose—the ethical edification of readers. But they are never boring or patronizing, in large measure due to Plutarch's genial and humorous personality. This shines through even his most sententious pieces, such as his advice for dealing with garrulous individuals in *On Talkativeness*.

Some of the essays include advice worth consulting today. Practicing patience when irritated with children, spouses, and close friends is inherently a good thing. But it is also the surest way to learn to control yourself when dealing with difficult people outside your immediate circle—this is Plutarch at his practical, ethical best in *On Containing*

Anger. He makes shrewd recommendations in *On Praising Oneself Inoffensively* about the contexts in which it is acceptable to praise oneself (for example, when being treated unjustly) and devices that can ameliorate the impression of immodesty.

Among Plutarch's essays, the one that most effectively combines a serious message with entertainment value is his *Gryllus*. This examines the nature of human society through the staging of a pseudo-Platonic debate between Odysseus, Circe, and Gryllus ("Grunter"), who has been transformed into a pig and does not want to be changed back into a man. Gryllus argues that he is correct in preferring his present existence. He achieves an impressive defense of zoomorphic being. Beasts are more courageous because they fight without guile. Female beasts are braver than female humans. Animals are more temperate and do not desire material possessions; animals have no need for perfumes; animals do not commit adultery deceptively; animals do not have sex except in order to procreate; they therefore avoid sexual perversions. Animals stick to simple diets, have the right amount of intelligence for their natural conditions of life and therefore must be credited with rationality. The life of the animal as defined by Gryllus resembles the life of an ascetic philosopher. Plutarch here entices the reader into serious thinking about human social and ethical life through the most charming and well-known of the stories in the *Odyssey*.

Although Plutarch's mainland Greece had been brought under Roman sway in the second century BC, some Greek-speaking cities remained independent of Rome for a longer period of time. The Attalid kingdom, centered at Pergamum, was bequeathed to Rome by the childless last Attalid king in 133 BC. The Seleucids survived in Syria until Pompey defeated them in 63 BC. Egypt, ruled by the Ptolemies, held out until the most famous of them all, Cleopatra VII, was defeated by Augustus at the battle of Actium in 31 BC. But even after these annexations, the cities of Pergamum, Antioch, and Alexandria and many others in Syria and Egypt remained Greek, sometimes defiantly, for centuries. Many possessed all the core institutions that defined Hellenism: town planning that provided central marketplaces, council houses, and theaters; regular institutionalized festivals featuring "sacred games" in which traveling musical performers as well as athletes would compete. Moreover, these Greek cities were still in existence, although not always flourishing, six centuries later when the Roman Empire, at least its westerly half, disintegrated.

This chapter therefore now moves south and east to conclude with three authors of incalculable influence who wrote in Greek yet came from the Roman provinces of Judaea and Syria. Their first languages were dialects of Aramaic. The most controversial by far is Josephus, whose full name was Titus Flavius Josephus (AD 37–c. 100), a Jersualem-born Aramaic-speaking Jew. But Josephus could never have written his seminal *Jewish Antiquities* without immersion in the Greek curriculum. His first book, *The Jewish War*, describes the Jewish revolt against the Romans in AD 66–73, in which he had led soldiers in Galilee. It includes his nail-biting account of the experiences in AD 67 of the last Jews alive (including himself) in the caverns of Jotapata, who were besieged by Nero's troops under the future emperor Vespasian. They discussed whether they had the right to commit suicide: Josephus, ultimately the sole survivor, proposed that each kill the other in turn. He came out last in the drawing of lots and negotiated his fate with the Romans. He then turned his back, to a certain extent, on his own people, and was appointed Vespasian's interpreter. When Vespasian became emperor two years later, he freed his Jewish protégé, who promptly adopted Roman citizenship.

We can catch a glimpse of how networks of intellectual Hellenism operated under the Roman Empire since Josephus was encouraged to write by Epaphroditus, an intellectual Greek freedman at Rome, who was also the owner of the Stoic slave Epictetus. Josephus's autobiographical defense of his actions in his *Life* makes uncomfortable reading. He clearly never relinquished his true attachment to the Jewish faith, but he expressed himself as an educated Greek and promoted Roman policies. He is the most significant spokesperson of the many communities of the Jewish diaspora residing in the Greek cities of the Roman Empire, the largest of which, besides Alexandria and Jerusalem, were at Sardis and Antioch.

Josephus's voice is profoundly original in that he combined Greek literary acumen with his distinctive vision of the role of the Jewish god in the unfolding of human history. But he is also a brilliant evoker of place, time, and experience, indeed "by far the most readable and appealing" of the Greek historians who went to Rome from the east, including Polybius. His historical works have from antiquity onward provided both Christians and Jews with essential information about their religious origins. In the Middle Ages, Josephus was consulted as an authority on chronology and provided Christian Crusaders with the seminal account of Alexander's apocryphal encounter with the High Priest at Jerusalem, for example in Gautier de Châtillon's twelfth-century epic *Alexandreis*. More recently, the writer Lion Feuchtwanger drew on Josephus's writings in his trilogy *Josephus, The Jews of Rome*, and *The Day Will Come*, first published in German between 1932 and 1942. These historical novels played a crucial role in alerting the world to anti-Semitism.

So Greek prose was used under the Roman Empire in serious descriptions of every aspect of life, but it also came to rival poetry as a medium for pure entertainment. When Diodorus of Sicily remarked that the sufferings of Perseus, the last king of Macedon, "were so great that his sufferings seem like the inventions of fiction," he had the new literary genre of the novel in mind, in which residents of the eastern Greek cities excelled. Suffering cruel imprisonment was one of the hazards faced by the fictional heroes and heroines of the half-dozen surviving Greek novels, at least the subgenre constituted by the romantic novel. But the villains who hold the Greek principal characters captive, in fiction at least, are never Romans. Although written by Greeks under the Roman Empire, their plots were nostalgically set in the free Greek past of long ago. All mention of the Romans is avoided. Married or affianced heterosexual and upper-class Greek couples are separated, undergo tribulations in exotic locations, and are ecstatically reunited at the climax. The longest and most influential is the *Ethiopian Story*, authored in the third century AD by Heliodorus of Emesa (now Homs), in Syria. An Ethiopian princess named Chariclea is born with white skin and given away by her black mother, who does not want to be accused of infidelity. Chariclea eventually becomes priestess of Artemis at Delphi but falls reciprocally in love with a Greek aristocrat named Theagenes. After countless ordeals including the threat of human sacrifice, the lovers are reunited in Ethiopia and wedlock. The ethos is escapist, exciting, and mildly titillating. Printed in 1534, and published in a French translation by 1547, Heliodorus's story fundamentally informed the themes adopted by the seventeenth- and eighteenth-century novel in Spain, France, and England—adventure, travel, erotic love.

But there were also realistic ancient novels in a burlesque key that tell a different story about being Greek under Roman rule. A summary survives of the Greek prototype of Apuleius's Latin novel *The Golden Ass*, in Greek simply called *Ass*. Apuleius's hero, Lucius, who is turned into an ass, was Greek. But in the Greek version, Lucius is Roman or thoroughly Romanized. He is also beaten, starved, and humiliated by the Greek underclass under Roman rule, to ludicrous effect. When the Lucius-ass is abducted by robbers, his first instinct is to summon the aid of the Roman emperor: He tries to call out, "O, Caesar!" but can manage only a bray. The Roman citizen's dependence on the imperial machine is subverted by its unsuccessful articulation in the mouth of an undignified animal. Here the novel inverts the real-life domination of Greece by Rome; the forces of local discontent and disorder embodied in the Greek robbers insult the dignity of the *Imperium Romanum*.

The subversive Greek *Ass* novel has come down to us under the name of my personal favorite among all the Second Sophistic writers, Lucian of Samosata, an artist of surpassing verve (AD 125–180). Samosata was home to both Greeks and ethnic Syrians, and Lucian belonged in the latter group, since he says that his mother tongue was "barbarian." Nearly a hundred essays are ascribed to him, all of them written in Greek. Lucian was an admirer of Menippus, a Cynic satirist of the third century BC from Gadara, in modern Jordan (which by Lucian's day was also in the Roman province of Syria). Menippus's hilarious treatises attacked other philosophical schools in a tone of scathing ridicule. But they have not survived, which makes Lucian our best evidence for the timber of all Menippean literature. Among Lucian's dazzling oeuvre, however, two works stand out for their influence. One is his *Death of Peregrinus*, a satire on Christianity that will be discussed in chapter 10. The other is his *True Histories*, the (totally untrue) history of a voyage to the moon. The ancestor of all science fiction writers, Lucian makes his reader accompany his entertaining narrator on an interplanetary cruise. The reader scrutinizes with him the moon-world and sun-world as parallel and analogical universes.

Greek articulacy colonized the Roman mind. Greek culture offered expressive ways to talk about the superpower that now ran the world. Strabo and Pausanias painted the word pictures of the Roman imperial territories and of old Greece under Rome that we have inherited. The writers of Greek romantic fiction, including the Syrian Heliodorus, pretended that the Roman Empire had never happened, while a burlesque novel attributed to another Syrian, Lucian, implicitly criticized it. Historians from Arcadia and Sicily, as well as Josephus of Jerusalem, wrote about the past in Greek, either criticizing or eulogizing Rome, depending upon their own subjective viewpoints. Greek remained the unchallenged language of all the dominant philosophical schools. It was also the language in which all our best sources on ancient medicine and the subjective experience of disease under the empire were composed. The most vivid insights into the minds of all the inhabitants of the Roman Empire were produced by the great celebrities who wrote in Greek. Their thoughts have had an incalculable impact on cultural and intellectual life since the Renaissance and still influence us today. Hellenism was so powerful precisely because it "was a medium not necessarily antithetical to local or indigenous traditions. On the contrary, it provided a new and more eloquent way of giving voice to them."

St. Paul preaching in Athens. Nineteenth-century engraving based on an oil painting by Raphael (c. 1515). (*Author's personal collection*)

10

Pagan Greeks and Christians

The last two chapters of Revelation describe John's vision of the New Jerusalem, experienced when he was on the eastern Aegean island of Patmos, possibly exiled from Ephesus, around the end of the first century AD. A new heaven and a new earth appeared to replace the old ones, "and the sea was no more." It seems symbolically appropriate that the sea, the home of so many glamorous nymphs and spectacular monsters, the place where the Greeks swam and sailed their swift ships, the element inseparable from pagan Greek intellectual and cultural identity, is erased from the revolutionary new Christian utopia. It was not Roman imperialism that put an end to the ancient Greeks, with their caustic wit, sculpted gods, inquiring, independent minds, philosophy, and love of sensual pleasures (the last of the characteristics I argue defined them, and which they were reluctant to relinquish). It was something different—a new religion, which offered, to those who followed its simple rules and austere lifestyle, many advantages: a detachment from pleasures of the external world, the body and the senses, a profound emotional engagement with fellow believers and their single god, the forgiveness of sins and immortal life. This chapter brings down the curtain on the dramatic two-millennia-long chronicle of the pagan Greeks by looking at some of their responses, from the first to the late fourth centuries AD, to the strange new religion practiced by the early Christians—responses that ranged from the tolerance and even mild admiration of some pagan intellectuals to the defiant defense of the Greek way of life by the last pagan emperor, Julian.

Christianity grew exponentially. There were fewer than ten thousand Christians in AD 100, but eleven times that number a century later. Despite intermittent persecution, which reached a climax under Diocletian at the turn of the fourth century, Christian communities became established from Portugal to Cologne, from the Danube to the Nile, and along most of the coast of North Africa. In 301, the Armenian king Tiridates the Great became the first national leader to proclaim Christianity the official religion. Just eleven years later, the emperor Constantine campaigned victoriously under standards that apparently displayed the cross or the *chi-rho* monogram of Christ; his soldiers carried the same signs on their shields. Christian commentators claimed that these Christian symbols were revealed to the emperor in visions and dreams, which directed him to "conquer by this sign" before a battle on the Tiber. In 325 he convened hundreds of bishops at the Council of Nicaea, in northwestern Turkey. The die was cast. Christianity everywhere was openly adopted and promoted by the emperor. It was not legislatively rubber-stamped as the official religion of the Roman Empire until 391, under Theodosius I, but after Constantine the old religion, if not yet dead, was in permanent decline. Its death warrant was signed when Theodosius forbade all forms of divination and closed down the oracles, including the most illustrious one at Delphi, which had been in operation for more than a thousand years. Although Hellenism lingered in some parts of the eastern empire, by the arrival there of Islam in the seventh century, the hallmarks of Greek civic architecture in Syria—theaters, marketplaces, and council houses, adorned with fluted columns, smiling statues, and painted porticoes—had already disintegrated. These Hellenized cities began to acquire the familiar appearance of agglomerated *souks* divided by narrow streets that their traditional quarters retain today.

Our evidence for the conversion of the Greeks and the Romans to Christianity begins in AD 50, when the Jewish Christian Paul of Tarsus wrote a letter in Greek, the first Epistle to the Thessalonians. It is probably the earliest Christian document to have survived. Having established a Christian community among the gentiles of Thessalonica, Paul wrote to them from Athens or Corinth to encourage them in their new faith. Now that they have "turned to God from idols to serve the living and true God," and "wait for his Son from heaven, whom he raised from the dead," they are to persevere in avoiding evil:

> May your whole spirit, soul, and body be preserved blameless at the coming of our Lord Jesus Christ. He who calls you is faithful, who will also do it. Brothers, pray for us. Greet all the brothers with a holy kiss. I solemnly command you by the Lord that this letter be read to all the holy brothers. The grace of our Lord Jesus Christ be with you. Amen.

Although the Christian converts of Thessalonica could not yet have known it, Paul's mission heralded the end of the glittering pagan Greek world. But the relationship between Hellenism and Christianity can't be fully understood without a brief retrospective detour into the three centuries before the birth of Jesus, to Ptolemy I. He had ruled over both centers of the Jewish religion, in Egypt (Alexandria) and Palestine (Jerusalem). Under the dynasty he founded, Greeks in Alexandria were tolerant of Jews, and vice versa; it was in the third century BC that the labor of the translation of the Old Testament into Greek, the Septuagint, commenced. Jewish thinkers such as Aristoboulos even argued that the Greek philosophical pioneers Pythagoras and Plato had borrowed all their ideas from the Law of Moses. Jewish poets even converted biblical stories into delightful Greek tragic meters.

Affairs in Jerusalem were never so harmonious, but it was only when the city passed into the hands of the Seleucid Antiochus IV in 175 BC that antagonism between Jerusalem's Jews and Hellenes erupted. Exploiting tension among Jews, expressed in their divergent attitudes to Hellenization, Antiochus entered Jerusalem. He looted the temple, enslaved women and children, and set about destroying the Jewish religion to impose the Greek one instead. The first book of *Maccabees* describes Jewish despair when he introduced idols of the heathen gods, ordered the sacrifice of pigs, and banned the Sabbath. The circumcision of baby boys was outlawed, and the threatened penalty was death. The reaction of the heroic Jewish resistance army, led by the family of the Maccabees, was to expel the Seleucids and establish Jewish self-rule under the Hasmonean dynasty.

When Jesus was alive and preaching, Jews in his homeland were therefore antipathetic to Greek thought, while between the Jews and Greeks of Alexandria, for the most part, there was mutual tolerance and even admiration. After Jesus's death, the Jews in Jerusalem and Alexandria who had converted to Christianity could not agree upon whether they were supposed to be converting Gentiles, including Greeks, or just Jews. But Paul had no doubts at all. The enterprising apostle knew what would please a Greek audience: According to the Acts of the Apostles, he quoted from Greek poetry, and even alluded to Aeschylus's *Eumenides* when he addressed the Athenians at the Areopagus, where Aeschylus's Orestes had sought justice in the play (Acts 17). Paul's experience in Athens, whether historical or not, is worth pausing over, because it encapsulated the different reactions of the Greeks to the Jewish-Christian apostolic mission, at least as an intelligent Christian writer saw it (Acts 17:16–21):

He reasoned in the synagogue with both Jews and God-fearing Greeks, as well as in the marketplace day by day with those who happened to be there. A group of Epicurean and Stoic philosophers began to debate with him. Some of them asked, "What is this babbler trying to say?" Others remarked, "He seems to be advocating foreign gods." They said this because Paul was preaching the good news about Jesus and Anastasis [Resurrection]. Then they took him and brought him to a meeting of the Areopagus, where they said to him, "May we know what this new teaching is that you are presenting? You are bringing some strange ideas to our ears, and we would like to know what they mean." (All the Athenians and the foreigners who lived there spent their time doing nothing but talking about and listening to the latest ideas.)

These Athenians responded to Paul's promise of resurrection by dividing into three groups. The first merely scoffed at him. A second group said they would like to hear more. But a third group was converted, among them an important man named Dionysius and a woman called Damaris.

The New Testament says little on the topic of the hedonistic old religion that Dionysius and Damaris now abandoned. It mentions only Zeus, Hermes, and Artemis at all, and it was Artemis who was seen, especially in the eastern Aegean and Turkey, as the most potent symbol of paganism. Pagan authors such as Artemidorus of Daldis in Lydia (Asia Minor) attest to the continuing authority of the cult of Artemis in Ephesus in the second century AD during the age of the Antonines: One of the hundreds of dreams he records in his five-book *Interpretation of Dreams* (the ancient book that inspired Sigmund Freud) was dreamed by a prostitute in Ephesus who wanted entry to the temple. Inscriptions confirm the regional importance of the goddess: One, found on the island of Patmos, shows how seriously Artemis was still being taken by her priestess, Vera, in the third century AD: "Artemis herself, the virgin huntress, herself chose Vera as her priestess, the noble daughter of Glaukias, so that as water-carrier at the altar of the Patmian goddess she should offer sacrifices of the fetuses of quivering goats which had already been sacrificed." Patmos, described as "the most sacred island" of Artemis (Artemis of the Ephesians) in Acts 19:28, was under Ephesian governance. But it was also the site of some of the principal early Christian activities and traditions. In Glaukias's proud description of his daughter's selection as priestess to carry the lustral water, and her bloodthirsty sacrifice of pregnant goats and their fetuses, we can hear the defiance of the old pagan religion against the perceived encroachments of the new Christian faith.

Certainly, when Paul arrived in Ephesus, sacred to Artemis, he encountered intense opposition. He was imprisoned at least once and feared for his life (2 Corinthians 1:8–10). The most dramatic evocation of any pagan cult in the whole New Testament is the account, in Acts of the Apostles 19, of the riot of the silversmiths, provoked by the spread of Christianity during Paul's time there. A silversmith named Demetrius, "who made silver shrines of Artemis," providing business to silversmiths and craftsmen in allied trades in the city, organized a meeting and told the assembled artisans that Paul would hurt business. Paul had been claiming "that gods made by hands are not gods at all," which, argued Demetrius, would damage the reputation both of the temple of Artemis and the province of Asia. His audience "became enraged and began to shout, 'Great is Artemis of the Ephesians!'" There was an uproar, and two of Paul's companions were dragged into the theater: When a Jewish lawyer named Alexander was put forward to address the situation, the crowd became further enflamed, shouting in unison (Acts 19:34–41):

> "Great is Artemis of the Ephesians!" for about two hours. After the city secretary quieted the crowd, he said, "Men of Ephesus, what person is there who does not know that the city of the Ephesians is the keeper of the temple of the great Artemis and of her image that fell from heaven? So because these facts are indisputable, you must keep quiet and not do anything reckless. For you have brought these men here who are neither temple robbers nor blasphemers of our goddess. If then Demetrius and the craftsmen who are with him have a complaint against someone, the courts are open and there are proconsuls; let them bring charges against one another there. But if you want anything in addition, it will have to be settled in a legal assembly. For we are in danger of being charged with rioting today, since there is no cause we can give to explain this disorderly gathering." After he had said this, he dismissed the assembly.

It was not going to prove easy to convince the inhabitants of the province of Asia to give up their alluring but ferocious goddess, regardless of whether they were motivated primarily by religious conviction or perceived threat to their income. In AD 268, two centuries after Paul's visit, the temple was destroyed by fire. But the arsonists were not Christians: They were a marauding army of Goths, barbarians from Germany. The temple was then restored. We can sense the continuing struggle between the pagan worship of Artemis and Christianity in an inscription set up by a Christian named Demeas in AD 354. Demeas emphasized, with the sign of the cross, that he had taken down "the false image of the *daimon* Artemis" that stood in front of the doors. But it took another hundred years after Demeas took down that statue for the Ephesian cult finally to be scrapped, in AD 450.

The collection of documents we know as the New Testament, however, had begun life at around the same time that Paul visited Ephesus in the first century AD. In around AD 61, a Jew who had become a Christian wrote the account of the life, ministry, and death of Jesus of Nazareth, which we know as the Gospel according to Mark. Although the author of this extraordinary document may have had access to a compilation of the sayings of Jesus in a Semitic language, the language he wrote in himself was the everyday Greek spoken across all of the eastern Roman Empire. By the end of the first century, all the texts comprising the New Testament, including the letters of Paul, had been written and had begun to be collected. By AD 170, the four gospels are mentioned together; with the introduction of the codex, far more texts could be assembled than had been possible previously in rolls. The Bible in a single huge book, including the whole of the Old and New Testaments, became a physical reality by the mid-fourth century. Amazingly, two examples survive, one held in the Vatican and most of the other, the Codex Sinaiticus, in the British Library.

The Gospels and the Acts underpinned the spread of Christianity in the second century, when it ceased to be dominated by Jerusalem and was taken all over the Roman world, including Greece and the eastern provinces of the Roman Empire, by proselytizing bishops. Over the course of the four centuries between the birth of Jesus and Theodosius's edicts, the relationship between Christianity and Hellenism was varied and constantly evolving, as we can see through the figures of two prominent women pagans. At the peaceable end of the spectrum, a shared Greek education and culture could allow Christians, Jews, and Arabs not only to coexist but to conduct civilized debates face-to-face. Zenobia, the Hellenized Arab queen of Palmyra in the third century, invited dazzling intellectuals to enhance the cultural life of her luxurious city, built at a lush oasis in the heart of the Syrian desert. They included a Greek orator named Kallinikos and a Christian bishop of Antioch—a significant theologian—named Paul of Samosata; a third was one Longinus, who may even be the author of the brilliant work of literary criticism *On the Sublime*, a profound attempt to explain how the beauty of literary art can make the heart of the hearer beat faster with excitement. It is written in Greek but its discussion of Genesis suggests that its author was Jewish. Hellenism made such intellectual internationalism possible. But at the other end of the spectrum stands the violent death of Hypatia, dramatized in the movie *Agora*, directed by Alejandro Amenábar and starring Rachel Weisz (2009). Hypatia was an outstanding Egyptian Greek scholar in the fourth to fifth centuries AD, the daughter of the Euclidean mathematician Theon, alongside whom she worked at the Alexandrian library. She was murdered when the Roman administration allowed angry Christians to destroy the library as one of the institutions symbolizing what they regarded as abominable pagan lore.

There are surprisingly few references by pagans to Christianity during its first two hundred years. Epictetus, the Stoic discussed in the previous chapter, did remark that the Christians, whom he calls Galileans, were unafraid of death. As a Stoic he would have found this commendable. The physician Galen also mentioned Christians in the late second century AD. His views were largely positive, which means that he may have had contact with the kindness of Christian individuals or a whole community. In his summary of Plato's *Republic* he paid the Christians a high compliment, not unlike that of Epictetus, in saying that their conduct, especially in their attitude to death, sexual self-control, and cultivation of virtue, made them "not inferior" to philosophers. But he was frustrated by their willingness to accept information on faith rather than requiring evidential proof. This was a serious intellectual failing to any Greek critical thinker; in resting their faith on "parables and miracles," Christians showed themselves to be no more capable than the general mass of the population of following an argument based on demonstrative steps. At one point Galen makes a reference to a passage in the Gospel of Matthew 3:9, which reports that John the Baptist said that God could break the laws of nature and make people out of rock. Galen saw the Christians' belief in such scientifically impossible marvels as evidence that they were intellectually impoverished.

While Christians are mentioned in the writings of several Roman emperors, including Trajan, Hadrian, and Marcus Aurelius, there are few sources that allow us to see how the sort of Greek-speaking people who enjoyed their time-honored way of life, and actively jeered at Paul in Athens, reacted to the Christians in the second century. The richest, wittiest text shows Lucian the satirist taking aim at the new religion and its obsessive adherents, although by a rather roundabout route. In his *Death of Peregrinus,* he tells part of the life story of a Cynic philosopher called Peregrinus Proteus, originally from Parion in Asia Minor, who, says Lucian, had in his youth temporarily converted to Christianity. In later life, after embracing Cynicism, Peregrinus became interested in Indian ideas. He was impressed with the story of the near-legendary Indian philosopher Kalanos, who had been cultivated by Alexander the Great and had burned himself to death at Susa in 323 BC. So Peregrinus, Lucian tells us, had imitated Kalanos by publicly immolating himself by fire at the close of the Olympic Games in AD 165.

Lucian uses this event as the opportunity to relate Peregrinus's experiences with the Christians, one of the inspirations behind Monty Python's *Life of Brian* (1979). Lucian paints a portrait of Peregrinus as a self-publicizing charlatan, and the Christians as puritanical, stupid, and ridiculous. (For this reason Lucian's text has found itself banned more than once by established churches.) The man with the Christian past had originally joined the pious community after strangling his own father and committing two sexual misdemeanors, adultery and corrupting a young boy. Fleeing to Palestine, he fell in with some Christian priests and scribes who were so gullible that he could convince them that he was a prophet. He became their leader, interpreted and wrote Christian books, and was honored by them second only to the man "whom they still worship, the man who was crucified in Palestine because he introduced this new cult into the world."

The local authorities arrested him, seeing that he was a fraud, but his Christian flock still believed in him and camped outside the prison. They brought food, read out their "sacred writings," compared him with the imprisoned Socrates, and invited supporters from all over Asia, "sent by the Christians at their common expense." The speaker in Lucian's text, who is a man he had heard speak at Olympia, provides us with a summary of how humorous pagans talked about the earnest Christians they saw around them in the second century AD: "The poor wretches have convinced themselves, first and foremost, that they are going to be immortal and live for all time, in consequence of which they despise death and even willingly give themselves into custody. Furthermore, their first lawgiver persuaded them that they are all brothers of one another." They become Christians "by denying the Greek gods and by worshipping that crucified sophist himself and living under his laws. Therefore they despise all things indiscriminately and consider them common property, receiving such doctrines traditionally without any definite evidence. So if any charlatan and trickster, able to profit by occasions, comes among them, he quickly acquires sudden wealth by imposing upon simple folk." These sentences crystallize the contemptuous pagan Greek vision, seasoned with Lucianic wit, of the Christian in the second century. Christians are unintelligent ascetics who volunteer for self-deprivation and even prison. They ludicrously believe that they are immortal, that they are all brothers, that material possessions are of no account and to be shared communistically. It is particularly interesting that the common belief about Christians was that they actually worshipped Jesus, held by most pagans to be just another Sophist: In another dialogue, Lucian lumps Christians together with two other groups he dislikes, Epicureans and atheists.

The Christians, however, did pose a threat to the time-honored ethos of Hellenic civilization, precisely because they denied the old gods and refused to join in the definitive core ritual of public sacrifice and all the fun and partying that accompanied it. Besides satirical caricature, other ways were found to defuse the challenge they presented, such as refutation of their doctrines in the venerable medium of the orderly treatise or systematic dialogue. A contemporary of Lucian, a Greek philosopher (perhaps an Alexandrian) called Celsus, composed such a work, entitled *The True Word*. Unfortunately, the text itself only survives in long quotations embedded within another treatise designed to refute it point by point, the work of a Christian named Origen written a few decades later. But the outlines of Celsus's arguments are clear enough. Christianity involves secret, illegal meetings. It is barbarous, uses sorcery, and demands irrational belief. It stems from the religion of the Jews, which is to be condemned because it insists on their separateness from other peoples. Christianity is mainly practiced by lower-class, ignorant people (although Celsus did acknowledge that there were intelligent and cultured individuals among them).

Celsus, then, interestingly, invents a Jewish speaker to put the Jewish case against Christianity, which raises the question of whether his intended readership included Hellenized Jews. Celsus's fictional Jewish voice states several objections. Jesus could not have been the anticipated Messiah because he was not divinely born (Celsus says his father was a Roman soldier) and not acknowledged by God. Jesus was forced by poverty to hire out his labor in Egypt, where he and John dreamed up the new religion as a scam, and practiced juggling tricks to aid in the manufacture of miracles. He was not the Messiah because he was betrayed by his own followers. He could not save himself from death and did not arise from the dead. If he had, he would have displayed himself to the judges rather than to a half-demented female acolyte.

Returning to his own pagan, philosophical voice, Celsus argues that Christianity is itself is contrary to reason. This can be seen by Christians' use of terrifying images of punishments in the future to intimidate people into conversion. Celsus particularly objects to the attraction of Christianity to self-professed sinners, and its claim that it can absolve sin. Like the good Greek philosopher he is, Celsus is clear that the only remedial course of action for someone who habitually sins is to try to change his whole attitude to life. When it comes to God, why would the supreme being want to become flesh and mingle with mortals, who are inferior? To undermine the whole background of the new Messianic faith, Celsus then launched a broadside against the beliefs of the Jews. Today it is an unpleasantly intolerant diatribe to read, but it reveals his intimate grasp of the Old Testament.

He saves his most acerbic rhetoric for the doctrine of the resurrection of the body:

They are irrational to suppose that when God, like a cook, introduces the fire that is to devour the world, all the rest of the human race will be incinerated, and only they will survive—not only the ones who are alive at the time but also those who have been dead for a long time, who they suppose will rise from the earth with exactly the same flesh as when they were alive. This would be a good thing for worms to hope would happen, but what kind of human would long for a body that has suffered from decay?

Yet for all the biting language against the beliefs of both Christians and their Jewish forebears, Celsus's aim was apparently not so divisive. He did express the hope that the pagans and at least the cultured Christians could come to an agreement by which the Christians kept their faith but cooperated with the affairs of state and held office in government. This would include, if necessary, the support of state religion. Celsus intended to write a sequel in which he would lay out practical proposals for achieving such a tolerant and cooperative model. Regrettably, his guide to multicultural living was apparently never written.

Celsus's opponent Origen, like most intellectual third-century Christians, blended his radical new religion with large doses of Platonic philosophy. The contemporary pagan Platonists who informed their Christian theology were in the nineteenth century labeled Neoplatonists, and their significance in the Italian Renaissance makes them one of the most influential groups of ancient Greeks. Although they were not directly responding to the advent of Christianity, the Neoplatonists played a critical role in reformulating one of the most important constituents of the "pagan lore"—the works of Plato—for the evolving sensibility of the late Roman Empire, which found Christianity so inviting. Their interpretations of Platonism have also been much used by thinkers in the Islamic and Jewish intellectual traditions.

The key figure here was a third-century Egyptian Greek named Plotinus, who in Alexandria had studied with the same teacher of philosophy as Celsus and was interested in Indian and Persian philosophy as well as Greek. Plotinus moved to Rome to work and write his fifty-four treatises. They are called *Enneads* because they were divided by his student and biographer Porphyry into six groups of nine (the Greek for "nine" is *ennea*). Plotinus's reading of Platonic metaphysics interpreted the universe as comprising three essential elements (a trinity, which heavily influenced Christian doctrine): the One (the unitary, single, and transcendent nature of God), the Mind (*nous*), perhaps better translated as Intelligence or Contemplative Reason, which contemplates or encompasses the realm of Plato's forms; and the Soul. The Soul has two parts, one of which is superior to the other. The upper part, which is closely related to Intelligence, watches the lower part as it becomes materialized and passes through life, vulnerable to physical desires, pleasure and pain, sorrow and vice, forgetful of the pure realm from which it emanated. The Myth of Er in the last book of Plato's *Republic* was central to this Neoplatonic narrative. The only way a human soul can get back to the pure immaterial realm is through cultivating virtue and practicing philosophy. It is not difficult to see how this mind-body dualism, and the idea of the return to immortal life in an immaterial realm at one with God, appealed to Christian intellectuals as well as to other esoteric groups who influenced and sometimes overlapped with them, those commonly referred to as Gnostics.

Plotinus's biographer Porphyry, a Hellenized Phoenician, was an eminent Neoplatonist in his own right. It was his Platonic writings that inspired Augustine of Hippo to believe in the reality of the incorporeal realm of the spirit, thus reconciling him to orthodox Christianity. Through Augustine, Porphyry contributed seminally to the foundation of Western theology as practiced to this day. He would, however, have been appalled to hear this. He had himself once been a Christian, and after abandoning the faith became one of its most brilliant critics. Around the time of Diocletian's persecutions, he wrote a treatise called *Against the Christians*. Its exposure of what he perceived as their intellectual confusion was so deadly that it was later banned by the Christian emperors from Constantine onward and has been almost totally lost.

The Neoplatonists handled other pagan texts than those of Plato. One of their favorites was the Homeric *Odyssey*. Even before Plato, the early Pythagorean philosophers, whose doctrines included reincarnation, developed an allegorical interpretation of the *Odyssey* that encompassed epistemology and metaphysics as well as the abstemious ethics propounded by the Cynic-Stoic tradition. An echo of their allegorizing method can be heard in the Platonist Plutarch's *Sympotic Questions*, where the topic is the Sirens. Plotinus, however, suggested that Odysseus's desire to go to his beloved homeland and away from Circe and Calypso, despite their charms, is Homer saying "with a hidden meaning" that man needs to return to his spiritual fatherland, tearing himself away from the beautiful sensory world. Ithaca thus metaphorically represents union with the divine. Plotinus's student Porphyry wrote the most dazzling allegory of the *Odyssey* of all in his treatise *On the Cave of the Nymphs,* which begins by quoting the description of the Ithacan cave in book 13 of the *Odyssey,* where Athena tells Odysseus to hide his goods. This cave is an allegory, according to Porphyry, of the physical universe—it is lovely but it is also murky. The olive tree represents the divine wisdom that informs the universe and yet is separate from it. When Athena tells Odysseus to hide his goods in the cave, Homer is saying that we need to lay aside our outward possessions in order to think about how to cut away all the destructive sensual desires and passions of the soul.

Neoplatonists helpfully allegorized the major pagan myths in ways that would subsequently make them palatable to abstemious Christians, who were content to relinquish sensual pleasure but did not want to give up reading their lovely old books. The fusion of Christian and pagan minds can also be seen in the impact of many mythical story lines on early Christian narratives concerning the apostles' journeys and tribulations. The *Odyssey* underlies the apocryphal New Testament Acts of Andrew, an exciting narrative about one of the more shadowy disciples, which was translated into numerous languages and read in early Christian Africa, Egypt, Palestine, Syria, Armenia, Asia Minor, Greece, Italy, Gaul, and Spain. The Acts of Andrew featured seafaring, shipwrecks, pirates, and cannibals, as well as an encounter with dead souls similar to Odysseus's encounters in the underworld. Andrew's loyal wife, Maximilla, waits at home like Penelope, resisting the advances of a predatory suitor. The hero is a fisherman who possesses extraordinary powers of endurance (he takes four days to die after being crucified). The story of Odysseus, the traveling hero, was part of the most elementary education of all the inhabitants of the ancient Greek and Roman worlds. Since everyone knew it so well, they tended to shape all their other stories about traveling heroes on similar lines to Homer's epic *Odyssey.* The disciple Andrew is in this sense a Christianized Odysseus.

The myth that underlies the narrative of the female apostle Thekla in the New Testament Apocrypha is the escape from the Black Sea of Iphigenia and Orestes, who bring the cult icon of Artemis with them. Thekla was converted to Christianity and perpetual chastity by St. Paul in Iconion, the central Anatolian city where she had been born into an upper-class family. The Thekla narrative relates how she resisted a suitor, was sentenced to be burned alive, but was saved by a storm sent by God to quench the flames. She traveled with Paul to Antioch and successfully resisted the attempts of an aristocrat named Alexander to rape her. Condemned to be eaten by wild beasts, she was saved again by divine intervention (she was often associated, like Artemis, with an entourage of animals). No wonder early Christians like Tertullian, opposed to women preaching and conducting baptisms, claimed that the story of Thekla was fraudulent. No wonder Thekla is important as a foremother to women in the Christian churches today.

But an appendix to her story tells of Thekla's later life, and death; she traveled "in a bright cloud" to Seleucia, converting many; she lived as a virgin priestess in a cave. The cave had such power that even approaching it produced miraculous cures. The pagan doctors of Seleucia plotted against her because she had damaged their business by healing everyone. They assumed that Thekla was a priestess of Artemis. Since the gods would remove her power if she lost her virginity, even at the age of ninety, the doctors organized a gang rape. But God opened up a rock cavern for her to enter, thus saving her virginity even as she died a death worthy of canonization. In this story the courageous, much-traveled holy virgin, connected with healing, whose memory is preserved in her miraculous cave, is inevitably assumed by the pagans of western Asia Minor, the epicenter of the cult of Artemis, to be a priestess of that goddess. It is in a cave high above the ruins of Ephesus that an astonishing Christian painting of Thekla and Paul was discovered by Austrian archaeologists. They are indeed often depicted as a pair, united not sexually but as travelers who announce the arrival of a new god.

We must be careful in assuming that even pagan myths about sex were objectionable to the early Christians. Like the *Odyssey*, they could be read by Christians who could not bear to abandon the old education. One solution to myths about sex was to interpret them as allegories containing moral examples that proved the benefits of Christian ethics. In the late fifth or early sixth century, the Christian Procopius of Gaza, an expert on the Old Testament, describes a series of new paintings that had just been installed in a public building. Procopius offers a Christian interpretation of the scenes, which were all from classical mythology, showing the moral lesson underlying the ancient story. The stories of Phaedra, who wanted to seduce her stepson Hippolytus, or of Ariadne, who betrayed her fatherland to sleep with Theseus, reveal the *danger* of erotic passion. It was particularly common to accommodate pagan Greek myths and narratives to Christianity in the figure of Dionysus, a process exemplified in dazzling mosaics found at Paphos in Cyprus and in a massive Greek epic poem called the *Dionysiaca* by the well-read Nonnus of Panopolis in Egypt in the fifth or sixth century AD. The poem tells how Dionysus won many victories in India before returning to the Near East in a triumphant procession, and includes the pagan mythical foundation stories of many of its Greek cities. By Nonnus's date, pagan worship was actually against the law, and so some scholars have seen the *Dionysiaca* as a serious defense of the old religion at a time when it was in terminal decline. But Nonnus also knew the Gospel of St. John and indeed paraphrased it in verse, which may mean he converted to Christianity after writing the epic about Dionysus. But there is a third interpretation, which is that the poem is a lighthearted and rather secular work, intended to be entertaining, and could have been written by a cultured Christian, much as a Christian today could at least theoretically write a popular novel about Jason and the Argonauts without betraying his or her faith. The pagan texts were still read and reworked in the Byzantine Empire, after all.

The question of Nonnus's Hellenism only presents a problem because in late antiquity, the idea of Hellenism had always implied for Christians the whole culture and literature of the Greek past, especially its religion and philosophy. In both pagan and Christian writings, the term "Hellenes" meant what we call "pagans." The verb "to behave like a Greek," *hellenizein*, included the sense "to practice the pagan religion." Yet Nonnus's fondness for Greek myth reflects a persistent strain in eastern Christian communities, a reluctance to forfeit a secular interest in the wonderful books of the ancients just because they had embraced a new faith. The issue came to a head with Julian, the last pagan emperor of all, whose brief reign lasted from AD 361 to AD 363. He is a figure who has always appealed to individuals disaffected with Christianity, among them Gore Vidal.

Julian fought a rear-guard action against the Christianization of the empire but had actually been brought up a Christian before embracing the old religion (which is why he was called "the Apostate"). He revoked the policies of the dynasty of Constantine, of which he was a member, indeed the last member to be emperor. He based his own policies on his convictions that Constantine and Constantius II (the two successive Christian emperors, his uncle and cousin, respectively) had been mistaken in thinking Christianity was the true religion. His own brand of paganism was esoteric, monotheistic, and philosophical, with Neoplatonic tendencies. He did not reject Christianity because he was addicted to pagan bodily or sensory pleasures—far from it. He openly despised material wealth and practiced asceticism, which meant he had more in common with serious-minded Christians than with most pagans, especially at the decadent end of the spectrum. But he believed that Christianity posed a serious political threat, since in his view it had the potential to alienate the very gods on whose favor the prosperity of the empire depended. Christians, in Julian's eyes, could not be trusted with the state because they did not participate in the ancient rites of the state religion.

Julian was a reasonable man. His instinct was to tolerate the Christians, meanwhile reinvigorating pagan religion. But eventually he went on the offensive, realizing that one of Christianity's strengths was that it did not require its educated followers to give up the beautiful intellectual culture to which they were passionately attached. He therefore attempted to prevent Christians from teaching the pagan curriculum, arguing that if they repudiated Hellenism in terms of the pagan gods, they were being inconsistent in clinging to it culturally. This infuriated many Hellenized Christians, especially the outspoken Gregory of Nazianzus in Cappadocia, who was later to be for a short time Archbishop of Constantinople. Gregory published vituperative invectives against the apostate emperor that show how desperate some Christians were to cling to their pagan books: "Julian has wickedly altered the very meaning of 'Greek' so it means not a religion and not a language; he has therefore stripped us of our speech [*logoi*], like a robber stealing the property of another." The Christians needed to distinguish the parts of the Greek heritage that they did want (the rhetorical and literary tradition and the emphasis of the philosophical schools on virtue and reflection) from the parts that they did not (cult, the more scandalous myths, images of the pagan gods, especially statues, entertainments, and the celebration of drinking and sex). Bishop Basil of Caesarea, also a Cappadocian, understood the problem. He wanted to inculcate in his nephew the importance of the Greek classics. In *To the Young*, Basil recommends a discriminating reading in which they plug their ears whenever the text they are reading mentions polytheism, as Odysseus's crewmen do in the presence of the Sirens. And when it comes to gods' erotic adventures—these obscene matters are not for Christians but actors on the stage.

Basil's disparagement of actors brings us to the element in the pleasure-loving pagan culture that Christians found most reprehensible —theatrical entertainments. By the fourth century AD, the center of theatrical performance was the magnificent city of Antioch, on the Orontes. Founded by Seleucus I in about 301 BC, Antioch functioned as the symbolic gateway between the cultures of the West and of the East. In New Testament times it became the chief center of Christianity in the East, and it remained important in Byzantine times. From the moment when Julius Caesar confirmed the freedom of the city in 47 BC, it saw itself as the eastern Greek equivalent of Rome, insisting proudly that it had been founded by Greeks from Argos, Crete, Cyprus, and Macedon. According to one Antiochene, Libanius, his fellow citizens imagined these ancestors "paying the accustomed honors to the gods, living in all happiness in the midst of barbarians, producing a city which was a true Hellas, and keeping their way of life pure in the midst of so much corruption all round them." The Greek Antiochenes also enjoyed live performances so much that they had two theaters. Antioch's exceptional mosaics, given to an astonished world when they were excavated in the 1930s, present a colorful impression of the lively visual and performance culture enjoyed by its inhabitants. It was against the decadent shows of Antioch that the Christian John Chrysostom directed his puritanical *Against Games and Theatrical Entertainments*. It was for the professional performers of Antioch that the pagan Libanius wrote his dignified defense *On Behalf of the Dancers*.

Libanius was born in Antioch in about AD 314 and received his higher education in the Greek classics at Athens before returning home to an appointment as the head of the best school. As the city's official Sophist, his duties included writing on its behalf to the Roman emperor. In 340 he went to Constantine's new capital on the Bosporus, where he worked as a private teacher until he was expelled after Christian factions rioted over the selection of a bishop. He took up posts elsewhere. In 349 he returned, reluctantly, when he was summoned to work as Sophist of Constantinople—Christian rulers still required pagan rhetorical expertise. But by 354 he had gone home to Antioch and settled there until his death in around 393.

The last great pagan orator and thinker, Libanius was a good and pleasant man: It is difficult to dislike someone so devoted to the slave woman with whom he lived, or who suffered such anxiety about the legal status of the son she bore him. His works convey his love of the decadent old city where he resided, with its entrepreneurial culture and addiction to recreational entertainments. Libanius saw no contradiction between Antioch's suitability as a place for an educated man to pursue serious interests and its undoubted status as a party city, a place to have a good time.

Through three speeches of Libanius, composed under three emperors, we can trace the struggle between Christian and pagan during the death throes of the old religion in the mid- to late fourth century. In AD 344, Libanius was required to write a posthumous panegyric on Constantine that also praised his sons, especially Constantius. The Sophist reproduces the official picture of Constantine as the energetic, righteous emperor. Libanius even brings himself to speak in monotheistic terms, refers to God as the "creator" of the world, and states that Constantine was himself sent to earth by God and later returned to him. But the lacunae in the praise of Constantine are telling. Libanius never even mentions that Constantine had fostered Christianity, let alone adopted it.

Nineteen years later, in 363, Libanius became the official Sophist of Antioch. He wrote an obituary oration for his friend Julian the Apostate. The emperor had died on military campaign in Persia; his last words are said to have acknowledged that he had been defeated in battle by the founder of Christianity: "You have beaten me, Galilean." We will never know whether Julian might have delayed the triumph of Christianity by a few more decades had he lived beyond his early thirties. Although Libanius felt Julian's death keenly, having approved of his support of paganism, he also found that praising the apostate to the Antiochenes presented a challenge. The emperor had not made himself popular during his nine months there from mid-summer 362. Julian had moved to Antioch to muster an army to deal with military problems on the eastern border of the empire and was also no doubt attracted by the proximity of the pagan oracle of Apollo at Daphne. But there was an inevitable collision between the luxury-loving, laissez-faire citizens of Antioch and the earnest, reforming emperor, whose family members were Hellenized but originally austere northerners from the faraway Danube. The Antiochenes regarded him as gauche, badly groomed, and intent on spoiling their fun.

Julian had offended pagans and Christians alike. He was seen as interfering in domestic matters when he tried to stop rich merchants and landowners from keeping the cost of food artificially high. He outraged the Christian community by having the bones of a dead bishop removed from where they had been buried near the temple of Apollo. His disdain for imperial protocol shocked everybody, as did his egalitarian instincts, which led him to converse with people of all social ranks. No Antiochene could understand a cerebral emperor who did not enjoy watching the games or shows in the theater. The refined, clean-shaven men of Antioch expressed their resentment of Julian's interference in their affairs by reciting in the marketplace comical poems focusing on the feature they felt symbolized his boorish, ascetic ways: his beard. They enumerated all the things he could do with the hairs—for example, make ropes. Julian's response was to write a speech in his own defense, called *Misopogon*, or Beard Hater, which displays his own command of the Greek literary tradition. He had the oration pinned up in public for all to read.

Julian counters satire with satire. At times his self-deprecating, parodic critique of his own appearance and habits is pleasantly humorous. But he was offended by the reception he had been given at Antioch, and the underlying emotion is anger. Julian's old friend Libanius had to take all this into account when he wrote Julian's funeral oration. But the Sophist's heartfelt response to the loss of the last defender of the old religion gleams through his defensive prose: "What fault had you to find with his intentions? Which of his actions did you not approve of? Did he not raise up your fallen altars, did he not erect new ones to your honor? Did he not worship magnificently, gods, heroes, ether, the heavens, the earth, the sea, fountains, rivers? Did he not wage war against those who warred against you?" Libanius's speech reaches a climax with the emotive question, "Did he not restore the world to health when almost at the last gasp?"

The untimely death of Julian the Apostate, the "restorer" of the dying pagan world and its magnificent rituals at the last gasp, brought one of his generals, Valentinian, to the imperial throne. Valentinian split the empire in two, giving his brother Valens the eastern provinces. His sons succeeded him. This family were committed Christians, and the theological conflict between them was centred on doctrinal disputes within the new religion. Valentinian I hated aspects of pagan belief and punished practitioners of magic, fortune-telling, and some types of sacrifice. But it was not until Theodosius I became emperor in 379 and reunited the two halves of the empire that Christianity officially prevailed. In a series of edicts between 380 and 391, Theodosius proscribed pagan sacrifices and prayers, conversion from Christianity to paganism (which was clearly still happening), divination from entrails, and worship of pagan idols and in pagan temples. On June 16, 391, he finally made it illegal for anyone to enter a pagan temple at all. We can hear the pagan anguish in response to these edicts in Libanius's speeches of this era, especially *In Defense of the Temples*, in which he begs the emperor to allow offerings of incense and to prevent fanatical Christians from assaulting the pagan shrines.

The voice that best defines the fourth-century pagan Greek world-view belongs to the acerbic poet Palladas, an Alexandrian author of taut epigrams. These combine the worst and best elements of the sensibility of the pagan males who had thought in Greek for the previous two thousand years. They are misogynistic, intelligent, and mordantly funny. Palladas is unhappy about the situation in which he finds himself: "We Hellenes [that is, pagans] are men reduced to ashes, holding to our buried hopes in the dead; for everything has now been turned on its head." In the same poem, he complains that at the age of seventy-two, he has been consigned to poverty and death. As a schoolteacher, he had lived off the glories of Greek literature, but now he has lost his job and is obliged to sell his copies of Pindar and Callimachus and even his Greek grammar. Palladas laments the pagan cult statues that have been toppled or melted down. Palladas even ascribes human consciousness to statues, humorously suggesting that they have been able to convert to Christianity as individuals themselves. One of his most striking epigrams encapsulates the dilemma of the pagan at this turning point in history. Is he living in a dream, or is it that death has actually come to the old way of life itself, with its beautiful statues and canonical poetry? "Surely we are dead and only seem to live, we Hellenes, having fallen into misfortune, pretending that a dream is in fact a way of life. Or are we alive while our way of life is dead?" He writes an acerbic epigram on the doctrine of the physical resurrection, and another that attacks Egyptian monks. But Palladas, however much he disliked Christianity, believed that Greek philosophy had also failed.

It was difficult to police the vast Roman Empire, divided permanently when Theodosius I died in AD 395. Even Theodosius's edicts could not destroy the old religion in areas of the east. As late as the sixth century, Greeks were still worshipping their bloodthirsty Artemis on the south coast of Turkey under her resonant title Artemis of Freedom; in the uplands of Tralles, more than fifteen hundred pagan shrines still flourished and were visited during annual festivals by many thousands of participants. The philosophical schools were not finally closed until 529, by the Emperor Justinian. But the "ancient Greeks" were now running their last lap, and it was destined to be the Christians who mediated much of our knowledge of them.

Our earliest sustained critique of Christianity from the Greek philosophical perspective, Celsus's *True Word*, comes to us in quotations selected by his Christian opponent. It was in the libraries of the Christian Byzantine Empire that pagan texts were either preserved or left to disintegrate. Even the last oracle ever dispensed by Apollo at Delphi was transmitted via early Christian historians. When Julian wanted to reinvigorate the old cult centers, he sent his personal physician to Delphi to offer his support as emperor. But the god of the bow, the lyre, and philosophy knew that time was up for paganism. His response to the incipient silencing of the priestess at the epicenter or "navel" of the Greek-speaking world surely had a wider application. It symbolizes the final muzzling of all the argumentative, inspirational, beauty-loving, and hedonistic pagan Greeks to whom I hope this book has done justice:

> *Tell the king that the hall with its sculptures has fallen to the ground.*
> *Apollo has no chamber any more, and no prophetic bay-leaves,*
> *No speaking spring. The water that had so much to say has dried up*
>   *completely.*

A Note on Sources

I have drawn on the work of many scholars during my research into the ancient Greek world, and some of that work is included in the suggestions for further reading below. The translations from ancient Greek authors are almost all my own, but in a few cases I have used others' translations.

On page 94, the description of the riotous symposium at Akragas is by an ancient writer, Athenaeus, and the translation of his *Deipnosophistae* 2.37 is that of Charles Burton Gulick in the Loeb Classical Library version of Athenaeus, vol. 1 (Cambridge, MA: Harvard University Press, 1927). The metaphors "half seas over" and "ship came in" are those of W. J. Slater, in "Symposium at Sea," *Harvard Studies in Classical Philology* 80 (1976): 161–70.

On page 116, the definition of a philosophical paradox is that of Charles A. Kahn, in "The Thesis of Parmenides," *Review of Metaphysics* 22 (1969): 720. The description of the ancient Mediterranean world as a "mosaic of highly individual and distinctive cultures" on page 122 is that of Amélie Kuhrt, in "'Greeks' and 'Greece' in Mesopotamian and Persian Perspectives," *The Twenty-First J. L. Myres Memorial Lecture* (Oxford: Leopard's Head Press, 2002), 9–10. The suggestion on page 138 that the Athenian Council "could thus have contained a fair cross-section of the citizen body" comes from P. J. Rhodes, *The Athenian Boule* (Oxford: Oxford University Press, 1985), 4. Paul Cartledge defines the Sparta of the mid-fourth century BC as "reduced to the status of a mere Peloponnesian squabbler," which I quote on page 163, in his *Agesilaos and the Crisis of Sparta* (London: Duckworth, 1986), 3. The description of the hoplite's sense of purpose on page 174 is that of Victor Hanson, in *The Western Way of War* (New York: Knopf, 1989), 220. Larry Tritle considers the possibility that ancient Spartans sometimes suffered from PTSD in "Xenophon, Clearchus and PTSD," in Christopher Tuplin, ed., *Xenophon and His World* (Stuttgart: Franz Steiner Verlag, 2004). Richard Owen's praise of Aristotle's zoology, quoted on page 195, is from Richard Owen, *The Hunterian Lectures in Comparative Anatomy* (May and June 1837), edited by Phillip Reid Sloan (Chicago: University of Chicago Press, 1992), 91. The translation of Galen on page 234 is a passage from his treatise *On Examinations by Which the Best Physicians Are Recognized*. The passage is preserved only in an Arabic version, here reproduced from the English translation of Albert Z. Iskandar, *De optimo medico cognoscendo* (Berlin: Akademie-Verlag, 1988), 103–5. Tessa Rajak's praise of Josephus's readability and appeal, on page 248, is quoted from *Josephus*, 2nd edition (London: Bristol Classical Press, 2002), 9. G. W. Bowersock's remark about Hellenism on page 250 is quoted from his *Hellenism in Late Antiquity* (Ann Arbor: University of Michigan Press, 1996), 7.

Suggestions for Further Reading

PREFACE

Bernal, Martin. *Black Athena: The Afroasiatic Roots of Classical Civilization*, Vol. 1. London: Rutgers University Press, 1987.

Hall, Edith, Richard Alston, and Justine McConnell, eds. *Ancient Slavery and Abolition*. New York: Oxford University Press, 2011.

Haubold, Johannes. *Greece and Mesopotamia: Dialogues in Literature*. Cambridge: Cambridge University Press, 2013.

Knox, Bernard. *The Oldest Dead White European Males: and Other Reflections on the Classics*. New York & London: W. W. Norton, 1993.

Lefkowitz, Mary, and G. MacLean Rogers, eds. *Black Athena Revisited*. Chapel Hill & London: University of North Carolina Press, 1996.

Lewis, D. M. *Sparta and Persia*. Cincinnati Classical Studies. Leiden, Netherlands: E. J. Brill, 1977.

West, Martin. *The East Face of Helicon: West Asiatic Elements in Greek Poetry and Myth*. Oxford: Clarendon Press, 1997.

INTRODUCTION: TEN CHARACTERISTICS OF THE ANCIENT GREEKS

Enos, Richard Leo. *Greek Rhetoric Before Aristotle*, rev. ed. Anderson, SC: Parlor Press, 2011.

Fantham, Elaine, Helene Peet Foley, Natalie Boymel Kampen, Sarah B. Pomeroy, and H. Alan Shapiro, eds. *Women in the Classical World: Image and Text*. New York: Oxford University Press, 1994.

Hair, P. E. E. "The 'Periplus of Hanno' in the History and Historiography of Black Africa." *History in Africa* 14 (1987): 43–66.

Halliwell, Stephen. *Greek Laughter: A Study in Cultural Psychology from Homer to Early Christianity*. Cambridge and New York: Cambridge University Press, 2008.

Holloway, R. Ross. "The Tomb of the Diver." *American Journal of Archaeology* 110, no. 3 (July 2006): 365–88.

Konstan, David. *The Emotions of the Ancient Greeks.* Toronto and Buffalo, NY: University of Toronto Press, 2006.

Lloyd, G. E. R. *Polarity and Analogy: Two Types of Argumentation in Early Greek Thought.* Cambridge: Cambridge University Press, 1966.

Mitchell, Alexandre G. *Greek Vase Painting and the Origins of Visual Humour.* Cambridge: Cambridge University Press, 2009.

Moity, Muriel, Murielle Rudel, and Alain-Xavier Wurst. *Master Seafarers: The Phoenicians and the Greeks.* London: Periplus Publishing, 2003.

Morrison, John S., and R. T. Williams. *Greek Oared Ships.* Cambridge: Cambridge University Press, 1968.

Patterson, Orlando. *Freedom in the Making of Western Culture.* London and New York: Basic Books, 1991.

Rupke, Jorg, ed. *The Individual in the Religions of the Ancient Mediterranean.* New York: Oxford University Press, 2013.

Starr, Chester G. *Individual and Community: The Rise of the Polis, 800–500 B.C.* New York: Oxford University Press, 1986.

Wallinga, H. T. *Ships and Sea-Power before the Great Persian War.* Leiden, Netherlands and New York: E. J. Brill, 1993.

1: SEAFARING MYCENAEANS

Burns, Bryan E. *Mycenaean Greece, Mediterranean Commerce, and the Formation of Identity.* Cambridge and New York: Cambridge University Press, 2010.

Deger-Jalkotzy, Sigrid, and Irene S. Lemos, eds. *Ancient Greece: From the Mycenaean Palaces to the Age of Homer.* Edinburgh: Edinburgh University Press, 2006.

Desborough, V. R., R. V. Nicholls, and Mervyn Popham. "A Eubeoan Centaur." *The Annual of the British School at Athens* 65 (1970): 21–30.

Duhoux, Yves, and Anna Morpurgo Davies, eds. *A Companion to Linear B: Mycenaean Greek Texts and Their World.* 2 vols. Louvain-la-Neuve: Bibliothéque des Cahiers de l'Institut de Linguistique de Louvain, 2008–2011.

Evely, D., ed. *Lefkandi IV: The Bronze Age*, Supplementary Volume 39. London: British School at Athens, 2006.

Higgins, Reynold. *Minoan and Mycenaean Art*, rev. ed. London: Thames and Hudson, 2005.

Marinatos, Spyridon. *Excavations at Thera*, 2nd ed. Athens: Greek Archaeological Service, 1999.

Mee, Christopher, and Antony Spawforth. *Greece: An Archaeological Guide.* New York: Oxford University Press, 2001.

Morris, Sarah P. "A Tale of Two Cities: The Miniature Frescoes from Thera and the Origins of Greek Poetry." *American Journal of Archaeology* 93 (1989): 511–35.

Nakassis, D. *Individuals and Society in Mycenaean Pylos.* Leiden, Netherlands: E. J. Brill, 2013.

Tartaron, Thomas. *Maritime Networks in the Mycenaean World.* Cambridge and New York: Cambridge University Press, 2013.

Ventris, Michael, and John Chadwick. *Documents in Mycenaean Greek.* Cambridge: Cambridge University Press, 1959.

2: THE CREATION OF GREECE

Blegen, Carl W. *Troy and the Trojans*, rev. ed. London: Folio Society, 2005.
Burkert, Walter. *Greek Religion, Archaic and Classical*. Cambridge, MA: Harvard University Press, 1985.
Clay, J. S. *Hesiod's Cosmos*. Cambridge: Cambridge University Press, 2003.
Cline, Eric, and Jill Rubalcaba. *Digging for Troy: From Homer to Hisarlik*. Watertown, MA: Charlesbridge Publishing, 2011.
Graziosi, Barbara, and Johannes Haubold. *Homer: The Resonance of Epic*. London: Duckworth, 2005.
Hall, Edith. *The Return of Ulysses: A Cultural History of Homer's Odyssey*. London and Baltimore, MD: Johns Hopkins University Press, 2010.
Hall, Jonathan M. *Hellenicity: Between Ethnicity and Culture*. Chicago, IL, and London: University of Chicago Press, 1999.
Hooker, J. T. *Reading the Past: Ancient Writing from Cuneiform to the Alphabet*. London: British Museum Press, 1996.
Isager, Signe, and Jens Erik Skydsgaard. *Ancient Greek Agriculture*. London and New York: Routledge, 1992.
Lane Fox, Robin. *Travelling Heroes: Greeks and Their Myths in the Epic Age of Homer*. London: Allen Lane, 2009.
Montanari, Franco, Antonios Rengakos, and Christos Tsagalis, eds. *Brill's Companion to Hesiod*. Leiden, Netherlands: E. J. Brill, 2009.
Morgan, Catherine. *Athletes and Oracles: The Transformation of Olympia and Delphi in the Eighth Century B.C.* Cambridge: Cambridge University Press, 1990.
Morris, Ian. *Archaeology as Cultural History*. Malden, MA, and Oxford: Wiley-Blackwell, 2000.
Osborne, Robin. *Greece in the Making, 1200–479 B.C.*, 2nd ed. London: Routledge, 2009.
Powell, Barry. *Classical Myth*, with translations by Herbert M. Howe, 7th ed. Boston, MA: Pearson Longman, 2012.
Rosenmeyer, T. G. "Hesiod and Historiography." *Hermes* 85 (1957): 257–85.
Schein, Seth. *The Mortal Hero: An Introduction to Homer's* Iliad, Berkeley: University of California Press, 1984.
Segal, C. P. *Singers, Heroes, and Gods in the* Odyssey. Ithaca, NY, and London: Cornell University Press, 1994.
Snodgrass, A. M. *Archaic Greece: The Age of Experiment*. Berkeley: University of California Press, 1980.
Spivey, Nigel. *The Ancient Olympics*. New York: Oxford University Press, 2004.
Wallace, Jennifer. *Digging the Dirt: The Archaeological Imagination*. London: Duckworth, 2004.

3: FROGS AND DOLPHINS ROUND THE POND

Andrewes, Antony. *The Greek Tyrants*. London: Harper & Row, 1974.
Aubet, Maria-Eugenia. *The Phoenicians and the West*. Cambridge: Cambridge University Press, 1993.
Braund, David, ed. *Scythians and Greeks*. Exeter: University of Exeter Press, 2005.
Budelmann, Felix, ed. *The Cambridge Companion to Greek Lyric*. Cambridge and New York: Cambridge University Press, 2009.

Csapo, Eric. "The Dolphins of Dionysus." In Eric Csapo and Margaret Miller, eds., *Poetry, Theory, Praxis: The Social Life of Myth, Word and Image in Ancient Greece*, 69–98. Oxford: Oxbow Books, 2003.

Dougherty, Carol. *The Poetics of Colonization: From City to Text in Archaic Greece.* New York: Oxford University Press, 1993.

Graf, Fritz. *Apollo.* London: Routledge, 2009.

Hall, Edith. *Adventures with Iphigenia in Tauris: Euripides' Black Sea Tragedy.* New York: Oxford University Press, 2013.

Hartog, François. *Memories of Odysseus: Frontier Tales from Ancient Greece.* English translation, Edinburgh: Edinburgh University Press, 2001.

Kurke, Leslie. *The Traffic in Praise: Pindar and the Poetics of Social Economy.* Ithaca, NY: Cornell University Press, 1991.

Larson, Jennifer. *Ancient Greek Cults.* New York: Routledge, 2007.

Malkin, Irad. *The Returns of Odysseus: Colonization and Ethnicity.* Berkeley: University of California Press, 1998.

Morris, Ian. "The Eighth-Century Revolution." In Kurt A. Raaflaub and Hans van Wees, eds. *A Companion to Archaic Greece*, 64–80. Malden, MA, and Oxford: Wiley-Blackwell, 2009.

Murray, Oswyn, ed. *Sympotica: A Symposium on the Symposion.* New York: Oxford University Press, 1990.

———. *Early Greece,* 2nd ed. Cambridge, MA: Harvard University Press, 1993.

Stanislawski, Dan. "Dionysus Westward: Early Religion and the Economic Geography of Wine." *Geographical Review* 65 (1975): 427–44.

Stebbins, Eunice Burr. *The Dolphin in the Literature and Art of Greece and Rome.* Menasha, WI: George Banta Publishing Company, 1929.

Woodhead, A. G. *The Greeks in the West.* London: Praeger, 1962.

4: INQUIRING IONIANS

Curd, Patricia, and Daniel W. Graham, eds. *The Oxford Handbook of Presocratic Philosophy.* New York: Oxford University Press, 2008.

Freely, John. *The Flame of Miletus: The Birth of Science in Ancient Greece.* London and New York: I. B. Tauris, 2012.

Gould, John. *Herodotus.* London: Bristol Classical Press, 2000.

Guthrie, W. K. C. *A History of Greek Philosophy, Vol. 1: Earlier Presocratics and Pythagoreans.* Cambridge: Cambridge University Press, 1962.

Hall, Edith. *Inventing the Barbarian.* New York: Oxford University Press, 1989.

Hankinson, R. J. *Cause and Explanation in Ancient Greece.* New York: Oxford University Press, 1998.

Heath, Thomas L. *A History of Greek Mathematics,* Vol. 1. New York: Dover Publications, 1981.

———. *Greek Astronomy.* New York: Dover Publications, 1991.

Kahn, C. H. *Anaximander and the Origins of Greek Cosmology.* New York: Columbia University Press, 1960.

King, Helen. *Hippocrates' Woman: Reading the Female Body in Ancient Greece.* London: Routledge, 1998.

Long, A. A., ed. *The Cambridge Companion to Early Greek Philosophy.* Cambridge: Cambridge University Press, 1999.

Longrigg, J. *Greek Rational Medicine*. London: Routledge, 1993.

Seaford, Richard. *Money and the Early Greek Mind*. Cambridge and New York: Cambridge University Press, 2004.

Thomas, Rosalind. *Literacy and Orality in Ancient Greece*. Cambridge: Cambridge University Press, 1992.

———. *Herodotus in Context: Ethnography, Science, and the Art of Persuasion*. Cambridge: Cambridge University Press, 2000.

5: THE OPEN SOCIETY OF ATHENS

Beard, Mary. *The Parthenon*, rev. ed. London: Harvard University Press, 2010.

Boegehold, Alan L. *The Lawcourts at Athens*. Princeton, NJ: The American School of Classical Studies at Athens, 1995.

Bridges, Emma, Edith Hall, and P. J. Rhodes, eds. *Cultural Responses to the Persian Wars*. New York: Oxford University Press, 2007.

Hall, Edith. *Aeschylus' Persians*. Edited, with Introduction, Translation, and Commentary. Warminster, UK: Aris & Phillips, 1996.

———. *Greek Tragedy: Suffering Under the Sun*. New York: Oxford University Press, 2010.

———. *The Theatrical Cast of Athens*. New York: Oxford University Press, 2006.

———. "Comedy and Athenian Festival Culture." In Martin Revermann, ed., *The Cambridge Companion to Greek Comedy*. Cambridge: Cambridge University Press, 2014.

Hornblower, Simon. *Thucydides*. New York: Oxford University Press, 2000.

Jordan, B. *The Athenian Navy in the Classical Period*. Berkeley and London: University of California Press, 1972.

Lissarrague, F. *Greek Vases: The Athenians and Their Images*. New York: Riverside Book Company, 2001.

Neils, Jenifer. *Goddess and Polis: The Panathenaic Festival in Ancient Athens*. Princeton, NJ, and Hanover, NH: Princeton University Press, 1992.

Ober, Josiah. *The Athenian Revolution: Essays on Ancient Greek Democracy and Political Theory*. Princeton, NJ: Princeton University Press, 1996.

Osborne, Robin. *Athens and Athenian Democracy*. Cambridge: Cambridge University Press, 2010.

Parker, Robert. *Polytheism and Society at Athens*. New York: Oxford University Press, 2005.

Podlecki, Anthony J. *Perikles and His Circle*. London: Routledge, 1998.

Pradeau, Jean-François. *Plato and the City: A New Introduction to Plato's Political Thought*. Exeter: University of Exeter Press, 2002.

Pritchard, David M. *Sport, Democracy and War in Classical Athens*. Cambridge: Cambridge University Press, 2013.

Robson, James. *Aristophanes: An Introduction*. London: Duckworth, 2009.

Rowe, Christopher. *Plato*, 2nd ed. London: Duckworth, 2003.

Stone, I. F. *The Trial of Socrates*. Boston: Little, Brown & Company, 1988.

6: SPARTAN INSCRUTABILITY

Cartledge, Paul. *Sparta and Lakonia: A Regional History, 1300–362 BC*, 2nd ed. London: Routledge, 2002.

——. *Thermopylae: The Battle That Changed the World*. London: Pan, 2007.

David, Ephraim. *Old Age in Sparta*. Amsterdam: A. M. Hakkert, 1991.

Ferrari, Gloria. *Alcman and the Cosmos of Sparta*. Chicago, IL: University of Chicago Press, 2008.

Hodkinson, Stephen. *Property and Wealth in Classical Sparta*, 2nd ed. London: Classical Press of Wales, 2009.

Kagan, Donald, and Gregory Viggiano, eds. *Men of Bronze: Hoplite Warfare in Ancient Greece*. Princeton, NJ: Princeton University Press, 2013.

Kennell, Nigel. *The Gymnasium of Virtue: Education and Culture in Ancient Sparta*. Chapel Hill: University of North Carolina Press, 1995.

Parker, Robert. "Spartan Religion." In Anton Powell, ed., *Classical Sparta*, 142–72. Norman: University of Oklahoma Press, 1989.

Pettersson, Michael. *Cults of Apollo at Sparta*. Stockholm: Abm Komers, 1992.

Pomeroy, Sarah B. *Spartan Women*. New York: Oxford University Press, 2002.

Powell, Anton. *Athens and Sparta: Constructing Greek Political and Social History from 478 BC*, 2nd ed. London: Routledge, 2001.

Powell, Anton, and S. Hodkinson, eds. *Sparta: Beyond the Mirage*. Swansea: Classical Press of Wales, 2002.

Rawson, Elizabeth. *The Spartan Tradition in European Thought*. New York: Oxford University Press, 1969.

Talbert, Richard J. A. *Plutarch on Sparta*, rev. ed. London: Penguin Classics, 2005.

7: RIVALROUS MACEDONIANS

Barnes, Jonathan. *Aristotle: A Very Short Introduction*. New York: Oxford University Press, 2000.

Billows, Richard A. *Antigonos the One-Eyed and the Creation of the Hellenistic State*. Berkeley: University of California Press, 1990.

Campbell, Duncan B. *Ancient Siege Warfare: Persians, Greeks, Carthaginians and Romans, 546–146 BC*. Oxford: Osprey Publishing, 2005.

Carney, Elizabeth. *Women and Monarchy in Macedonia*. Norman: University of Oklahoma Press, 2000.

——. *Olympias, Mother of Alexander the Great*. New York: Routledge, 2006.

Cartledge, Paul. *Alexander the Great: The Hunt for a New Past*. London: Macmillan, 2004.

Ginouvès, René, ed. *Macedonia: From Philip II to the Roman Conquest*. Princeton, NJ: Princeton University Press, 1994.

Hammond, N. G. L. *Philip of Macedon*. London: Duckworth, 1994.

Heckel, W., and L. Tritle, eds. *Alexander the Great: A New History*. Oxford: Wiley-Blackwell, 2009.

Holt, Frank L. *Alexander the Great and Bactria: The Formation of a Greek Frontier in Central Asia*, 3rd ed. Leiden, Netherlands: E. J. Brill, 1993.

Janko, Richard. "The Derveni Papyrus: An Interim Text." *Zeitschrift für Papyrologie und Epigraphik* 141 (2002): 1–62.

Lane Fox, Robin. *Alexander the Great*. London: Penguin, 2004.

Mayor, Adrienne. *The Poison King: The Life and Legend of Mithridates, Rome's Deadliest Enemy*. Princeton, NJ: Princeton University Press, 2010.

McGing, B. C. *The Foreign Policy of Mithridates VI Eupator, King of Pontus*. Leiden, Netherlands: E. J. Brill, 1986.

Waterfield, Robin. *Dividing the Spoils: The War for Alexander the Great's Empire*. New York: Oxford University Press, 2012.

8: GOD-KINGS AND LIBRARIES

Blum, R. *Kallimachus: The Alexandrian Library and the Origins of Bibliography*. Madison: University of Wisconsin Press, 1991.

Canfora, L. *The Vanished Library*. London: Radius, 1989.

El-Abbadi, M. *The Life and Fate of the Ancient Library of Alexandria*. Paris: UNESCO, 1990.

Ellis, Walter M. *Ptolemy of Egypt*. London and New York: Routledge, 1994.

Evans, J. A. S. *Daily Life in the Hellenistic Age: from Alexander to Cleopatra*. Norman: University of Oklahoma Press, 2012.

Fraser, P. M. *Ptolemaic Alexandria*. Oxford: Clarendon Press, 1972.

Hansen, E. V. *The Attalids of Pergamum*, 2nd ed. Ithaca, NY: Cornell University Press, 1971.

Hutchinson, Gregory. *Hellenistic Poetry*. New York: Oxford University Press, 1988.

Irby-Massie, Georgia L., and Paul T. Keyser. *Greek Science of the Hellenistic Era: A Sourcebook*. London and New York: Routledge, 2002.

Ireland, Stanley. *Menander, the Bad-Tempered Man (Dyskolos)*. Edited with a Translation, Introduction, and Commentary. Warminster, UK: Aris & Phillips, 1995.

Jones, Alexander. *Astronomical Papyri from Oxyrhynchus*, 2 vols. Philadelphia: American Philosophical Society, 1999.

Lloyd, G. E. R. *Greek Science*, rev. ed., with an introduction by Lewis Wolpert. London: Folio Society, 2012.

Ma, John. *Statues and Cities: Honorific Portraits and Civic Identity in the Hellenistic World*. New York: Oxford University Press, 2013.

Parsons, P. J. *City of the Sharp-Nosed Fish: Greek Lives in Roman Egypt*. London: Weidenfeld and Nicolson, 2007.

Rice, E. E. *The Grand Procession of Ptolemy Philadelphus*. New York: Oxford University Press, 1983.

Toomer, G. J., ed. *Ptolemy's Almagest*. Princeton, NJ: Princeton University Press, 1998.

9: GREEK MINDS AND ROMAN POWER

Anderson, Graham. *Studies in Lucian's Comic Fiction*. Leiden, Netherlands: E. J. Brill, 1996.

Clarke, Katherine. *Between Geography and History: Hellenistic Constructions of the Roman World*. New York: Oxford University Press, 1999.

Easterling, P. E., and Edith Hall, eds. *Greek and Roman Actors: Aspects of an Ancient Profession*. Cambridge: Cambridge University Press, 2002.

Gigante, Marcello. *Philodemus in Italy: The Books from Herculaneum*. Translated by Dirk Obbink. Ann Arbor: University of Michigan Press, 1995.

Goldhill, Simon, ed. *Being Greek Under Rome*. Cambridge: Cambridge University Press, 2001.

Hall, Edith. "The Ass with Double Vision: Politicising an Ancient Greek Novel." In D. Margolies and J. Maroula, *Heart of a Heartless World: Essays in Honour of Margot Heinemann*, 47–59. London: Pluto Press, 1995.

———. "Playing Ball with Zeus: Reading Ancient Slavery Through Dreams." In R. Alston, E. Hall, and L. Proffitt, eds., *Reading Ancient Slavery*, 204–32. London: Bristol Classical Press, 2010.

Harrison, Tom, and Bruce Gibson, eds. *Polybius and His World*. New York: Oxford University Press, 2013.

Holzberg, N. *The Ancient Novel: An Introduction*. London: Routledge, 1995.

Israelowich, Ido. *Society, Medicine and Religion in the Sacred Tales of Aelius Aristides*. Leiden, Netherlands and Boston: E. J. Brill , 2012.

Kuhrt, S. A., and S. Sherwin-White, eds. *Hellenism in the East*. London: Duckworth, 1987.

Long, A. A. *Epictetus: A Stoic and Socratic Guide to Life*. New York: Oxford University Press, 2002.

Mattern, S. *The Prince of Medicine: Galen in the Roman Empire*. New York: Oxford University Press, 2013.

Petsalis-Diomidis, A. *Truly Beyond Wonders: Aelius Aristides and the Cult of Asklepios*. New York: Oxford University Press, 2010.

Pretzler, Maria. *Pausanias: Travel Writing in Ancient Greece*. London: Bristol Classical Press, 2007.

Rajak, Tessa. *Josephus: The Historian and His Society*, 2nd ed. London: Bristol Classical Press, 2002.

Whitmarsh, T. *Greek Literature and the Roman Empire*. New York: Oxford University Press, 2001.

10: PAGAN GREEKS AND CHRISTIANS

Benko, S. "Pagan Criticism of Christianity During the First Two Centuries A.D." In *Aufstieg und Niedergang der römischen Welt,* edited by Hildegard Temporini et al., 1055–1118. Berlin: Walter de Gruyter & Co., 1980.

Browning, Robert. *The Emperor Julian*. Berkeley: University of California Press, 1976.

Cameron, Averil, and Stuart G. Hall, eds. *Eusebius' Life of Constantine*. Introduction, Translation, and Commentary. New York: Oxford University Press, 1999.

Chadwick, Henry. *Origen, Contra Celsum*. London: Cambridge University Press, 1965.

Cooper, Kate. *The Virgin and the Bride: Idealized Womanhood in Late Antiquity*. Cambridge, MA: Harvard University Press, 1999.

Cribiore, Raffaela. *The School of Libanius in Late Antique Antioch*. Princeton, NJ: Princeton University Press, 2007.

Gleason, Maud. "Festive Satire: Julian's *Misopogon* and the New Year at Antioch." *Journal of Roman Studies* 76 (1986): 106–19.

Hall, Edith, and Rosie Wyles, eds. *New Directions in Ancient Pantomime*. New York: Oxford University Press, 2008.

Hall, Stuart G. *Doctrine and Practice in the Early Church*, 2nd ed. London: Society for Promoting Christian Knowledge, 2006.

Lane Fox, Robin. *Pagans and Christians*, 2nd ed. Harmondsworth and London: Penguin, 1988.

Lee, A. D. *Pagans and Christians in Late Antiquity: A Sourcebook*. London: Routledge, 2000.

Lynch, Joseph H. *Early Christianity*. New York: Oxford University Press, 2008.

Walzer, R. *Galen on Jews and Christians*. London: Oxford University Press, 1949.

Webb, Ruth. *Demons and Dancers: Performance in Late Antiquity*. Cambridge, MA: Harvard University Press, 2009.

Index

Page numbers in *italics* refer to illustrations.

About the Author

EDITH HALL is one of Britain's foremost classicists, having held posts at the universities of Royal Holloway, Cambridge, Durham, Reading, and Oxford. She regularly writes in the *Times Literary Supplement*, reviews theater productions on radio, and has authored and edited more than a dozen works on the ancient world. She teaches at King's College London and lives in Gloucestershire.